Grief
Growth
Grace

Neena is first and foremost a mother. A meaning-inspired person and scholarly practitioner, Neena is a 'Grief and Growth' specialist, counsellor and expert companion, Appreciative Inquiry and Positive Psychology practitioner and a Leadership & Life coach. She combines appreciative inquiry, positive psychology, logotherapy, poetry, therapeutic writing and expressive arts to facilitate meaning-centric deep growth. Neena is a Professional Member of the NTL Institute for Applied Behavioral Science, Professional Certified Coach from the International Coaching Federation and an Associate of the Taos Institute. Her grief memoir *A Mother's Cry .. A Mother's Celebration* has helped many bereaved people. Neena runs an independent library movement for underserved children.

Please reach her at drneenavermachimes@gmail.com

Dr. Neena Verma has authored a unique volume, integrating timeless and ubiquitous practices to restore us in the wake of grief. Through her inclusive and incisive writing, the reader will be guided through a transformative journey.

—**EK Rynearson**, MD
Clinical Professor of Psychiatry, University of Washington and Medical Director, Virginia Mason Grief Services

This book is both a timely and timeless precious gift. Through stories, concepts, meaningful guidance, inspirational insights, reflective exercises and poetic affirmations, Neena Verma shows the way to growth through grief, with grace. Grounded in her lived experience and professional expertise, and wrapped in her children's loving wisdom, the author's life-affirmative journey inspires.

—**Dr Jackie Stavros**
Professor, Lawrence Technological University and Author of *Conversations Worth Having* and *Thin Book of SOAR*

This book is an affirmation of strength amidst upheavals. It proffers a magical spur to honour the past, deal with pain, highlight the positive and precious moments and keep moving. The author has penned an awesome book which should be savoured by all.

—**Mona Mohanty**
Principal Commissioner Income Tax and Author of *Betwixt, Turns and Twists* and other best-selling books

Neena's amazing book is a timely help for those wanting to transform their grief and pain to compassion, grace and purpose. I highly recommend this conceptually sound and evocatively written book to those in grief, as also anyone interested in deep growth.

—**Dr Amitabh Varma**
Eminent Neurologist and Brain-Behaviour Expert
Former Honorary Neurologist to President of India

This book is a mindful and much welcome companion for those on a grief journey. Neena gently invites us to live purposefully by embracing our losses and unpacking the gifts that they offer. She interweaves her own remarkable story of resilience, with the wisdom of ancient and new concepts and practices.

—Jakob van Wielink
Leadership Coach and Grief Counsellor
Co-Author of *Loss, Grief, and Attachment in Life Transitions: A Clinician's Guide to Secure Base Counseling*

This book succinctly captures the essence of grief experience, and the art of transforming it into a growth and grace experience. Being a bereaved mother myself, and having counselled several bereaved people for organ donation, I find Neena's book deeply resonant for those desirous of a meaningful life after loss.

—Lalitha Raghuram
Country Director, MOHAN Foundation

Grief ... Growth ... Grace is a compelling read. It tells us that no grief is final, and no growth impossible. Written from the heart, it will appeal to those who seek the affirming path of growth and grace, in the aftermath of loss. Verma's words are literature for life.

—Ziya Us Salam
Author of *Women in Masjid* and other best-selling books
Associate Editor, *The Hindu* and *Frontline*

Grief
Growth
Grace

A SACRED PILGRIMAGE

Neena Verma, PhD

RUPA

Published by
Rupa Publications India Pvt. Ltd 2021
7/16, Ansari Road, Daryaganj
New Delhi 110002

Sales centres:
Allahabad Bengaluru Chennai
Hyderabad Jaipur Kathmandu
Kolkata Mumbai

Eminent thinkers' and authors' words are quoted with
due acknowledgement. Lapse, if any, is inadvertent.

Poetry, and process models inside this book are author's own creation,
unless wherever attributed otherwise. Please respect copyright and give due
acknowledgment if you use any.

The views and opinions expressed in this book are
the author's own and the facts are as reported by her
which have been verified to the extent possible,
and the publishers are not in any way liable for the same.

ISBN: 978-93-XXX-XX-X

First impression 2021

10 9 8 7 6 5 4 3 2 1

The moral right of the author has been asserted.

Printed at

for
my son
utkarsh

sometimes
a fragrant flower withers away before time
a profound poetry remains unfinished
a mellifluous song is left unsung
and a radiant evening star goes to sleep early

yet
the 'Presence' lives on
all light and grace

Contents

Foreword

Books on bereavement tend to fall into three genres: academic volumes that feature jargon-filled discourse for professionals; grief memoirs that pour forth the partially digested experience of the author in all of its painful particularity; and formulaic self-help guides that offer pop-psychological advice in a one-size-fits-all format. Remarkably and uniquely, Neena Verma's readable yet resonant volume avoids all of these extremes. Intimate but never indulgent, her well-crafted counsel draws on a deep well of world wisdom, blending eastern philosophical insights with western psychology.

The paradoxical legacy of loss and the reality of human resilience are brought to life with memorable vignettes of relatable people—including Neena herself—grieving and growing through myriad losses. In these pages the reader will encounter metaphorical maps of mourning and prompts for personal processing of the great range of losses that life includes, all illustrated by concrete narratives of tragedy and transformation on the part of protagonists with which readers will readily identify.

Drawing on the symbolism of the *mandala*, vivid imagery arising from encounters with the natural world in all of its mystery and majesty, and an engaging style of writing that is literary and alliterative without sacrificing personalism, Neena Verma provides the reader with verbal and visual orientation to the landscape of loss, and compassionate companionship for the journey. Without sugar-coating the bitter pill of life-vitiating bereavement, she gives voice to the experiences of loss that will be recognizable by any bereaved person who has felt alone and lost in the desert of despair. But crucially, she then, ushers readers into a deeper dialogue with grief that gently encourages them to pivot in the direction of affirming life, even or especially in the shadow of death.

From its nearly prayerful opening paragraph to the virtual prose poem of its closing coda, *Grief ... Growth ... Grace* offers to the broken heart, the sort of counsel that is both timely and timeless. In summary, I recommend this book to anyone seeking to find meaning in a life undone by loss, or looking for compassionate counsel for a friend, family member or client contending with the anguishing absence of someone they love. At the level of heart, mind and soul, this compact compendium delivers.

Robert A. Neimeyer, PhD
Originator of 'Grief Therapy as Meaning Reconstruction'
Author of *New Techniques of Grief Therapy:*
Bereavement and Beyond
Director, Portland Institute for Loss and Transition

In Appreciation and Gratitude

Utkarsh, my first-born, my soul, my anchor, my beloved child...
how can I ever put in words my love, appreciation and gratitude
for you. You amazed and inspired me with your selfless spirit,
quiet altruism, courage, abundant curiosity, unsatiating hunger
for learning, love for nature and more. You continue to light
my path, and evoke kindness, courage, strength and sense of
meaning in me. This book is inspired by you and dedicated to
you. Stay radiant my wondrous child, and spread your light in
the realm you have transcended to.

Pratyush, my second-born, my angel, my beloved child...
I can never thank you enough for guiding me on the path
of forgiveness. Our long jams leave me richer with many an
insight, several of which have found their way to this book. I
am in particular grateful for the rainbow-crow story that you
contributed. Your gentle and warm wisdom calms my grieving
heart and fills it with love. Stay abundant my beautiful child,
and share your strength with the world.

I am short on words to express my loving gratitude for
my husband. Many Thanks Yogesh Ji for all your support and
care, and for patiently putting up with my occasional absent-
mindedness as I worked on this book.

I am grateful to my clients and many wonderful people,
who have allowed me the privilege to join their grief journey,
witness and facilitate their inspiring growth, and learn from
their wisdom. Many thanks for sharing your stories, pain and
love with me, and in the process, helping me become a humbler
and more loving human being.

I offer a heart full of appreciation and gratitude to my mentors—Dr Robert (Bob) Neimeyer and Dr Ronald (Ron) Fry. A hearty thank you, dear Bob, for being the most amazing teacher, mentor, colleague and friend. Your signature creation of *'Grief Therapy as Meaning Reconstruction'* guides my work every step of the way. Many thanks for allowing me to share your life-story with the readers. It adds special meaning to chapter nine. A warm thank-you dear Ron for inspiring me to embody authentic appreciation, and teaching me the true essence of *'Appreciative Inquiry'*. Your presence in my life, and your influence on my work are deeply precious for me.

I thank all the pioneering experts whose inspiring body of work has deepened my understanding and practice, particularly—Carl Jung, Viktor Frankl, Carl Rogers, Robert Neimeyer, David Richo, Ronald Fry, David Cooperrider, Lawrence Calhoun, Richard Tedeschi and Joseph Campbell.

I am abundantly thankful to Ziya Us Salam for nudging me to write this book, and Jayaseelan Ganesan for his support and wise comments.

Importantly, this book wouldn't be possible if not for the trust and support of my publisher and editor. I am deeply grateful to Kapish Mehra, the Managing Director of RUPA Publications, for believing in the theme of this book, and taking the leap of faith. And I express warm gratitude to my editor Rudra Narayan Sharma, Deputy Managing Editor Nishtha Kapil, and the entire RUPA Publications team, especially Anjasi NN, Raj Kumari John and Amrita Chakravorty, for making this book happen.

My heart is filled with warmth and gratitude for you dear reader. Your interest in this book celebrates the sacred pilgrimage of 'Grief, Growth and Grace'.

Finally, I bow to the Supreme One. You are the design. You are the doer.

Invocation

Namaste.

As I invoke you to this book with the famous Indian greeting, I am deeply alive to its meaning—*the light in me honours the light in you.* The spirit of 'Namaste' is at the heart of this book. My loss affirms your loss. My pain holds your pain. My sorrow sobs with your sorrow. My fear sees your fear. My faith honours your faith. My strength reveres your strength. My growth avows your growth. My love celebrates your love. Together we invoke Mother Nature's grace, as we undertake the 'Grief ... Growth ... Grace' pilgrimage that this book takes us on.

Life, as we all learn at some point, is a symphony of sharp and melodious notes, a twilight of day and night, and a confluence of dark and light. These seemingly opposite phenomena do not just coexist—they complete each other. The same is true of 'Grief' and 'Growth'. The Sun shines on our sorrow and strength alike. Loss and bereavement are not the dead-ends of life. If anything, grief can and does spur growth. Unimaginably painful, indeed. Undoubtedly transformative, nonetheless. This book affirms the faith that 'loss and love', 'trauma and transformation', 'mourning and meaning', 'cry and celebration', and 'pain and purpose' are existential co-pilgrims. I have no way to prove this with reason or evidence. Those who take the 'Grief ... Growth ... Grace' pilgrimage somehow know this. Honouring the reality that pain has a higher calling, my metaphor for the grief and growth journey is 'pilgrimage'.

Invoking faith and compassionate courage, as we undertake the arduous grief journey, the sacred shrine of grace opens its door and blesses us with the nectar of growth.

This three-part book invites and shepherds you to discover each of the three entwined phenomena of grief, growth and grace. Part I affirms the inevitability of loss, death and grief in human life. The two chapters in this part lay the foundation by explaining the complex *Maze of Grief*. The first chapter talks of loss, death, bereavement and trauma, including bereavement during the COVID-19 pandemic era. Though I do briefly touch upon non-death losses as well, this book's purview is bereavement-caused grief. The second chapter explores the intricate phenomenon of grief. This chapter highlights the universality as well as individuality of grief, and explains that the grief journey is slow, chaotic and unique to each individual. There is nothing to be fought, fixed or treated. Grief is not a matter of getting-over. Instead, grief is to be transcended. Movement towards growth is both advisable as well as possible. Taking you through the labyrinth of grief, chapter two talks of the multi-layered effects of grief at physiological, mental, behavioural, relational and social levels, and offers a nuanced view of the entangled ball of emotions. As well as exploring the metaphors of grief, this chapter also clears the mist off various myths and misconceptions around grief. Finally, I emphasise that grief is a journey, of course with phases and aspects. But unlike some popular models, this journey is not stage-bound or sequential. To each, their own way of grieving and growing.

The seven chapters in Part II form the heart and the mind of this book, and unravel the *Mystique of Growth*. Chapter three introduces the 'Grief and Growth Eternal Spiral' and the 'GROWTH Mandala' models. Both are my humble creations. This chapter explores the phenomena of 'Post Traumatic Growth' (PTG) and 'growth wisdom', and outlines the six phases of the GROWTH Mandala model. This model is useful both for self-help, as well as professional application. Chapters four to nine offer a deep dive into each of the six phases, and accompany you on your GROWTH Mandala pilgrimage. I hope you find meaning and value in all the phases, particularly the ALIVE framework of 'grief affirmation' (chapter four), and the RISE framework of 'resilient adaptation' (chapter five) that I have created. While chapter six guides you to 'open up to the emergent' and create a new life-narrative that has space for both grief as well as growth, chapter seven devotes itself to facilitating your 'way to well-being'. Honouring the growth promise of the grief journey, chapters eight and nine usher you towards deeper 'transformation' and 'harmonious reemergence'. I must emphasise that all of these six phases are sovereign, and not necessarily sequential. Please feel free to start from whichever phase calls you the first or the strongest.

The book culminates with the soulful Part III of *Marvel of GRACE* that puts the spotlight on the almost invisible but essential aspect of 'grace'—the humble, gentle, calm and acceptant human spirit that helps us affirm the dark, and inspires us to seek the light. While chapter 10 shepherds you on the self-transcendent path of 'forgiveness', chapter 11 unfurls the five petals of the flower of GRACE—Gratitude, Reverence for life, Affirmation, Compassion and Essence of life.

The theme of this book is both timely and timeless. The high purpose is to bring to light the reality that grief is a normal human experience, and growth can be its natural companion. Grief is not sickness, neither physical nor mental. And it should not be made light of with clichés and sermons like 'time will heal', 'be strong', 'move on' and more. In fact, sometimes grief may have no closure. It comes to stay. And this too is fine, unless it has turned complicated, in which case, professional help should be sought. Most of us learn to affirm our grief, adapt resiliently to our loss-altered reality, and find a way to restore our well-being. Some of us grow even beyond, reaching a deeper level of transformation, and reemerging humbler, wiser and stronger. Each of us is naturally endowed to work through our grief and growth journey. A little help from well-meaning people, this or some other book, or any other resource can be of immense help. That said, if there is a convincing reason for therapeutic or medical intervention, the same should be sought.

This book has emerged from the collective wisdom of many people and resources—established research and theories, what I have learnt from my mentors, several experts' work, my professional practice and grief volunteering, and the lived experience of many bereaved people, including myself. I have made an earnest attempt to let my heart, mind and soul, touch and talk to yours. This book supports your healing, learning and growth in many ways. There are reflection prompts, therapeutic writing and expressive arts exercises, transformative tips and vignettes, including glimpses from my own story. All vignettes are abstracted accounts of real stories from my professional practice, personal connections or public domain. The names and identities have been changed to honour privacy, except in chapter nine where Robert (Bob) Neimeyer happily gave his consent, and in case of stories from the public domain. Each chapter ends by invoking you to create a **P**oetic **A**ffirmation to **T**ake **H**ome, where home means 'your inner abode'. It is not without meaning that this invocative exercise is called **PATH**. I encourage you to write/draw your reflections by hand in a dedicated journal or sketchbook, as you work through various exercises. Make it an embodied experience, not just digitally recorded content.

While this book intends to serve as a sincere self-help support to those in normal grief, I make no claim of this being a substitute for therapy or medical treatment. I encourage the reader to seek professional help, how ever needed, particularly in case of trauma, traumatic bereavement, complicated grief and medical issues.

This book invites you to come in faith, initiate your grief and growth pilgrimage, and experience the experience yourself. My noble intent is to support those in grief and trauma acknowledge, face and embrace their pain, and find a way to help themselves and others heal and grow. I hope and believe that fellow practitioners and helping professionals would also find this book of interest and value, especially my GROWTH Mandala model and various exercises.

There are various nudges I received from the universe to write this book. On the way, I met many people, forces and situations, that prodded me to deepen my grief and growth understanding, and offer it to the world as a self-help resource. I feel blessed to have received the call to write this book, and accepted the same with a sense of wonder and gratitude. It took longer than expected to complete this book, not without reason though. Each aspect and concept touched a chord within, and helped me grow beyond myself. Each phase of the GROWTH Mandala and GRACE pilgrimage that I take you through, first took me through myself.

Another pain embraced.
Another joy surfaced.
Another cry allowed.
Another celebration avowed.
Another wound healed.
Another wisdom revealed.
Another me discovered, all anew.

I hold the same invitation for you. With faith, care, thought, strength and love, I invoke you to your own healing capacity, growth wisdom and transformative potential.

We all know that a sunflower instinctively knows its source of life-giving energy, and follows it the whole day. Some of us believe that when it is dark and the Sun is hiding, the sunflowers turn to each other, and energize and strengthen each other. This faith is beautiful. I feel humble and grateful to have received the wisdom of 'Grief ... Growth ... Grace' that Mother Nature and many sunflower-like people have blessed me with. I lovingly share this gift of grace with you, and hope, you too would bloom like a sunflower in someone's life, and share your gifts with the world.

And so the pilgrimage begins.

Part 1

MAZE OF GRIEF

Life and Loss

'Death belongs to life as birth does.
The walk is in the raising of the foot,
as in the laying of it down.'

—Rabindranath Tagore

Anita was with one of her team members, Winston, whose mother had been on life-support after kidney failure, when she heard the unsettling news of her company's merger with a global MNC. After respectful closure of her conversation with Winston, as a well-meant supportive gesture, she leapt for the phone to gather more information. There was an imminent risk of many people, including herself and Winston, losing their jobs. She felt gripped by the fear of losing her job at a time when her family responsibilities were at their peak. On the drive back home, Winston remained on Anita's mind. He had, just hours ago, requested her for an expeditious release of an extraordinary advance to arrange for his mother's urgent kidney transplant. She felt both sad and concerned for him. She remained disturbed through the weekend, not knowing how to reach out and help him.

On a Monday, that felt more frightening than fresh, she had barely driven a few yards to her office, when she received a distress call for help from her cousin Maya whose daughter Sonya had met with an accident. Maya had already been in agony since her divorce and now she sounded traumatized because of Sonya's accident. By the time Anita reached the hospital, Sonya had been declared brain dead. Anita found her dear sister and childhood playmate, Maya, shattered to the core. She and her ex-husband John were being counselled by the hospital team to agree to donate Sonya's organs and corneas. Rising above their pain, the distraught parents decided to make a comprehensive donation of all the retrievable and usable parts of their darling daughter's body, which had turned lifeless, from being full of zest and liveliness, in a matter of a few hours. Just as Anita was trying to gain composure, her phone beeped with the message of Winston's mother's demise. She felt acute emotional and physical fatigue. Almost like Prince Siddhartha, she had witnessed suffering all around.

Loss was showing up with many faces—as Winston's grief and guilt over not being able to arrange for his mother's kidney transplant; as Maya's grief and anguish over such a colossal loss, further compounded by her ex-husband John's lament, holding Maya responsible for Sonya's accident; and Anita's own heightened anxiety over a highly probable loss of her job. She was overwhelmed with sadness, anguish, fear, anxiety, worry, despair and more. But the season of loss was still unfolding. An intense earthquake woke her up in the middle of the night. She learnt, shortly thereafter, that it had brought about massive devastation in her beloved hometown in the Himalayan state of Uttarakhand.

Anita sighed, 'Such is the fabric of life... loss woven intricately with every warp and weft.'

❖

LOSS
THE INTRICATE WARP & WEFT OF LIFE

'All the trees are losing their leaves,
and not one of them is worried.'

—Donald Miller

Loss is an integral part of life. It happens in many ways and at many levels—trauma, death or non-death, tangible or intangible, discernible or ambiguous, primary or secondary. It is inevitable that in our lifetime we will endure one or more losses, whether by bereavement or to non-death reasons such as sickness or loss of health, divorce, separation, loss of relationship, miscarriage, job-loss, disappearance, trauma, calamity and violence. While loss by death is permanent and irretrievable, some non-death losses are mild and passing. There is a possibility or hope of recovery and rebuilding. But non-death losses involving accident, violation, violence, disaster or a traumatic event can leave long-lasting, sometimes irreparable, damage and pain. The year 2020 unfolded with a uniquely devastating global calamity of the COVID-19 pandemic which has made, and continues to make, deep and lasting dents in the physiological, emotional and mental well-being of people at large.

One can still find a way to cope, adjust, restore and recover from tangible non-death losses. But some *intangible losses* like loss of trust, respect, love and security are hard to express, work around and resolve. Divorce and separation are often quite agonizing, but the pain which stems from marital infidelity and abuse can feel deeply distressing, even stigmatizing. No less complex is the pain of not being able to grieve over the *socially unspeakable loss*, such as the demise of a lover with whom the relationship had not been declared openly, solemnized or socially sanctioned; or *stigmatized loss*, such as demise by suicide or drug overdose. Loss of pregnancy and still-birth are often *socially negated losses*, even though women suffering such losses talk of feeling shattered.

When people go missing, it can create a sense of inexplicable *ambiguous loss*, leaving their loved ones in a complicated state, not knowing whether to wait and continue the search, or to accept and mourn the loss. An extreme example relates the disappearance of Malaysia Airlines Flight#370, that left the families and friends of those onboard the ill-fated flight, in an ongoing state of ambiguous grief. One may experience a similarly vague sense of loss and grief when a loved one is physically present but mentally and psychologically absent, such as in the case of medical conditions like Alzheimer's, dementia or comatose state.

In recent times, COVID-19 has emerged as a uniquely painful variant of *complex bereavement.* The dreaded virus is depriving people of parting contact with the deceased, and leaving the bereaved in a state of incomprehensible pain over not being able to see, touch, talk to, say a symbolic goodbye and have some sort of closure with their departing loved one. The guilt over not being able to offer a dignified funeral and perform parting rituals complicates the bereavement even more.

Not just limited to our personal life context, there is a range of *losses at the workplace* such as organization closure, lay-offs, missed opportunities, denied opportunities, workplace politics and injustice, manipulation, loss of identity and more. Very often the grief following such losses remains unacknowledged and unrecognized, and therefore unaddressed. Anita's grief over her imminent job loss, and the devastation caused by the earthquake in her hometown, is something that she finds difficult to make sense of herself, leave alone expecting others to understand.

There are several other *non-death losses* that can cause pain and grief to the affected person. Losing mobility or normal functioning capacity to prolonged or chronic sickness can be hard to come to terms with. Even diminished vitality and aging related health issues in the evening years of life, can feel daunting. Sometimes we can see a loss coming, such as in Winston's case. Witnessing her progressively degenerative medical condition, Winston experienced *anticipatory grief* even before his mother had passed away.

Separation, estrangement and heartbreak in relationship are losses that are hard to express in words, and even harder to understand. The emotional turmoil over the coming apart of their marriage, a life experience that is special and precious for most people, was painful enough for Maya and John. With the added pain of their only child's demise, they feel lonely and distant. Even in their shared loss, they feel deserted and lost in their brokenness.

In Eastern cultures, the institution of family continues to be more collectivist than individualistic, even though the onset of urban lifestyles has established the system of nuclear families. In such cultures, conflict, estrangement or relational split between siblings, or other family members can feel like a *loss of love and trust*. Similarly, loss of trust and respect between close friends can also feel quite hard to accept and resolve.

Sometimes a loss can trigger additional *secondary losses*, such as a widowed spouse feeling intense distress over loss of social and/or financial security, along with the grief of losing spouse who might have been the primary breadwinner. A similar secondary loss can be felt after divorce or separation like in case of Maya and John, who now have the added pain of their daughter's demise who died in a reckless road accident. Not all accidents or other such traumatic events, though, result in death. Sometimes people are left in permanent impairment or sustained medical conditions, thereby affecting their employment or livelihood prospects. The secondary loss of security and mobility in such events can cause as much, or sometimes even greater, grief than the trauma and impairment itself.

—◆—

TRAUMA

'There are wounds that never show on the body,
that are deeper and more hurtful than anything that bleeds.'

—Laurell K. Hamilton

We all experience or witness life events that are traumatic in nature and impact. Trauma often follows natural calamities and disasters that bring about massive devastation. On many occasions though, trauma is brought upon by humankind itself, through conflict, war, injustice, abuse, violation and violence. We are all vulnerable to trauma, which often springs up most unexpectedly in the unsuspecting alleys of life.

Sometimes, a traumatic event may not involve death, yet the severity of the trauma can feel acutely grievous, almost like bereavement. Common examples include devastating natural calamities or accidents that leave people with serious injuries, permanent immobility or in a non-functioning state, causing lasting trauma. Victims of crimes involving gruesome violence or violation are potentially high-risk cases for prolonged psychological trauma. People affected by such traumatic events sometimes develop **Post-traumatic Stress Disorder** (PTSD), showing symptoms like hyper-anxiety, depression, paranoia, intrusive rumination or other such conditions.

Irrespective of the gravity of the event, when trauma hits, it hits hard. There is shock, numbness, despair, crippling fear, pain, confusion, hopelessness, loss of faith and more. Some people have support systems. But some others find themselves broken and stranded on the highway of life. In the aftermath of the COVID-19 triggered lockdown, thousands of socio-economically disadvantaged people suffered acute trauma on account of having to walk hundreds of miles to their native places, running the risk of meeting with accidents while walking on highways. Some lost their lives and several lost their limbs.

One can experience a range of strong and intense emotions. It is normal to experience some amount of pain, anguish, grief, fear or any other psychological distress following a trauma, even when one is indirectly affected, like in the case of Anita. To an onlooker, the deceased was just her niece. But for Anita, given her close bond with Maya, Sonya's accident and death left her feeling badly traumatized. Though she quickly composed herself to offer needed support to Maya and John, she also felt an acute need herself for a shoulder to cry on.

Most people are able to deal with trauma with a fair measure of resilience—dusting off their brokenness, gathering themselves up, and getting on with life. But sometimes people get deeply shattered, develop PTSD and need clinical help. Their stress and pain notwithstanding, there is enough evidence to suggest that not only do some people emerge stronger, but they actually turn a traumatic event into a stimulus for growth.

—◆:◆—

DEATH
THE ETERNAL TRUTH OF LIFE

Death is the only abiding truth of life. Lord Krishna[1] avers in The Bhagavad Gita[2]—

जातस्य हि ध्रुवो मृत्युर्ध्रुवं
(jātasya hi dhruvo mṛityur dhruvaṁ)
Death is certain for one who has been born

—*Shrimad Bhagavad Gita* (Chapter 2, Verse 27)

Death is the first thing to become certain the very moment life is conceived, and it is the only reality that remains abidingly definite all through life. Benjamin Franklin famously quipped, 'nothing is more certain than death and taxes'. With due respect to the great leader, philosopher and scientist, I humbly seek to remove 'taxes' from the category, and insist that no other phenomenon is as absolutely true as death.

Life culminates in death.

The story goes that a young woman by the name of Krishna Gotami roamed about the city begging people for help to revive her infant child who had fallen sick and died. Most people ignored her, thinking that she had lost her mental balance in the wake of her grief. Some laughed at her delusionary state, but one wise person directed her to Gautama, the Buddha. She laid the lifeless body of her child at the feet of the Buddha who listened to her cry for help with immense compassion. He promised to help her

---

[1] The Hindu God-incarnate.
[2] The *Shrimad Bhagavad Gita* is the sacred Hindu scripture that chronicles Lord Krishna's sermon about dharma (duty), delivered on the battle-field of Kurukshetra.

if she could fetch a mustard seed from a house that had never known death. Desperate to bring her child back to life, she ran from one house to another but couldn't find one in the entire city that had never experienced a death. Realizing the message in the condition set by the Buddha, she understood the eternal truth of life—'impermanence indeed… in samsara[3] there is no house with no death and no suffering'—and accepted her loss.

It is easy to appreciate this story and understand its message if it concerns others, but extremely hard to bear the pain of death when it happens to oneself. I learnt the story of Krishna Gotami at a young age in my life. I must have recounted it in my heart and mind on several occasions, every time I encountered or witnessed a loss. But the story and its message became profound for me the day my young, healthy, bright son died suddenly of inexplicable cardiac arrest. Death felt like a cruel merciless joke of destiny, one that I didn't deserve. In a snapping moment, my life had come apart. In a flicker, I came face to face with the hard reality of life—its transience. And in a startling blow, I was exposed to the harsh reality of death—its finality. It took me a long time to appreciate and accept the essence of what Japanese writer Haruki Murakami said,

Death is not the opposite of life but an innate part of it.

Life, one ultimately learns, is nothing but an eternal cycle of birth, living and death. Nature is in a perpetual dance of impermanence. The Hindu faith represents this eternal truth as creation, sustenance and dissolution, as embodied and

---

[3]'Saṃsāra' is a Pali and Sanskrit language word that represents the 'material world'. In Hindu and Buddhist traditions it implies ceaseless cycle of existence, characterised by recurring circuitous run of birth, life, death, until one finds enlightenment and salvation.

symbolized by the Holy Trinity of Brahma, Vishnu and Shiva. All so good to say and hear, but so very hard to accept when death comes visiting you personally. And yet that is the irony that we must make peace with—what we love is what we must be prepared to lose. As Sogyal Rinpoche wisely advises, 'learning to live is learning to let go.'

BEREAVEMENT

'The death of a beloved is an amputation.'

—C.S. Lewis

Bereavement is the 'grievous loss' that ensues when we lose someone significant to death, someone whom we feel emotionally close and attached to. The word 'bereavement' evolved from old English word bereafian (be + reafian) or Middle English *bereven*, which meant to rob, deprive of, take away or tear away (Merriam Webster Dictionary). In a symbolic way, *loss by death* actually feels as if one has been torn apart, robbed and deprived.

In most cases, where death has happened under normal circumstances and/or was anticipated because of age or medical state, people find it less painful to come to terms with their loss, healthily integrate it and gain a sense of restoration. But when death is sudden, untimely or unexpected, bereavement can have complicated manifestations. Same is true in case of death by trauma, crime, violence or under suspicious circumstances. Bereavement researcher, Margaret Stroube, explains the relationship between trauma and bereavement.

Bereavement without trauma—A large percentage of death experiences are without any trauma symptoms, because most commonly the death is natural, timely, expected, and under normal circumstances. Though people do take time to adapt and restore, it is free of any trauma manifestations.

Traumatic bereavement—Sometimes the experience of death creates trauma. Bereavement can expectedly turn traumatic when something about death itself is traumatizing, such as in the case of death by violence, crime, accident or devastating natural calamity; and a sudden, unexpected or untimely death. In some other situations, the bereaved may feel traumatized by the death experience because of the relationship with the deceased. It could be either too close, important or special, leaving the bereaved feeling emotionally shattered. Or the bereaved might have had a heavily dependent relationship with the deceased, and feels abandoned, insecure and anxious having to face life alone post bereavement. In some less-common cases, it could be that the relationship with the deceased was close but conflicted. With much left unfinished, the bereaved may have intrusive ruminative feelings and thoughts, going through pangs of guilt, regret, sometimes even shame. In some extreme situations, the bereaved may experience bitterness towards deceased if there is a sense of victimization or violation suffered at the hands of the deceased. Trauma of bereavement could feel even worse when the death is without an apparent sign or clear reason, leaving things unanswered. Not that pain and grief become any less, but knowing what happened helps one accept the loss and work towards resolution.

Perhaps one of the hardest to talk about is the loss of a child. It is not without reason that such a traumatic loss is called the **ultimate bereavement**. No parent can ever be strong enough to contemplate the thought of outliving their child. It is just not in sync with the natural order of life, and the norm of parenthood that entrusts the parents with the responsibility to raise, care for and protect their children. The pain of performing a child's funeral is the worst burden to carry for parents in any culture or part of the world. It can leave the bereaved parents in acute prolonged grief.

'When parents die, they leave behind legacy.
When children die, they leave behind shattered dreams,
which pierce your whole "being" like sharp pieces of broken glass.'

—Neena Verma

Even in the impoverished parts of the world where poverty and poor health conditions cause high mortality for children, it is very hard to accept the loss of a child. In more privileged and medically endowed parts of the world, it can be seen as very wrong to lose a child. A child's death at any age is untimely and unacceptable to parents. Contrary to popular perception, the trauma can be even more pronounced, and pain even more persistent in case of the death of an adult child with whom a significant part of life has been lived and precious dreams nurtured.

MY STORY

My son had collapsed at home without an explicable medical reason. My husband who was home at that time noticed after some time had lapsed. By the time he rushed our son to the nearest hospital, which, incidentally, is also a reputed heart institute, critical time was lost. Nothing that the medics did could retrieve our beloved son. We, the distraught parents, were handed complex medical nomenclature hinting at an undetected cardiac condition, which could neither calm our agonized minds nor soothe our broken hearts. To us, the vulnerable family, all of this felt like a spooky drama that unfolded without an alert, except that the horror had been played on us. Months later I met the attending doctors, and some other specialists, yearning to know why my healthy son had cardiac arrest at the young and unlikely age of 22 years and three months. All in vain.

'What happened?'—the brutal question belonged to us and us alone, but we had to endure it again and again from many people, whether out of genuine concern or unhealthy curiosity.

Much water has flown under the bridge since 24th of September, 2014. With faith, compassion, gratitude, courage, strength and love, we have chosen to reconstruct life with meaning. My younger son and I are taking forward my transcended elder son's mission for inclusive learning, by serving marginalized children with our independent library movement. Our resilient adaptation and meaningful reemergence notwithstanding, the wound still feels raw and continues to ache. Even as desperate yearning has slowly made way for harmonious resurrection of my son's 'Presence' in spirit, the brutal 'What happened? And why?' still occasionally gnaws at me.

Whatever be the age of the child, *ultimate bereavement* is extremely difficult to bear. This pain feels no less in case of un-born child. Grief arising from loss of pregnancy and still-birth often goes unacknowledged, since these losses are mostly regarded as physiological events. 'Grief Therapy as Meaning Reconstruction' creator, Dr Robert Neimeyer, shares a moving story of a young mother who delivered a stillborn baby at seven months gestation. Shattered by her neonatal loss that made no sense, she found help in constructivist therapy. She could eventually affirm her child as having *'lived in my womb'* and poignantly reframed her loss by calling the child *'born still'* rather than stillborn. This is not just wordsmithing. An in-depth study of the case reveals the severity of grief that the woman experienced. But, as is often the case with women suffering loss of pregnancy and still-birth, she found no space or support to honour, express and process her grief. Agreed, it may not be appropriate to attribute her recovery entirely to the constructivist therapy support she got. But it can surely be said with some confidence, that there was a likelihood of her grief turning complicated in the absence of therapeutic support. I know this first hand, having miscarried thrice.

Pause and Ponder-1

In most cases, it is extremely painful to come to terms with the death of a loved one. But in some cases, the agony of acceptance is particularly pronounced. Think of a loss by death (your own loss or someone else's that you were a close witness to) that was exceptionally hard to accept. Recall your/their journey of acceptance.

- What was peculiar about this loss that made it harder than usual to accept?
- How did you/them eventually make peace with the reality, and accept the loss?
- What facilitative resources or processes helped?

If you were to guide/help someone through their acceptance journey—what stories, poetry, metaphors, literature, art or any other medium would you use? To what effect? And how?

—◆:◆—

BEREAVEMENT DURING PANDEMIC

Bereavement during pandemic, whether by COVID-19 or by any other manner of death, is causing a peculiar form of grief unlike any that we know. People who have been infected by the corona virus have to endure unclear prognosis. They suffer chronic physiological problems and immense psychological distress, not just on account of anxiety about their medical state, but equally and in some cases more so because of the punishing effects of isolation and loss of social connect. Being a corona survivor with a near-death experience, I learnt that however objective and resilient one may try to stay, the psyche tends to unconsciously fall prey to fear, worry, and mental and emotional stress. It is still worth enduring with the hope of recovery and reunion with family. But there is enough evidence to suggest that even after recovery, one is prone to secondary medical complications. Not to forget the stigma, that those infected and their families suffer.

The thick blanket of fear and anxiety also extends to people suffering from non-COVID medical conditions. Many people are avoiding visit to a medical facility for fear of catching infection. Even for those who are seeking help, the overwhelming pressure on medical systems is hampering due attention to non-COVID patients, many of whom are developing otherwise avoidable complications, leading to more deaths than should have been in ordinary circumstances.

In the harsh eventuality of a loved one losing the battle of life to COVID-19, the bereaved people are found to be experiencing a more complex kind of grief. Not just the pain of loss, but there is also guilt on account of not being able to see, meet and bid adieu to their loved one. Whether on account of COVID-19 or otherwise, the bereavement is turning traumatic in many cases. Sometimes, it is because of not being able to secure required and timely medical support. But mostly it is because of being deprived of a final tender touch, and not being able to offer a dignified farewell to the loved one. The funerals are without proper rites and rituals, and ruthlessly destitute. It is extremely disturbing to witness the horrifying visuals of bereaved people standing in stigmatized isolation, distanced from the mortal remains of their loved one. In many cases, they are not even able to see their loved one, leave alone giving them the ceremonial holy bath. Honouring their noble duty, the thinly staffed funeral workers are overwhelmed with the physical risk and the emotional torment, cremating or burying unknown bodies by the dozens each day.

I have been grief volunteering during this pandemic. The complex grief of the bereaved is further compounded by the intense psychological torment because of isolative disconnect with their loved ones in their last moments, and the surreal funerals devoid of a dignified goodbye. It was a revelation to know the indirect and secondary effects of COVID-19 deaths and cremations, when a journalist friend reached out for help. Having covered several stories of COVID and non-COVID deaths during the pandemic, he needed therapeutic support. He took three weeks off to recuperate from acute psychological distress, and regain some coherence and strength before being able to return to work.

Pause and Ponder-2

Do you know anyone who has suffered bereavement (whether by COVID or non-COVID death) during the pandemic? This could be anyone you directly or indirectly know, even yourself.

- Is there something peculiar about this loss?
- How does it feel to live with loss during the pandemic?
- Do you see a likelihood of this grief turning chronic?

- Traversing this journey of grief—what stories, poetry, metaphors, philosophy, or any other resources or process do you find helpful?

'Grief is a most peculiar thing.
It is like a window that will simply open of its own accord.
But it opens a little less each time;
and one day we wonder what has become of it.'

—Arthur Golden

At some point in life, we all have to navigate the maze of grief triggered by loss, trauma or bereavement. Grief can feel dense even when death is expected, timely and under normal circumstances. But it is more likely to turn complicated in case of traumatic bereavement; sudden, untimely and unexpected loss; ultimate bereavement on account of loss of a child; socially negated, unspeakable or stigmatized losses; and bereavement during the pandemic. Grief under such circumstances can turn complex—acute and persistent over a prolonged period of time.

In the following chapter, we will talk about the many faces of grief, the myths and misconceptions associated with grief, metaphors of grief that fill bereaved people's consciousness, the labyrinth of grief reactions that we have to navigate, and the entangled ball of difficult emotions that we must work with. Before that, here is an invitation to create a poetic affirmation of your own.

PATH 1

Poetic Affirmation to Take Home

'Love is the song of life.
And grief, the cry of love.'

—Neena Verma

Celebrate the song called life.
Affirm the cry called grief.

Grief ... The Cry of Love

'Grief, like love, is the song of the soul.
Not all songs bring joy though.
Some are songs of cry.
Cry your loss.
Celebrate your love.'

—Neena Verma

Returning to college after missing almost an entire term, Tanya looked distraught and disheveled—a far cry from the always smiling, and well-turned-out person that her friends knew her to be. They were expecting her to be sad, having lost her mother three months ago to a degenerative neurological condition. But, no one expected to find her so distraught and self-isolative. Even after a fortnight of rejoining college, she was mostly silent, and distant.

Tanya's mother had been the family's anchor, even in her sickness. Hiding her own pain behind a mask of poise and strength, she continued to attend to her responsibilities towards a large family. More importantly, she continued to shower Tanya and her sister Tisha with abundant love and care, sheltering them from the pain of a complex dysfunctional family. But she was gone now.

Even in their shared loss, the response of Tanya's younger sister, Tisha, was radically different from hers.

Tisha felt relief for their mother, whose agonizing pain and progressively debilitating condition were almost reducing her to a vegetative state. Having expended all means and ways of treatment, they knew that death was imminent for their mother, and the medical treatment was only making brief uncertain extensions in her time. Her sadness, pain and grief notwithstanding, on another plane, Tisha felt gratitude that they could bring their mother home, just in time before she breathed her last in her own bed, just the way she wanted.

In contrast, Tanya felt let down by doctors and medical technology. She was upset with their father who continued to remain private and detached as ever. Neither did he express his feelings, nor did he make himself available for the emotional needs of his daughters. Even with their father around, Tanya felt orphaned and abandoned. She felt as if a massive earthquake had ripped apart their life and home.

Her faith shaken; Tanya secretly felt angry at God. Overwhelmed by a heavy and knotted flock of emotions, she felt struck, anguished, fearful, hapless, anxious and guilty on one hand, and responsible for her sister's well-being on the other. Unable to handle her grief and her responsibilities at the same time, she slowly slipped into a depressive state. With each passing moment her grief felt denser than before, and spiraled inwards.

Yet, even while she felt swamped by her emotions, she intuitively knew that there must be a light somewhere on the other side of the dark tunnel of her grief and pain.

—◆—

Is there a definite way to describe and understand the phenomenon of grief that would represent a universal meaning, and speak to us all! Hard. Very hard.

Legendary psychologist, Gordon Allport, asserted that human beings are as unique as they are universal. Adapting Allport's famous quote to the realm of grief, the renowned grief expert William Worden avers—

'Each person's grief is *like all other* people's grief;
Each person's grief is *like some other* people's grief; and
Each person's grief is *like no other* people's grief.'

The experience of grief is uniquely personal, as is amply clear from the contrasting stories of Tanya and Tisha despite their shared loss. Yet, it is both possible and desirable to form a basic understanding of the phenomenon that can guide us in most cases, if not all.

—◆—

GRIEF—THE UNWELCOME GUEST

Simply put, grief is a natural and normal response to loss, bereavement or trauma. Except that it isn't simple at all. It entangles one in a complex maze of feelings. There is shock, sadness, pain, anger, yearning, fear, anxiety, guilt, loneliness, fatigue and more. There is no escape from the intensely painful effects of grief. Those in grief exhibit a range of states and behaviours—daze, panic, despair, paranoia, depression, sickness, absentmindedness, insomnia, silence, hysterical crying, social withdrawal, sometimes even delusion, and more. As I shared in my grief memoir, *A Mother's Cry .. A Mother's Celebration*—

'Sometimes there is a deadening silence,
and sometimes there is a deafening wail.'

It can behave like a wayward storm that breaks-in anytime. For Tanya, her grief was one such devastating storm that had hit her like a hapless wave, thrown and beaten on the rocks. However hard she tried; she couldn't see through the bottomless pit of her emotions. Her grief came layered with guilt, anger, fear and anxiety. She felt guilt over what she thought was her failure to save her mother from dying. She was angry with her father for his disengaged attitude. She felt fearful and anxious for her sister and herself. Unable to get a sense of her feelings, she didn't know what to tell others, and thus, isolated herself. And the more she did so, the more she felt abandoned, uprooted and lonely.

Grief can also feel like the gentle shepherd who guides the sheep with care and wisdom, through slopes, cliffs, passages, and meadows, safely bringing them back home. For Tisha, her grief became her guide. She noticed her mother's pain. As much as her loss haunted her, she also felt some sort of relief and gratitude that death brought an end to her mother's pain. She appreciated the efforts of the medical team. She loved her sister Tanya for the sensitivity and responsibility with which she handled things at hospital and home. She even respected her father's way of being and acting the way he did. As young as she was, she understood the transient nature of life, accepted her loss, and grew more appreciative of life.

Grief is a sovereign phenomenon. It happens of its own will, pace and rhythm, sometimes appearing intrusively, sometimes remaining hidden in layers beneath other emotions, and suddenly surfacing, all blown up. Its journey is slow, gradual and unique to each individual. Grief is not a sickness or a disorder. There is nothing to be fought, fixed or treated. It has no final destination, and no predictable course. Grief charts and directs its journey itself. Grieving, in contrast, can be a conscious process. Though hard, it is very much possible to choice-fully direct our grief journey with self-awareness and/ or support from others. When it is contemplated by choice, and mindfully lived with faith, compassion, courage, strength and wisdom—grieving can be an immensely transformative experience.

It is important to understand the difference between grieving and mourning. *Grieving* is an internal and personal process. We experience grief within, and mostly deal with it in our inner world. *Mourning* in contrast, is a social and external process. Most cultures and societies have rituals and social ceremonies to mourn the loss in a shared way. Mourning has an important purpose. When we receive genuine compassion, care and support from others, our sadness, pain and fear get lightened to some extent. That said, grief remains a personal journey. Each of us walks it our own way.

Grief is a universal phenomenon across all cultures, as old and as true as human history. Surely, all communities and faiths must be having their own mourning practices. The Sikh community has a pragmatic and restorative approach to mourning that intends to help the bereaved people and families restore and return to the routines of life, at least in a basic way. Before returning home from the crematorium, the bereaved family is first taken to the Gurudwara (Guru's abode—the Sikh place of worship) where they offer ardas (the Sikh way of praying) and partake of kadha-prasad (the Sikh holy food offering). The purpose is to ensure that the family begins eating before the social mourners leave. As is normal and expected, once the social buzz fades away, the bereaved generally tend to miss on food and other routine bodily needs. Partaking of kadha-prasad before returning home is an existential reminder to the bereaved that life must go on, at least in a basic sense. Unlike Hindu and Jain communities that generally hold the prayer meeting on the fourth, tenth, thirteenth or seventeenth day of the death, Sikhs typically organize theirs on the Sunday following the death. The guiding belief once again is that life must go on. And it is assumed that on a Sunday, most of the social mourners' normal routine wouldn't be disturbed. The message is clear—acknowledge death, accept loss, mourn, grieve, and return to life with poise and strength.

In some sense, grief plays a facilitative function for our healthy adaptation and regeneration. It serves the noble mission of helping the griever accept, mourn and integrate the loss, restore and regenerate, without denying, hiding, suppressing or getting drowned in the crushing effects of loss. If grief hits, it also heralds growth. If it is the bearer of pain, it is also the harbinger of meaning and purpose. If it traumatises, it also transforms at psychological, behavioural, existential and spiritual levels.

—◆:◆—

MANY FACES OF GRIEF

Loss and bereavement are never easy to live with. Grief is essentially a painful experience. That said, if grief is a natural fall-out of loss and bereavement, so is the innate human resilience and sense of meaning. Most people are able to navigate grief without professional help—reconciling their loss, integrating their grief and adapting to their loss-altered life. Not so when the bereavement is complicated or traumatic, which I talked about in the previous chapter. Even in normal, timely or expected loss, the bereaved can experience acute grief. But in case of bereavement by accident, sudden, untimely or unexpected loss, death of a child, traumatic death by violence, crime or in an unnatural way—there is a much stronger likelihood of the bereaved slipping into what is known as *complicated grief*—chronic and persisting over a long period of time.

There is a chance of *ambiguous grief* arising when the loss is on account of someone gone missing. It happens with people whose family members get lost, or desert the family and go untraceable, or disappear during a war or socio-communal violence. I hope you remember from chapter one the case of ill-fated Malaysian Airline flight MH-370 that went missing. The search is inconclusive. In cases like these, the family members are forever left to wonder if and when should they stop waiting, even as, in some sense, they might have begun grieving. While one part of the griever may be holding on to hope since there is no sight of mortal remains, another part may want to bring the wait to a closure.

Another form of grief called *anticipatory grief* can arise while tending to a terminally-ill loved one. A mishmash of emotions such as fear, sorrow, despair and guilt, is common in such a case. But what may go completely unnoticed or unacknowledged are the caregivers' physical and compassion fatigue, sometimes even irritation. It is possible that the caregivers may even secretly hope or wish for their loved one's passing, either because they can't stand the sight of their pain and debilitating condition, or because they are feeling spent in various ways. If you have not yet watched, I would encourage you to watch the Hindi movie *Waiting*. It is a classic case of anticipatory grief which is enmeshed with several difficult emotions.

The wait in both ambiguous and anticipatory forms of grief, are uniquely painful and carry a chance of getting complicated.

❧

'One is in "waiting", whether or not it is over.
Grief comes to stay, never up for closure.
There is no escape, one is always yearning.
Grief envelops those left behind in mourning.
Struck with pain, writhing deep in heart.
Let go! Yes! But how to make a new start.
One has to live in the dark blind blackhole.
Until light would grace, rekindling the "whole"'

—Neena Verma

❧

Sometimes socially-negated loss (miscarriage, still-birth), stigmatized loss (suicide, death by drug overdose) or socially-unspeakable loss (demise of someone with whom the mourner had a secret or socially-unsanctioned relationship) can trigger what the grief pioneer Dr Kenneth Doka conceptualized as *disenfranchised grief.* In such circumstances, the bereaved or mourners do not get social support or sanction to grieve their loss. They feel forced to shut their grief within, which can prolong and solidify their grief, triggering various psychological and physiological complications.

◆

METAPHORS OF GRIEF

Grief has different symbolic and figurative meanings for different people. To each, their own unique metaphor of grief. Jandy Nelson has put it so beautifully—

> Grief is a house where the chairs have forgotten how to hold us, the mirrors how to reflect us, the walls how to contain us. Grief is a house where the doors no longer let you in or out.

For quite some time I felt as if I was being pulled into a *blackhole* from where I would never return. I had almost lost all sense of my surroundings. All that I saw and felt was darkness outside and within that seemed to suck my whole being deeper and deeper. On some other occasions, I felt swept away by a *tsunami* of multiple complex emotions. Slowly and gradually, witnessing my grief with affirmative eyes and an open quiet heart, I could see myself reaching a *new galaxy* on the other side of the blackhole of my grief. A time came, when with a rekindled '*will to live*', I felt the desire to resurrect my devastated self, just as people affected by a real tsunami, rise from their mourning and rebuild their disappeared homes and habitats.

Many people whose grief and growth journey I facilitate, talk of grief in similar metaphorical ways. One widowed woman I counselled, likened her grief to a *desert sand-dune*, never-ending and constantly changing form and shape. The more she walked with fortitude, the more she felt stuck and covered in the piercing sand of her grief. She felt dry and parched within, and unrecognizable outside. Over time, with counselling and self-work, she reframed her internal talk, and created a new metaphor for her unfolding growth, calling it an *oasis-in-the-desert*.

Recall the story from the start of this chapter. For Tanya, her mother's death felt like an *earthquake* that had thrown her life upside down. Even though physically intact, her home looked wrecked to her. She felt the earth beneath her feet had cracked open. Her secure base had been lost, and so was her self-belief. Over time, after working with an art-therapist, she found a way to express her feelings. Expressive arts and writing helped her construct new metaphors for life. The heat of her pain notwithstanding, she started to find a way to transform this heat into something therapeutic. She started to feel as if her grief was a *hot water spring* that heals, rather than burns.

A particularly painful story of acute complicated grief belongs to parents who lost all of their three children to a rare blood disorder. A medico social worker had contacted me for contribution towards the medical treatment of their youngest daughter. The next day, when I called her to inform that I and a couple of my friends had transferred money, she informed me of the child having passed away the previous night, even as she was being prepared for her next chemotherapy. I remained disturbed and in sorrow for several days. There was no way I could even begin to imagine the pain of these thrice bereaved parents. A few weeks later, I accompanied the medico social worker to meet the parents who were expectedly buried under heaps of shock, anger, pain, guilt, fear and grief. The father remained mostly silent. But beneath his seemingly stoic appearance, his dazed eyes conveyed his pain. Muttering incoherently, he lamented about being 'totally robbed' by the 'heartless thief called God'. The mother, on the other hand, cried hysterically. She looked completely overcome by her pain and sorrow. Her will to live severely shaken, she didn't seem willing to get out of what she called the *quicksand* of her grief and pain. Grief for them has come to stay, as it does with many bereaved people, mostly so with bereaved parents. Yet, they are carrying their grief with fortitude and grace, having dedicated their life to supporting parents of children with rare blood disorders. They call life a game of *snakes-and-snakes* and *no-ladder-except-love*. The calm courage and warm wisdom with which they carry on living, loving and serving is a rare virtue.

Call it by any name—a blackhole, a tsunami, a desert sand-dune, an earthquake, a hurricane, a swamp, a whirlpool, a cyclone, a roller-coaster, a web, a dark wood, a dingy cave, a gorge or whatever else—grief is a labyrinth that we all must walk through.

Pause and Ponder-1

Recall a personal loss or someone else's that you closely know and understand—

- What metaphor did grief represent for you (or the person in your mind)?
- What did this metaphor say of the nature and intensity of your (or the person you are thinking of) grief?
- What impact did this metaphor create on your/their ability to accept your/their loss and navigate through the grief?
- Looking back, would you/they like to reframe your/ their grief? Why? How?

MYTHS AND MISCONCEPTIONS

The phenomenon of grief is shrouded in many myths and misconceptions. Perhaps one of the most common misconception is that 'time heals'. Well, not quite. Time doesn't heal. We heal over time, albeit not as per a set timetable. In fact, in some cases, grief may become more chronic over time. And in some other cases, time just stands still. We often hear people say to the bereaved—'just give it time'. Of course, we should—but not with a fixed expectation. In grief there is *no predictable timeline or trajectory*.

A common misconception about a normative trajectory emanates from a flawed understanding of the famous Elizabeth

Kubler-Ross stage model, which suggests that those dying go through the five stages of denial, anger, bargaining, depression and acceptance in a linear order. While her model contributed uniquely to raising the understanding of the process of dying and the various stages that dying people go through, its relevance in the context of grief has been blown out of proportion. Her model is specifically in the context of those dying, not post-loss grief. While the experiences associated with her five stages are normal in the course of grief journey, there is nothing universally fixed or linear about them. Grief can be random, clumsy, even messy. It has no clear timeline or end-point. There is no one definite sequence or process that would work for all. As C.S. Lewis poignantly wonders,

> For in grief nothing 'stays put'. One keeps on emerging
> from a phase, but it always recurs. Round and round.
> Everything repeats. Am I going in circles, or dare I hope
> I am on a spiral? But if a spiral, am I going up or down
> it? How often—will it be for always?

More important is that we embrace the unfolding feelings and allow them their due time and space in life. What we suppress, hide or neglect does not go anywhere. It continues to lurk and shows up most unexpectedly, engulfing us like a swarm of stinging bees. As David Richo wisely avers, 'Grief unravels and returns in an ever-surprising and often distressing variety of feelings and forms'. We need to allow our feelings due acknowledgment and expression, even if quietly within ourselves. This expression doesn't need to be externally verbalised. Like Tanya, who found a healthy release of her feelings in expressive arts, we can express our feelings through a variety of media. Instead of keeping a vigil on time and waiting for it to make things easier for her, Tanya sought solace and healthy resolution in arts. Though she is an engineer by education and vocation, now, she regularly volunteers to help terminally ill patients and their caregivers heal their pain through expressive arts.

Another common misconception is that all bereaved people would necessarily experience and exhibit distress and depression. This is not universally true. People experience grief in varying intensity. Different people have different ways of engaging with and resolving their grief. In most cases where death is normal, timely or expected, it isn't too hard to accept the loss. The feelings of grief are naturally less intense when the deceased have lived a long, full and generally happy life. In many cases, even if grief takes up a significant space, it doesn't always drown the bereaved. Grief is indeed likely to be chronic and prolonged in the event of untimely, unexpected, traumatic, violent or not-natural death. In such cases, the bereaved are likely to experience much more intense and intrusive feelings. Distress and depression are normal and to be expected in such cases, but not in all cases. Let us remember, grief is not sickness. It is not a mental health condition either. True that it can trigger depression in some odd cases, but mostly it is just grief, and needs no fixing or cure.

It is important to highlight that there is *no one correct way to grieve.* There is no one single grief pathway that all of us can take. To each their own. The intensity of distress and other emotions depends on various factors, one of which is the psychological make-up of the bereaved. Some people are naturally more resilient. People who tend to focus more on the present and the future than on the past, are less likely to experience acute distress for long. For some practical grievers, accepting the loss and reconciling with reality may be less of a struggle. But not necessarily always so.

Sometimes it is assumed that keeping busy would help one deal with grief in a better way, as if grief is something to be dealt with. The underlying assumption here is that grief can be worked-out. Not really. Grief is *not a task or problem* to be dealt with. It is to be allowed its due course, which differs from person to person. It is true that getting busy with work or pursuing something else can provide good solace and diversion, but only for some time. We can't forever go on distracting ourselves away from grief by engaging in outwardly activities. Ignoring the inner churn is a form of escapism which may provide temporary relief but will not provide abiding solace.

Often bereaved people are advised by others to 'move on'. Of course, movement in life is both advisable as well as possible, especially if it is in the direction of growth. That said, the truth is that there is *no moving on* by forcefully closing the grief. Sometimes, grief may have *no full closure*, especially in ambiguous, traumatic or unnatural losses, or in case of loss of a child. And it is okay if grief has not found a closure, as long as it has not turned acute or complicated, in which case therapeutic help should be sought. My younger son, Pratyush, emphasized wisely while speaking at an international conference as a not-yet-19 young and non-expert presenter, 'Grief is to be transcended, not gotten-over'.

Finally, a strange misconception is that if a bereaved person avoids using the word 'death', it means denial or incoherence. It is unwise to apply such thumb rules. There is nothing wrong with gentler references like 'passed on', 'left the mortal world' or 'left for eternal journey'. I myself say—'my transcended son'—whenever I talk of him. We should be empathetic in understanding and respecting bereaved people's choice of expression, unless there is convincing reason to doubt their mental health.

◆◆◆

LABYRINTH OF GRIEF

Grief is much more than experiencing and expressing emotions. It has manifestations at physiological, mental, emotional, behavioural, spiritual, relational and social levels.

PHYSIOLOGICAL REACTIONS

While the effects of grief at heart and mind levels are widely known, its severe impact on the body is not as commonly recognized. The truth is that grief affects the body as harshly or sometimes even more than it affects the heart and mind. Vague aches, low-grade fever, nausea, fatigue, upset stomach, hypertension, loss of appetite and sleep disorders are common physiological upshots of grief. But there can be more severe manifestations like diabetes, cardiac stress, reduced brain functioning or even organ malfunctioning.

MY STORY
How grief hit my body

Within three months of my son's demise, I had lost a lot of weight and much of my hair, so much so that a neighbour gently expressed concern over my 'ghostly appearance'. I was so completely absorbed with my grief that neither his positive intent, nor his somewhat negative and extreme description (ghostly appearance) registered with me.

Though I gradually regained some weight and hair, some other medical complications showed up without apparent signs. I had a troubling and painful menopausal phase, combined with sudden development of full-blown type two diabetes. I was put on a treatment protocol meant for high-risk diabetes, but my body rejected such heavy medication, which in turn triggered bouts of hypoglycemia (low blood sugar count) one of which even turned serious. My eyesight deteriorated and I became iron deficient.

Nothing of my professional background could keep me from being swamped by my grief. Attending as usual to my life responsibilities, I outwardly appeared functional. But beneath the mask of strength, my body, mind and heart protested. My grief demanded to be acknowledged, experienced, expressed and addressed. And in the absence thereof, my body took the brunt.

As if my grief was not trying enough, an attack by some unknown persons, seemingly with an intent to rob, left me with an extremely painful neurological injury, the traumatic upshot of which got aggravated because of my already grievous heart and mind. Thankfully, the resultant medical issue has been managed very well by my neurologist, who acknowledges the positive impact of my affirmative life-view in helping me cope and recover.

I once heard a mourner complain of finding even his most favourite food tasteless, and his most loved flower fragrance-less. It is not uncommon for some people to find their sensory experiences go bland. Some people tend to develop hyper-sensitivity to light or sound. I myself did. Sometimes, without a clear reason, the throat may feel choked, the nasal tract congested and breathing rendered short, rapid, shallow or erratic in some other way. Some people even develop endocrinological issues. Occasionally, a peculiar grief spasm may surge suddenly and intensely, triggering momentary, or in rare cases, even longer seizures. While women are commonly prone to menstrual irregularities and/or reproductive malfunctioning, men also tend to develop some problems.

There is enough research evidence to suggest that what we know as broken-heart syndrome is real. A counselee, I worked with, had sustained three major losses at a young age—her father and both her grandparents whom she was quite attached to, all within two years. There were secondary losses by way of financial, emotional and social insecurities. The circumstances of her life required her to dedicate her youth and subsequent life to support her family, that comprised her homemaker mother and two younger siblings. For 23 long years, since her losses, she had inexplicable cardiac arrhythmia (irregular heartbeat). Now that she has harmoniously integrated her grief and begun to reconstruct her life with meaning, her cardiac arrhythmia and a couple of other bodily issues have begun to settle. I would hesitate to attribute this entirely to grief therapy, but the correlation is noteworthy.

The point of explaining possible physiological reactions to grief is not to scare you, but to sensitize you about the same so you can help the bereaved people in your personal and social circles, and god forbid yourself, if and when grief comes calling, which it does at some point in life.

MENTAL REACTIONS

It is common for bereaved people to feel their minds go numb, especially in the immediate aftermath of loss. The dazed brain takes time to process the sudden upsurge of an array of physiological and emotional reactions. The reptilian (primitive) brain goes hyper-alert, causing the bereaved to react with default primal instincts of fight (deny, disbelieve, question, feel anger, lament, and more), flight (hide away from the reality, feel fearful or insecure, and more) or freeze (go numb). The thinking and problem-solving parts of the brain, in contrast, seem to go into hibernation. The mental functioning, as a result, gets affected, and in some cases, seriously or even permanently so. But milder effects are quite common. I used to be regarded highly for my mental math ability. Since my loss, I sometimes feel the need to use the phone-calculator. Perhaps it is not odd in general. It certainly is, given my history. Over time, my mental math ability has got restored to a good extent. But it is still far from what it used to be originally.

Many people complain of their memory acting wobbly. Sometimes they need the same information repeated several times, and still miss out on it. Some people tend to lose their way to the places (including their homes) that they have been habituated to visit. While the old memories come gushing, the new information doesn't register.

Mental fuzziness, confusion, distraction and absent-mindedness is common. Bereaved people tend to remain preoccupied within. Their ability to process and think gets affected in varying degrees. Sometimes they even miss out on things, or find themselves stuck in the middle of things, wondering what they were up to.

It isn't surprising for some people to have their self-confidence shaken. Before my loss, I was considered to be the best driver in my family. In fact, both my children looked up to me more than their father, for driving proficiency. But in the aftermath of my loss, I suddenly started to feel frightened of traffic on the roads. The attack by unknown persons, that I mentioned previously, only worsened my confidence. I felt an overall sense of doing poorly in everything, be it cooking, family responsibilities, household chores, professional matters or driving.

It is often not noticed at workplace that grief can affect mental functioning, at least temporarily, if not on a sustained basis. If someone's mental functioning has been affected by grief (let us hope temporarily), they may have difficulty coping with their workload and meeting performance expectations. It is unfortunate that most organizations lack a dedicated bereavement care policy, whereby people can be allowed some paid time off from work to recuperate, at least from initial shock and pain. Nobody would dispute that bereavement of any nature needs time and space to restore a basic level of functionality. In case of traumatic or complicated bereavement, such a need is even more pronounced. And yet, most organizations do not recognize the need to extend therapy, counselling or at least focussed employee care support to the employees going through grief and trauma.

BEHAVIOURAL REACTIONS

Bereaved people tend to react in a myriad of ways. Sometime shock, daze and numbing last long and strong. My younger son remained in a daze for nearly a fortnight after the demise of my elder son. His stony silence and frozenness worried me. There were days when I had to, literally, feed him. Finally, on the seventeenth day he broke down and cried inconsolably. His despair and sense of uneasy emptiness within continued for many months. It was after nearly one and a half years of our loss, that my younger son emitted a sense of peace and warmth while placing his certificate of a remarkable accomplishment before his big brother's picture. Finally, accepting his loss, he let his brother's mortal absence become 'Presence' in spirit.

One of my counselees, Rubin, went through a crisis of faith after the demise of his mother. He had no clear memory of his father, who had died in a road accident when he was just a toddler and his younger brother an infant of few weeks. His mother had single-handedly raised the two boys, arranging for the best education for them, despite her modest earnings. As Rubin started to earn, he hoped to give respite to his mother. But it was not to be. She soon died of renal failure. For many years thereafter, Rubin remained in fierce anger towards God. Sometimes he even felt bouts of envy towards those with complete families. His disillusionment with life and his silent anger slowly turned unhealthy. Overwhelmed by intrusively ruminative memories of his mother's struggle-filled life, Rubin found an escape in alcohol. Thankfully, his sense of responsibility towards his younger brother prevailed, and he quit before turning into an addict. In our early meetings, all that I did was to hold space for him to give voice to his disillusionment, the shattering of his faith and his anger. It was a long journey for both of us before Rubin restored his sense of coherence and accepted his loss. He has since been re-working his life design. His anger still shows up occasionally, albeit with less intensity.

Quite often, bereaved people tend to have a sense of 'Presence' of their deceased loved one. This could be by way of hearing voices, seeing silhouettes, or even feeling touch, or thinking, '*I saw!*' Well, seeing a 'face in the crowd' is a very common experience, and not surprising at all in the early months of bereavement. It would be insensitive and unwise to dismiss this behaviour as hallucination or delusion before being certain of it. Such a pronouncement, may turn the bereaved into self-isolative silence. Sometimes, all that the bereaved need is an empathic listener and non-judgmental understanding. We should be patient and supportive to help the bereaved express their true feelings.

At the same time, it is important to stay observant. If you notice in someone, a clear pattern or convincing evidence of recurring delusionary thoughts that continue for too long, then therapeutic help should be firmly advised and arranged. God forbid, if you are the one going through this experience, have courage to seek feedback and advice or help.

RELATIONAL AND SOCIAL EFFECTS

The social life of the bereaved tends to go haywire. Sometimes even relationships do. Even in shared loss, different people have different paces and ways to grieve, cope, heal and recover. This is particularly relevant in the case of bereaved parents. It is not surprising to see the bereaved couple feel distant from each other, finding it difficult to relate to each other's way of grieving and coping. Similar dynamics can be found in other types of bereavement as well. As we saw in the opening story of this chapter, the two sisters had a very different engagement with their grief even in their shared loss. While they were both pained with their father's continued lack of engagement, Tisha found it easier to ignore his peculiar ways. For quite some time, until she started to restore herself through art-therapy, Tanya did not like Tisha's forgiving attitude, which led to (thankfully temporary) misunderstandings between otherwise dearly attached sisters.

Being a natural introvert and social recluse, my social life has never been vibrant. With grief, my discomfort in social settings became rather pronounced. Earlier my home used to be constantly abuzz with visiting relatives and my husband's friends. Despite my socially passive nature, people used to love my warm and efficient hospitality. But in the aftermath of my loss, this constant swarming at my small house started to leave me ill at ease. On occasions I even resented their business-as-usual buzz and banter. I tended to withdraw and isolate myself, and unwittingly created a double whammy for myself. While some entitled relatives became upset, some genuinely concerned friends interpreted my outward behaviour as a signal for privacy. So I ended up losing good sympathisers, while continuing to serve those who I wanted respite from. C. S. Lewis puts it so succinctly in his classic *A Grief Observed*—

> There is a sort of invisible blanket between the world and me. I find it hard to take in what anyone says. Yet I want the others to be about me.

Sometimes, a bereaved person's life may be so entwined with that of their deceased loved one, that death may even trigger an identity loss, at least in a limited sense. It is quite common in case of widowed spouses who had an intimate and/or socially and financially dependent relationship. This is likely to be more pronounced in societies where the identity of married women is attached to the identity of their husbands, and they are dependent on their husbands in more ways than one. But such identity loss is possible in other relationships as well, especially in case of bereaved mothers. My son was unquestioningly the most important person in my life. I used to (and still do) call him my anchor. Though it is more a fond symbolic reference, his going literally left me feeling uprooted, even orphaned as I described in my grief memoir *A Mother's Cry .. A Mother's Celebration*. An equally close and dear relationship with my younger son notwithstanding, my heart continues to yearn for the unique way my elder son adorned me with motherhood, a role that is at the heart of my very being, and defines my identity in a precious way.

Not all relational effects of grief are bad though. Bereaved people tend to value the idea of relationship at a deeper level. They become gentler, and more loving, caring and forgiving. In the wake of loss, sometimes we need to make fresh alignments with other people in our life. Some bonds get strengthened and deepened, while some relationships call for reduced engagement, if not complete letting go. Sometimes a relationship is built afresh with new meaning and depth. For my younger son, his brother meant the world. To him, my elder son wasn't just his big-brother, but also a playmate, friend, confidant, peer, guide, role-model all rolled in one. In some sense, he even found a parent figure in his brother, more dearly loved than my husband or me. It was natural for him to feel lost and lonely. Occasionally he even felt angry at his brother for 'abandoning' him. Over time, with my gentle care, but more importantly through his own transcendent life-view, he began re-sculpting his relationships, starting with me. Today, we are much closer than we were before my elder son's passing on. And it is not merely out of necessity of our grief, but more because of our affirmative engagement with our own and each other's grief.

'Embrace your pain
A tear at a time
A moan at a time
A lament at a time
A prayer at a time'

—Neena Verma

ENTAGLED BALL OF EMOTIONS

Grief, by nature, is an emotional experience and process. It has the power to deluge us with a barrage of difficult emotions. One can feel knotted like an entangled ball of emotions that appear in a thousand guises and varying intensities.

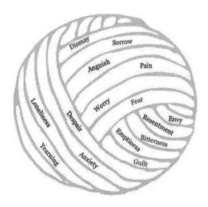

Many bereaved people tend to give an outward impression of strength. They either hide their feelings or seem to be stoic about them. Sometimes such stoicism may be natural and in sync with their temperament. More often though, various personal, familial or societal pressures, or cliched sermons place an expectation on bereaved people to suppress or hide their feelings. The masked smile of 'all is well' is often incongruent with deeply personal and intimate feelings. But no matter how neatly we hide or suppress our emotions, they just lurk behind as our shadow, and show up as physiological problems. It is, therefore, very important to recognize, understand and address the flurry of entangled emotions that show up in the wake of loss and grief. No wonder, Shakespeare, the great bard of tragedy, wisely says—

> 'Give sorrow words; the grief that does not speak knits
> up the over wrought heart and bids it break.'

Let us delve deeper into some of the most common emotions triggered by grief.

Sadness is a natural and expected face of grief. True— love must endure loss. But on the hard ground of enduring, there is nothing philosophical about pain. If anything, sorrow and pain are physical experiences. Sadness has many faces. It can show up as despair, loneliness, even depression. It is however, important to understand that grief-triggered sadness is not necessarily depression. Of course, it can and often does feel depressive. But, unless professional assessment suggests so, grief related depressive sadness should not be mistaken as depression, which can be a medical condition or a combination of medical and psychological conditions.

Depending on its form and manner, loss can cause feelings of betrayal, disappointment or injustice which in turn can evoke *anger* which is the psyche's natural response to hurt, pain or fear. Rubin felt disappointed by doctors and cheated by God. His muted anguish soon turned into bitter anger and a lament against God. It is not surprising if the bereaved carry a sense of anger towards their deceased loved one only, especially if their loss has left them feeling abandoned in a literal or symbolic way. Many bereaved spouses or young children feel so. For a brief while, my younger son felt angry at my demised elder son, lamenting that 'the chair on my side has gone vacant'. Sometimes the bereaved carry a vague anger at the world at large for going about the normal business of life when they are hurting so badly. They yearn for their own happy life when they see others enjoying theirs.

It is important that the personal or professional carers and companions hold space for the bereaved in a gentle yet attentive way. One of your noble duties is to help them express and resolve their anguish in a healthy way. As we saw in Rubin's case, timely help saved him from falling prey to his anger and turning into an alcoholic.

Anger hides many other emotions, *fear* being a dominant one. In grief, it may feel as if one is trapped in a deep, dark, dry, bottomless well where fear crawls all over. If it sounds too frightening, let me tell you, it can get so. Engulfed by the grief of losing his beloved wife, the famous litterateur C. S. Lewis bemoaned, 'No one ever told me that grief felt so like fear'. There can be fear of being left alone, of abandonment, of more loss, of having to face the altered future and changed circumstances all alone, of social and financial insecurity, of loss of identity, of losing grip on life, and of one's own death.

A painful 'G' that often tags alongside grief is the feeling of *guilt*. It is understandable if one has a passing feeling of guilt over not being able to save one's loved one from dying, like what Tanya or Rubin felt. In some cases, though, guilt can gnaw painfully. For bereaved parents especially, the *survivor guilt* is enormous, since their loss violates the assumptive belief that parents are supposed to protect their children. When parents outlive the child, they find it extremely hard to forgive themselves even though they might have done everything possible to save the child. Something called *recovery guilt* also tends to haunt the bereaved who find it difficult to give themselves permission to return to normal pleasures of life. Guilt is more likely if the bereaved had some *unfinished business* with their deceased loved one, especially if the relationship had some negative undercurrents. It is natural that the bereaved might feel guilty if they have said or done something harsh towards the deceased. But it is possible that the bereaved may feel guilt over some passing *ordinary regrets* as well.

On the fateful day of my son's demise, just as I was stepping out for work in the morning, he had asked for one of his favourite dishes for breakfast. Since I was already running late that day, I promised that I would cook it in the evening and left in a hurry. He nodded smilingly. The evening never came. An undemanding, simple, content and uncomplaining boy, he rarely, if ever, used to ask for something special. By some strange unconscious design, after a very long time, he had asked for something on the very morning of the day that was to be his last. His last wish of me, a small simple wish, and I didn't fulfil it. I loathed myself for a long time before I could reframe '*I did not fulfil*' to '*I could not fulfil because of paucity of time*'. Thanks to my younger son's support, an associate's help, and the advantage that my background as grief practitioner bestows on me, I could find my way out of the *guilt loop*. Not everyone, though, may find it easy. As carers, companions and well-wishers, we should be willing, ready and able to help the bereaved stay clear of such guilt traps.

Often the bereaved feel overwhelmed by a sense of *yearning*. The disbelief and pain of loss are so intense that even though they might have mentally accepted the loss, at a deeper level, they may still be longing and searching for their loved one. This longing, at times, can get so strong that they may experience something called *face in the crowd syndrome*. It is quite common to feel the presence and hear the voice of the deceased loved one. But most bereaved people prefer to keep quiet about their feelings and experiences, fearing unkind judgment or sermon. Such behaviours may be termed by others as delusions or hallucinations. True, it may be so in some odd cases, but in most cases, it might actually be intense yearning, which is likely to lessen slowly with self-compassion and empathetic support. If suppressed for too long, the feelings of emptiness and yearning can create psychosomatic ill-effects. We should, therefore, hold space for the bereaved, and gently facilitate them to allow expression of such feelings and move towards a healthy integration of their grief.

The range of bodily, emotional and other reactions associated with grief is vast. I have explained some of the most common ones above. Most of these happen as a normal and natural reaction to loss, and slowly wane in intensity. However, one should definitely seek clinical advice if any of these reactions persist or seem oddly acute.

Pause and Ponder-2

Referring back to your (or of the person you thought about, referred hereto as OP) loss that you reflected upon in 'Pause and Ponder-1'—

- What, if any, bodily reactions showed up? How did you (or OP) deal with these physiological upshots of grief?
- In what way did grief affect your (or OP's) mental functioning, behaviour, relationships and social engagement?
- What emotions did you (or OP) experience? With what effect?
- What personal qualities helped you (or OP) to maintain optimal level of health, functionality, and harmonious relationships?
- How did you (or OP) manage the difficult fall-outs, if any?

—◆—

GRIEF IS A JOURNEY

'Grief is like a long valley, a winding valley where any bend may reveal a totally new landscape.'

—C.S. Lewis

I hold the view that grief is a journey whereby one goes through various phases, albeit in a uniquely organic way. There are various models of grief. One of the popular ones is Elizabeth Kubler-Ross' five-stages model which, as I mentioned earlier in this chapter, she conceptualized in the context of death and dying. It is limited in scope and application in so far as grief context is concerned. Grief expert William Worden conceptualized a tasks model which advises four non-linear tasks to work through grief. These can happen in any order, even simultaneously—

1. Accept the reality of the loss.
2. Process the pain of the grief.
3. Adjust to the world without the deceased.
4. Find an enduring connection with the deceased in the midst of embarking on a new life.

Based on my own grief journey, and experience as a grief and growth practitioner, I have come to understand grief as an ongoing journey that encompasses all stages, phases and tasks, but not necessarily in a sequential order, nor bound by any one of these. This journey happens with an uncertain ebb and flow—sometimes moving about quietly and subtly, like gentle waves, and sometimes loud and thundering like rocking tides or even a tsunami. To each their own waves and tides. Grief journey is no ordinary journey. I call it a pilgrimage where every pilgrim (griever) must choose their own destination, make their own path, and follow their own pace and rhythm.

We will talk about post-traumatic growth, the *pilgrimage* metaphor of grief journey and its phases in the next part of the book that has a chapter for each of the phases of the growth journey. Until then, create your take-home poetic affirmation.

—◆—

PATH 2

Poetic Affirmation to Take Home

'I... a happy fly,
If I live,
Or if I die.'

—William Blake

Affirm your innate deep quiet happiness,
that is neither dimmed by loss,
nor bounded by worldly trappings.

Part 2

MYSTIQUE OF GROWTH

3

GROWTH Mandala

'In the midst of winter, I found there was, within me, an invincible summer.'

—Albert Camus

Sujoy was two weeks shy of turning 18 when his father died of cancer, barely five months into his superannuation from work. With the most immaculate health habits in their entire clan, his father was actually a health and fitness role model for everyone. The sudden surfacing of his aggressive cancer didn't allow the family any time to absorb the shock. They had to immediately get into action. But despite the best treatment, his father died within three months of the diagnosis.

A late child and the youngest in the family, Sujoy had led a sheltered, comfortable and almost pampered life. Overnight, the shy, protected, easy-going and laid-back teenager had to become the man of the family, handling so many complex things, including absorbing the pressure of looking after his arthritic mother and partially visually impaired elder sister. Though she was well-educated and employed, her physiological challenge required some support from the family which was mostly being taken care of by their father.

All of a sudden, young Sujoy found himself struck by such a profound loss, and overwhelmed by anxiety on account of his family responsibilities and worry about his own future. Heartbroken and fearful, Sujoy was taken over by emotional and mental stress. It wouldn't have surprised anyone to see him getting drowned in the ocean of his grief, fears and despair.

Instead, it was heartening for everyone to see how Sujoy accepted his loss, embraced his fears, lived up to his responsibilities towards self and family, and chose to let his pain inspire a purposeful life. He sought therapy to deal with his intrusive emotions and thoughts. His therapist credited Sujoy's regeneration more to his own emotional resilience and ability to healthily engage with his grief. From being an average performer, Sujoy completed his college with above average grades, and followed it with competitive examinations. He secured admission into an MBA program at a coveted B-School, and working hard throughout the course, landed himself a good job. Though the family was not in acute financial stress, they had been mostly living off Sujoy's father's family pension, his elder sister's modest salary, and savings from good days. With Sujoy's handsome salary adding on, things got better. But he still had the arduous job of helping his mother make peace with her grief. The way Sujoy facilitated his mother to not just accept and restore, but even inspired her to join him in his community outreach service, filled his therapist with admiration for Sujoy. He had not just turned his grief into reason for growth, but also deepened his relationship with his sister, and helped his mother recover and restore her well-being.

—◆—

How did Sujoy bloom like a lotus in the swampy waters of grief, pain and fear?

How can one find or create the way to phoenix-like resurrection, while engulfed in the scathing embers of loss and sorrow?

—◆:—

SEASON OF GRIEF, REASON FOR GROWTH

'Every season is one of becoming, but not always one of blooming. Be gracious with your ever-evolving self.'

—B. Oakman

We often see children undergoing something called *growing pains.* Some of us may even have vivid memories from our own childhood of experiencing vague muscular pain in legs, especially in the calf area. Though these pains may not have a medically proven connection to growing bones, they are commonly called growing pains. What do we see most parents do when their children are troubled by such pains? They explain to the kids that growth is the gift of nature, and that it comes with stretch, stress and pain. They gently massage the kids' sore muscles, nudge them to resiliently endure pain, and let it settle naturally. They help the children learn that pain is the harbinger of growth, and prod them to affirm their inherent capacity to bear pain, heal and grow.

Life is one such compassionate and wise parent, that asks us to kindle our natural instinct to endure, heal and transcend our pain, when grief, trauma and adversity come calling. Certainly, one should not have to go through the excruciating passage of grief to be on the journey of growth. But when it does come about, as it eventually shall to everyone, grief has a way of finding an unlikely but affirmative companion in growth. The ironical partners of grief and growth can put up a fascinating dance on the floor of life, if only we embrace grief and choose the path of growth.

⊙⊛⊙

'A season of grief
Unfolds invitation for growth'

—Neena Verma

⊙⊛⊙

Sujoy took the daunting journey by seeking the path of growth without suppressing his grief. He recognized and embraced his pain, fears and worries, rather than staying in denial or shock, avoiding, escaping or succumbing. Eventually, he prepared himself to seek therapeutic help, transcending the taboo associated with it in his society. Even as the therapist played his part well, Sujoy took charge of his journey, staying open, hopeful and resilient no matter how hard it got.

Most people are able to bear the pain of grief, adjust and recover in a natural gradual process. Not everyone may need professional help to live through their grief journey. But those who do, often find it hard to even sense and acknowledge their need to themselves, leave alone getting over the social stigma and seeking help. Sujoy felt the need and honoured his inner sense, seeking therapeutic support to give voice to his feelings. One step at a time, he engaged with his pain, fear and worries, and discovered the resilience, compassion, hopefulness and courage that he probably already had. It is also likely that he cultivated these psychological resources all anew upon coming face to face with his grief. In any case, his loss provided the spur for his personal growth. But he could make the most of it, only because he was willing to endure the growing pains, and believed in the prospect of emerging stronger and wiser.

Not everyone in grief, though, goes through the same

experience. Unfortunately, sometimes people are torn apart by grief like some trees get uprooted by storm. Some people are shattered badly for life, and some barely cope and survive. That said, like most trees bend to the punishing winds but do not break, most people also gradually accept the loss, make peace with their grief, and adjust to their altered world. It is also important to know that sometimes what appears on the surface to be good adjusting, might be a stoic suppression of grief. This may help to cope for some time, but it is likely to trigger physiological and/or psychological complications in the long-term. Most people, though, resiliently get on with life, with or without significant change or growth.

And then there are some who actually go beyond such resilient adaptation. Tapping into their deeper instinct to heal, they nurse and transform their pain. These are the people that the post-traumatic growth (PTG) researcher, Dr. Stephen Joseph, likens to a tree that does bend, yet finds a way to not just regrow the storm-struck parts, but actually sprouts new greens and blooms at places which were bare before. This tree chooses to accept, adapt, restore and grow anew, transcending the grief and pain of being mauled by the brutal storm.

Pause and Ponder-1

Recall a time of loss when all your strength and inner resources felt crushed like the trees lashed by the storm. Think about—

- Which tree were you like—the tree which got uprooted; the one that was bent but recovered; or the one that recovered and grew anew?
- What was it like to be the tree that you were?
- Looking back, would you rather prefer to be another tree? Why?

- Which qualities of yours made (or could make) a positive difference? How?
- What is your one (or more) special life lesson?
- If you were to help someone else going through a similar loss, which tree would you help them choose to be? Why? And how?

PROMISE OF POST-TRAUMATIC GROWTH

'That which does not kill us, makes us stronger.'

—Friedrich Nietzsche

There is enough evidence from real-life accounts, research and clinical practice to suggest that traumatic experiences that shake us to the core also spark deep transformation. It's true indeed that, sometimes, trauma could be so all-encompassing that even survival and a minimal functionality may be hard to come by. Survivors of the holocaust, war, terrorism, socio-communal conflicts or violence, partition, may find it hard to recover. The enormity of their trauma and pain notwithstanding—many transcend their grief, brokenness and despair, and choose to affirm life. A holocaust survivor and Logotherapy[4] pioneer, Viktor Frankl, who lost his father, mother, brother and pregnant

---

[4]Logotherapy was created by legendary psychiatrist Dr. Viktor Frankl, whose lived experience as a Nazi concentration camp survivor, guided his work. Not just a form of psychotherapy, logotherapy is a life philosophy that affirms that in all circumstances, life has meaning (*logos* in Greek), and we are free to choose our *will to meaning* even when all other freedoms are taken away from us. Logotherapy is renowned for helping people in trauma, grief or any other suffering. It is known for having had a profound effect by helping people find meaning in their suffering, and meaning of their life.

wife to the horrors of Nazi concentration camps, avers in his acclaimed book *Man's Search for Meaning*—'Everything can be taken from a man but one thing... the last of all the human freedoms... to choose one's attitude in any given set of circumstances, to choose one's own way.'

One vital factor that influences our response to loss, grief and trauma is the *story we tell ourselves*. Their loss, suffering and lament, notwithstanding, some people's self-talk is rich with healing and resilience. We all can create a narrative of hope, meaning and growth, like Viktor Frankl chose to do. He attributes his capacity for survival to the internal questions that beset him. While most people in the concentration camps were succumbing to the unimaginable tortures of Nazi brutality, Frankl found himself wondering—'If there is meaning in life at all, then there must be meaning in suffering.' He nurtured a world-view of meaning and possibility, and focused on affirming life, despite all the horrors and uncertainty. He looked for and appreciated goodwill and gestures of kindness, however small or rare. And he imagined a future of meaning beyond the infinite expanse of suffering.

What Viktor Frankl chose to pursue, is by all means possible for us all. Although there is no set formula that can predict or direct people's responses to loss and trauma, many turn it into a catalyst for deep transformation. In the process, the existential growth that ensues is what eminent trauma researchers, Lawrence Calhoun and Richard Tedeschi, christened as **Post-traumatic Growth (PTG)**. They describe the phenomenon of PTG as the 'positive change that the individual experiences as a result of the struggle with a traumatic event.' Their research confirms that a wide range of people, from those showing mild symptoms to those with full-blown post-traumatic stress disorder (PTSD), seek the path of and foster PTG, whether by themselves or with professional help.

Their pioneering work opened up a brave and much needed paradigm beyond PTSD. As their work explains, trauma can actually inspire an existential need to review and reconstruct one's core beliefs that get torn apart in the aftermath of loss or traumatic event—a much valued trigger for deep growth. The life of the great literary maestro and first Indian Nobel Laureate, Guru Rabindranath Tagore, is an unparalleled testimony to this very phenomenon of post-traumatic growth.

> *Tagore's life bore witness to several intimate and profound losses one after another. Losing his mother at just 14 years of age, he found solace in literature, the love for which he shared with his sister-in-law who was very dear to him. Her death by suicide affected Tagore deeply. To help him cope with his grief, Tagore's father sent him on work to a rural region. Tagore was filled with awe and inspiration seeing ordinary people's ability to live with resilience and contentment despite their trying circumstances and unrelenting misery. He returned to literature. The next few years ensued immense growth in his literary gifts. His progressive philosophy began to influence the common citizens of not just Bengal but entire India. Unfortunately, his own trials wouldn't abate. He lost his wife and daughter in quick succession within the same year. Three years later his father passed away, and two years farther in time his son passed away on his wife's fifth death anniversary. While nursing his ailing daughter and son, Tagore used to sing lullabies and hymns which eventually found way to several of his anthologies, most notably the legendary Gitanjali that won him the Nobel Prize for Literature. The first Indian Nobel Laureate, Tagore's humility and equanimity even in the face of the coveted honour, astonished people around him.*

How does one make sense of the relentless losses that besieged Tagore's life? If not for his strength to accept, endure and transform his grief, how else could Tagore make the revolutionary contributions that he did as a litterateur, artist and social reformer. He penned and painted his pain. He mourned through his music. He sang his sorrow. He motivated people of Bengal to raise their voice against brutal colonial orders, and inspired them to join hands, rising above the communal and religious diversity. He immersed himself in arts and literature, and devoted his life to founding and developing the Shanti Niketan, the first University of integral learning in India.

Tagore's life is a profound salutation to what I expressed in my grief memoir *A Mother's Cry .. A Mother's Celebration* as the mesmerizing dance of paradoxical partners of dark and light, that ensues when we choose to affirm life in its wholeness.

'Grief invokes Grace
Woe invokes Wonder
Lament invokes Love
Cry invokes Celebration'

—Neena Verma

Contrary to common misconception that loss, grief and post-traumatic stress only have adverse effects, they often provide just the right spur that we need for existential rebirth. It is possible to transcend beyond, and rise above the dark clouds of grief and pain. The promise of PTG doesn't in any way suggest that we ignore PTSD. Neither does this insist that PTSD be fixed before growth can be initiated. Both PTSD and PTG are natural human responses to loss and traumatic experience. They can and often do, co-exist.

Post-traumatic growth may not begin in the immediate aftermath of loss and trauma. In fact, it should not be prompted or initiated in a hurry. It is essential to acknowledge and affirm the trauma and grief, and allow ourselves the time and space we need. The rawness of grief and pain needs to go through the organic experiencing and expression, in our journey from trauma to transformation and pain to purpose. Growth may or may not ensue, whether or not grief finds closure. Even when one is able to make peace with the loss, not everyone may experience growth. Similarly, grief may still live with you even when growth has begun to unfold. To each their own. Recall Sujoy's story. He did not just find a way to accept and resolve his grief, but also found meaning in his pain, and grew as a person. His sister reconciled and moved forward, albeit with no particular growth. For their mother in contrast, grief is an ongoing part of her life, though with gradually waning intensity.

MY STORY

My son, Utkarsh[5], is my first child. He blessed me with motherhood. From the time he came in my womb, through the complicated pregnancy and difficult delivery, his childhood, growing years, and up until his transcendence to the other world—he held me warm and strong, way more than I did as his mother. I felt unconditionally accepted and loved by him in a quiet but sure way. And also, objectively critiqued whenever needed. We had, rather, we have a rooted and deep relationship.

[5]*Utkarsh'* is a Hindi word with many meanings, the most common being excellence and exaltation. The deeper meanings though are awakening, essence, emergence and transcendence.

I call Utkarsh my anchor. He continues to anchor me with his Presence that will always be alive and conscious in my heart, my mind, my soul, my life.

What do you expect of a bereaved mother who felt orphaned at the sudden demise of her 22-year-young beloved son! Is it possible for her to make peace with her loss, leave alone transcend her grief, grow at a deeper level, and choose the path of a higher mission? Unbearably painful and unimaginably hard indeed. Possible nonetheless. And advisable very much so. As we progress through the book, you will see some glimpses of my grief, growth and grace journey.

MANY FACES OF GROWTH

'Perhaps all the dragons in our lives are princesses who are only waiting to see us act, just once, with beauty and courage. Perhaps everything that frightens us is, in its deepest essence, something helpless that wants our love.'

–Rainer Maria Rilke

The phenomenal research of Lawrence Calhoun and Richard Tedeschi establishes that PTG happens in five broad ways, although there may be individual differences in the specific way and extent to which different people experience growth. Sujoy's story offers practical insight about how to make deliberate strides to grow in one or more of these ways.

First is the possibility of cultivation or enhancement of *personal strength*. Tedeschi remarks wisely that just as adversity is the mother of invention, 'trauma may be the mother of strength'. In the aftermath of trauma, it is common for people to realize greater strength within. People in Sujoy's life were amazed to see his transformation from a sheltered teenager to a strong self-facilitative young man. More than others, Sujoy was, himself, surprised to discover his inner strength which might have been hiding in the comforts of a protected life, and showed up when he found the ground beneath his feet ripping apart. It is also likely that he developed it all anew.

The second way growth happens is by way of *improved relationships with others.* Sujoy's relationship with his elder sister prior to their father's demise was that of a pampered younger sibling. Later, as he took up his father's role to help his sister manage her restricted mobility, they didn't just develop a deeper intimacy as siblings but also found great friends in each other. What more, she became a sounding board and barefoot counsellor to Sujoy. He sometimes wonders what all he would have missed in their relationship, had their loss not brought them closer.

It is amazing how loss invokes humility and greater *appreciation for life.* Having witnessed death up close and personal inspired Sujoy to value and feel gratitude for the privileges he enjoyed in life. It was heart-warming for his family to see Sujoy transform from being a comfort-loving person who took things for granted and complained often, to an appreciative and grateful human being.

For some people, loss also helps them see life with new eyes, thereby opening *new possibilities.* His loss jolted Sujoy out of his smug reliance over his father. It also awakened him to his own hidden smartness. Given his not so impressive grades, he had limited options. He chose to make up for it through the route of competitive entrance examinations, and worked extra hard to secure admission at a reputable B-School. His mother and sister were happily surprised to see a new Sujoy—aspirational, focused, gritty and committed. Sujoy had chosen to look around with new eyes, identifying a range of possibilities, rather than succumbing to adverse circumstances.

Loss, trauma and grief sometimes prove to be a harbinger of deeper existential realization. People develop a new understanding of the *meaning and purpose* of their life. Inspired by his sister, Sujoy began practicing meditation. It wasn't easy to come by. But he kept at it. Eventually as his practice deepened, so did his inner calm. His friends found him so much more patient and warmer, a welcome change from his earlier irritable self. Not just this, inspired by his voluntary teaching of socio-economically disadvantaged children, some of them even joined him at the community outreach program that Sujoy was serving at.

Pause and Ponder-2

Go back to the incident you recalled under 'Pause and Ponder-1'.

- Notice the changes you experienced in your way of thinking, being, relating to and approaching life.
- In which aspects (personal strength, improved relationships, appreciation of life, seeing new possibilities, finding meaning and purpose) do you experience a sense of growth and renewal?
- How would you like to build on and accentuate your growth?
- Is there something to learn from others? How would you like to use their example, wisdom and feedback?
- If you were to help someone in similar state, how would you facilitate their growth?

We must note that Sujoy is special in the way he could grow in such a wholesome way. Not everyone though may manifest growth in all aspects or to such an extent. Different people experience growth in different ways and to different degrees. Yet, the promise and the prospect are open for all those who choose the path of healing, resilience and transformation, affirm their grief and seek to reemerge with meaning.

GRIEF AND GROWTH—ETERNAL SPIRAL

'For a seed to achieve its greatest expression,
it must come completely undone.
The shell cracks, its insides come out
and everything changes.'

—Cynthia Occelli

Organic and ongoing, the phenomenon of growth is as old as human civilization. Decay and regeneration are simultaneous biological processes. New cells keep growing in place of old dying ones. The imaginal cells that give birth to the butterfly emerge from the gooey remains of the disintegrating caterpillar. Likewise, the case of psychological and existential growth. Its promise and possibility are alive till our last breath.

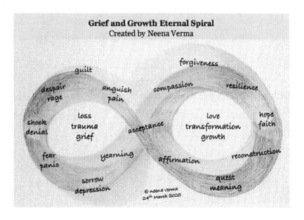

The complex maze of grief has shock, denial, sorrow, despair, fear, pain, anguish and yearning at every twisting turn and blinding corner. We go through a thousand difficult emotions. It feels as if we might forever remain stuck in a dark dingy tunnel that has no opening. But there is, indeed, light at the other end of every tunnel, grief being no exception. Each one of us takes our own time and way. But we do reach a point when acceptance happens.

Invoked by the mystique of growth, we begin to affirm our grief and honour its sacred space in our life. It, ultimately, finds a way to transcend towards the other side of the infinite cosmic loop, where we are greeted by our inherent faith, hope, resilience, compassion, gratitude, forgiveness, meaning and love. We welcome and flow with the unfurling growth that knows how to seed from and live alongside our grief.

Like many other seemingly paradoxical opposites, grief and growth too are existential partners. The anguished dance of loss and trauma, and the liberating dance of love and transformation, form a confluence and cocreate the *eternal spiral of grief and growth*, as depicted in my model and pictorial above.

We have an abundance of mythological and classic literature, and movies with post-traumatic growth and deep transformation at the heart of their narrative. There is great poetry that honours grief and celebrates growth. All religions propound that suffering leads to higher wisdom. The *Shrimad Bhagavad Gita* explains the eternal churn of life and death, and shows the way to transcend grief and take the path of noble karma (deed). Buddhism teaches the way to accept and endure suffering, and seek enlightenment beyond it. The Christian consciousness celebrates resurrection of Jesus Christ. The hallmark of Sufism is annihilation of the material-self and emergence of the conscious-self. Whether literature, religion or psychology—all endorse the sacredness of grief on the journey to growth.

The people who undertake the treacherous journey and meet their pain in the face, are able to go beyond resilient adaptation and restoration of well-being, and emerge deeply transformed and all anew. They healthily integrate their grief as an abiding truth of life, and often discover or create a deeper calling in life. For them pain becomes the pivot for profound transformation. Their grief invokes them to a *pilgrimage of growth and grace.* Inspired by such a prospect, this book seeks to explore and explain the mystical relationship between *grief* and *growth*, with *grace* forming the transcendent backdrop.

Pause and Ponder-3

Recall a time of grief when you yourself felt or saw someone feeling hopelessly stuck, yet being able to affirm grief, and choosing path of growth.

- What was it like to feel stuck in the dark tunnel of grief? How did it affect you or the other person (OP) you have in mind, at physical, psychological and behavioural levels?
- What helped you (or OP) see or seek light? How did you (or OP) endure?
- How did you (or OP) come to choose growth, despite and alongside grief?

GROWTH WISDOM

Growth is an ever-unfolding phenomenon. It is not an object or a destination to chase. Legendary humanistic psychologist,

Abraham Maslow, maintains that human beings are inherently endowed with *growth wisdom* which guides them on the path to self-actualization and transcendence. Growth wisdom is about our instinctive will and ability to accept the pain, harmoniously weave it into our whole being, and use it as a spur for growth. Inspiring us to become more affirmative, kind and compassionate towards ourselves and others, growth wisdom shows the way to acceptance, transformation and renewal. In my personal and professional experience, one can consciously cultivate or enhance growth wisdom. It helps us navigate through grief and trauma by preparing us to—

Embrace pain and fear—When confronted with trauma or danger, our primal instinct is to take flight (avoid, escape, succumb), fight (resist, dismiss, react) or freeze (go numb). In contrast, growth wisdom, as co-created by a mindful brain, a compassionate heart and a loving soul, enables thought-through and reflective responses. It prepares us to face reality and engage with it, rather than fighting or taking flight. It helps us acknowledge the reality, understand its full effect and actively engage with it.

Take responsibility—As we see the reality in wholeness, we are better able to own responsibility to make peace with it, integrate it with the rest of who we are, and reconstruct our life with meaning and purpose.

Open up—Seeing anew and wholesomely, changes and expands our perspective. A whole new vista unfolds where we can see faith, resilience, hope, compassion and other growth-inspiring human strengths, coexisting alongside the grief manifestations of pain, fear, anguish and sorrow.

Reflect affirmatively—Without denying, hiding or suppressing our pain, we begin reflecting about and searching for more affirmative choices and invitations that life still holds for us, beyond our loss and trauma—including those that are triggered by our loss and trauma.

Create a new narrative—The beauty of growth wisdom is that it inspires and enables us to author a new life narrative. A narrative that respects our grief and sorrow, allows it the sacred space it deserves in our consciousness, and yet helps us transcend beyond our pain, and towards transformation and higher purpose. This honours the non-duality law of nature that affirms the simultaneity of light and dark, life and death, and other such existential partners that we humans in our limited understanding view as opposites.

Pause and Ponder-4

Revisit 'Pause and Ponder' 1, 2 and 3.

- Think of the ways your growth wisdom shows up and enables you to accept, heal, transform and grow.
- If you were to help someone in a similar life-journey as yours, invoke their growth wisdom, how would you help them?

MANDALA

'In all chaos there is a cosmos, in all disorder a secret order.'

—Carl Gustav Jung

The word, mandala, has its origin in the Sanskrit language. The concept of mandala can be traced to the *Rigveda*, one of the oldest Hindu scriptures, although mandala gained prominence more as a Buddhist practice. It has a revered place, and abundant pictorial and text presence in Tibetan Buddhist scriptures. Over time, mandala has been adopted all over the world by various sects and communities as a meditative practice. With its rich visual appeal, it has also become popular as a form of art.

Typically round in shape, mandala symbolizes the eternal cycle of life. There are many circles within the mandala circle, which I personally interpret as several journeys within one life-journey. The outermost circle is known as the *'ring of fire'*. It represents wisdom in the midst of chaos. Drawing the first ring symbolizes consciously choosing to step on the threshold of *samsara* (material world outside of oneself). The middle circle is known as the *'ring of vajra'* (thunderbolt). It represents eternal truth and power, and ushers us towards the inner essential self. The next circle is called the *'ring of lotus'*. It signifies the start of the journey towards *bodhi* (essential knowing). While the *Self* (the awakened knowing state) sits at the center, the *self* (the mortal non-knowing state) exists and evolves in the realms (circles) in between the sacred center where the *Self* resides, and the circumference which represents the *samsara* (the material mortal world). Mandala forms the confluence of the *self*, the *samsara*, and the *Self*.

Mandala is believed to have many meanings, of which 'cosmic circle' and 'essence' are most common. All its supposed meanings together bring alive the metaphorical significance of mandala which, to me, represents the Buddha-field (the space of supreme wisdom) where fear, chaos, sorrow, ignorance coexist with courage, creativity, peace and enlightenment. Every existential dilemma and struggle of the mortal *self*, its relationship with the world around (*samsara*), and the deep wisdom of the enlightened *Self*, can be contemplated and represented within a mandala. The legendary psychoanalyst, Carl Jung, pioneered the adaptation of mandala symbolism for self-growth. He insisted that true

Mandala is always an inner image, created gradually through deep contemplation and active imagination.

—◆:◆—

GROWTH MANDALA

'The lotus is the most beautiful flower,
whose petals open one by one.
But it will only grow in the mud.
To grow, first you must have the mud,
the obstacles and suffering ...
sadness, loss, illness, dying and death.'

—Goldie Hawn

It is not without meaning that the innermost ring of a mandala is named after the mystical flower lotus, that seeds and flowers in the same moment. The lotus manifests grief, growth and grace all at the same time. It emerges from the womb of muddy waters, unfurls with majesty and grace, and kindles sacred feelings. I have combined mandala consciousness and lotus symbolism with my personal and professional experience to create a model that guides and facilitates the transformative journey of grief and growth. I call this model the GROWTH Mandala.

My metaphor for grief and growth journey is *'pilgrimage'*. A pilgrimage is a deeply personal experience. So is the case with grief and growth. There is no one single path that would serve all. The GROWTH Mandala offers you a guide map that you would find helpful. That said, each of us has to make our pilgrimage our own way. There is no known path. We make our own by choosing to walk. We heed our soul's call of courage, and choose to take the trail of our pain, our fears, our sorrow, our trauma, our grief. We go through the ravines of our fear and the *Great Pass* of our sorrow, enter the dense scary woods of our pain, soak in the beauty of the meadows of love that nature continues to shower on us, take shelter in the serene hermitage of emerging wisdom, trek up the mighty mountain of our suffering, and find ourselves at the shrine of transformation and growth that we had little or no hope of reaching.

GROWTH Mandala
Created by Neena Verma

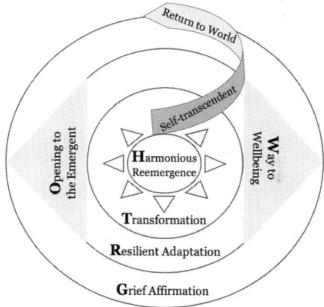

There is no deity or priest here. We are the pilgrim, we are the priest, and we are the deity. We meet a new healed self. We partake the holy nectar of transformation. Our pain and misery dissolve and we reemerge with meaning. We have the choice to end our pilgrimage with our healing and growth. But some of us choose to serve others, and share the nectar of our transformation with the world. With love, care and wisdom we choose to hold space for others, and live for a deeper calling and higher purpose.

☙

'Chosen are those who become the pilgrim
Granted the healthy return mid-way into the journey
They nonetheless choose to go the treacherous uphill way
To the shrine that they know nothing about
Just an imaginal feeling in their heart and soul
There is no path, not even a trail
They walk in faith, and make a path
Trekking to the shrine of their grief
They make life a pilgrimage
And return with the sacred nectar to share with the world
They choose the way of grace'

—Neena Verma

☙

Meditating over a mandala is thought to inspire wisdom and equanimity to simultaneously embrace both ignorance and knowing, loss and love, pain and purpose, and life and death. It is believed that no mandala is like another. All are individually unique and different. In the context of human growth, it would mean that each of us has to contemplate and carve our own unique mandala of growth. And this is both trying as well as transformative.

Mandala Art

Expressive Meditation

This is a meditative arts exercise. Please do it when you can be in a quiet reflective state by yourself.

- Think of a loss, trauma or adversity that you have undergone, and draw a mandala representing:
  - your experience of suffering—in the outermost circle
  - realization, resilience and courage—in the middle circle
  - transformative journey—in the innermost circle
  - regenerated and knowing Self—at the center
- Now reflect about the following and write down your reflections:
  - How was the experience of drawing this mandala?
  - What does this mandala mean to you?
  - Notice what shapes, elements of nature, and colours emerge on your mandala. What do they represent?
  - What would someone looking at your mandala think of you and your GROWTH Mandala pilgrimage?

GROWTH MANDALA PILGRIMAGE

'All we have to decide is what to do with the time that is given to us.'

—J.R.R. Tolkien

Chapters four to nine present different phases of the **GROWTH Mandala pilgrimage**. Each phase has a full chapter devoted to it. Before I briefly introduce them here, I want to emphasize that each phase is sovereign and sacred. The presentation of the phases in the GROWTH Mandala is in a particular order so as to ensure coherence of the model, and to honour the wholeness of the grief and growth process. In no way does it suggest that these phases need to happen in a linear order. While all the phases have an organic relationship with each other, they are not sequentially bound to each other.

It is true indeed that taking the entire pilgrimage helps us return home healed and grown, and ready to share the nectar of our transformation with the world. However, not all pilgrims take the same path, or walk the entire journey. Different phases may hold different meaning and relevance for different people. We all intuitively know where lies the way to our healing, well-being, adaptation and growth. It is for you to decide which phase you want to skip and which one you want to experience more deeply. You may even choose to pursue two phases simultaneously. For example, I have seen some people preferring to work through *'resilient adaptation'* and *'way to well-being'* phases simultaneously. To each their own. Each one of us has to decide for ourselves which phase resonates the most with our specific context and needs in life.

I share below a tiny glimpse of each phase, and invite you to start your pilgrimage the way you want.

GRIEF AFFIRMATION

Recall the story of Krishna Gotami from the first chapter. She learnt from her loss that there is no house without loss and suffering. In affirming her loss, she got enlightened, realizing and understanding the transience of life. The *'grief affirmation'* phase of the GROWTH Mandala pilgrimage is about accepting one's loss and embracing one's pain and sorrow. It is about facing and honouring one's grief without force-closing pain or getting overwhelmed by suffering. This phase would take one through the process of recognizing and understanding various manifestations of grief, and the way to accept and affirm grief. In the GROWTH Mandala this phase is represented by the outermost circle (aka ring of fire). We choose to start the journey of grief and growth, and step on the threshold of our pain. This chapter will guide you to traverse grief one moment at a time—accepting, facing, coping, understanding and honouring one's own grief, and helping others do the same.

RESILIENT ADAPTATION

Perhaps one of the most poignant tributes we can offer to our deceased loved ones is to honour life despite our loss. And to do so we have to adapt to our loss-altered life. Loss doesn't just shatter us emotionally, but can also leave us feeling destitute or helpless. We find it difficult to rearrange life on a practical plane. The *'resilient adaptation'* phase is about helping ourselves find or kindle courage within, and picking ourselves up with all the strength at our command. In the GROWTH Mandala, the middle circle (aka ring of thunderbolt) represents this phase, where one holds on to one's truth with poise and grit. This phase would guide you to resiliently adapt to life beyond loss.

OPENING TO THE EMERGENT

The post-loss life unfolds many new realities before us. Sometimes, very basic questions of life like financial or social security need immediate attention. Sometimes, relationships need to be reconfigured. And sometimes, more stark challenges need resolution. In essence, life calls us to seek and accept a new reality. The *opening to the emergent* phase is about recognizing, acknowledging and embracing our loss-altered new reality. It is about being willing and able to create a new life-narrative. This phase is represented by the consciousness triangle in the GROWTH Mandala that nurtures the life-energy to direct us towards what is still possible, despite and beyond our loss. This phase seeks to help the person in grief or trauma rediscover and mindfully develop the ability to notice the emergent, flow with it and redesign life.

WAY TO WELL-BEING

Grief hits body, mind, heart and soul in varying ways and degrees. Some people get badly affected at body level, while some others have their mental, emotional, behavioural or relational functioning more badly affected. The *way to well-being* phase is about restorative journey towards healing and holistic well-being. This phase is represented by the affirmative triangle in the GROWTH Mandala that holds the nourishing energy to heal and recover from the bio-psycho-social-relational fallouts of grief. The focus of this phase is on healing, restoring well-being and holistic revival.

TRANSFORMATION

Several existential philosophers and psychologists' works guide the notion that it is both possible and advisable to transition from sorrow to strength and trauma to 'transformation'. Sufi poet Rumi's profound words, 'wound is where the light enters', inspire this phase. The innermost circle of the GROWTH Mandala (aka ring of lotus) epitomizes this phase of phoenix-like resurrection of self. In this phase, we become the *lotus* that accepts the dark muddy waters of pain, blooms nonetheless, and spreads open to the infinite grace of nature. The lotus honours its muddy base yet transcends it with affirmation and grace. With compassion, courage and creativity, you may find this phase guiding your butterfly like metamorphosis, which honours the gooey remains of the caterpillar, and grows from it.

HARMONIOUS REEMERGENCE

Death doesn't happen to the dead alone. Those left behind, die too, in parts and ways that don't come back to life easily. Yet, some people find a way to regenerate themselves all anew, harmoniously re-weaving the fabric of their life, moving from 'misery to meaning' and 'pain to purpose.' The sixth and last phase of the GROWTH Mandala is about finding, creating and pursuing a higher calling. The centre (the awakened-knowing *Self*) of the GROWTH Mandala embodies this phase, that guides the way to '*harmonious reemergence*' from grief, and the self-transcendent return to the world with grace.

Words Create Worlds

The Pilgrimage Begins

This is a therapeutic writing exercise. Please do it when you can be in a quiet reflective state by yourself. I encourage you to write your reflections—(a) by hand because growth is an embodied experience and the more you make it sensory, the deeper would be its effect; and (b) in a dedicated notebook since following chapters have similar exercises, and having all your reflections in one place would help you make deeper meaning of your growth pilgrimage.

◆

Think of various grief experiences you have faced in life, whether about death or non-death loss, trauma or adversity. Try to be fully aware in your body, heart and mind of the feelings and thoughts that you had while going through the experience. Now write about the GROWTH Mandala pilgrimage you seek for yourself. If you need help, you may use the following prompts.

1. Your metaphors for grief and growth. What do they signify?
2. How would you like to bring the growth metaphor alive through your thinking, being, doing and living?
3. When overwhelmed by grief, how do you stay in touch with your growth wisdom? To what effect?
4. Which phase of the GROWTH Mandala pilgrimage is calling you?

'सोना आग में तपकर ही कुंदन बनता है'
(sona aag mein tap kar hi kundan banta hai)
'It is only by burning in fire that
raw gold becomes pure fine gold'

This popular Hindi saying suggests that the transformative journey of gold from raw metal to kundan (pure fine gold) calls for it to surrender itself in faith to the annihilating fire, the hammering blows, the grinding, the chiseling, the sculpting and the polishing. The pilgrimage of grief and growth also tries, tests, humbles, cleanses, heals, shapes and transforms us. We have to offer ourselves in faith to the sacred fire of sorrow, pain, lament, cry and mourning, before we emerge stronger, wiser, purer, and invoke love, grace and meaning in life.

Before we move to the next chapter which offers a deep dive into the 'grief affirmation' phase of the GROWTH Mandala pilgrimage, please remember to create and take home your poetic affirmation.

PATH 3

Poetic **A**ffirmation to **T**ake **H**ome

'Womb of night
Nurtures light
Life pulsates'

—Neena Verma

Feel your way through the dark night of soul
And keep your light awake

4

Grief Affirmation

'A full soul not only copes with painful, even terrible losses;
it emerges with a greater fullness,
and most essential of all
with a new blissfulness of love.'

—Friedrich Nietzsche

It was New Year's Eve. Sheeba and Raman were heartily planning their annual lunch party to usher in the new year, which also happened to be their only son Aryan's birthday. Undeterred by the cold, they were busy reviewing arrangements, while waiting for their son to return home from work. This year was special because their elder daughter Sana was going to visit them for the first time since her marriage five weeks ago. As fog had reduced visibility to near-zero, they advised Aryan to stay overnight at his friend's home who lived close to his office. But in his excitement, he decided to return home.

As evening grew into night, the happy parents began to worry for their son. Their attempts to reach him on the phone went in vain. It was 12 a.m. already. Just as they decided to seek help, the police called to inform them of their son's accident. Blinded by fog, his car and a truck had collided. The two-hour drive to the hospital through the dark, foggy night felt longer than a lifetime. By the time they reached, the birthday of their young son had turned into his death day. He had been declared brain-dead. Both parents collapsed with shock. As Sheeba regained consciousness after a few minutes, she found Raman stone-numb.

Broken to the core, the distraught mother had to act brave on the outside. As if looking after Raman, who needed cardiac first-aid, and informing their newly married daughter was not traumatic enough, her shock worsened when a special hospital team approached her with an organ donation appeal, since Aryan was brain-dead and his young body held the promise of healthy organs. Slowly, Raman regained consciousness, but in view of his cardiac stress, Sheeba didn't tell him about the organ donation appeal. Instead, she requested the on-duty police officer to expedite the discharge process, so they could take their beloved son home. But a distress call from the officer's home required him to rush for urgent hospitalization of his daughter who had malfunctioning kidneys. His family was desperately hoping for a kidney donor before it was too late to save her. Yet, he did not leave the hospital without personally comforting Sheeba, speaking to the hospital authorities about honouring her decision, and instructing his deputy to ensure the needful. Though in her dazed state she didn't remember to thank the kind officer, she couldn't get the thought of his ailing daughter off her mind.

Caught between her grief and fear of family backlash on one hand, and compassion on the other, Sheeba's sense of humanity won and she gave consent for donation. Minutes turned into hours and hours stretched to the following morning. Aryan's organs and corneas helped four people. Raman had initially refused, owing to religious beliefs and emotional reasons. Counselled by their daughter Sana, *he eventually agreed to sign the consent form, albeit with distress.*

Eleven months since their loss, the otherwise happy couple had grown distant. Even in their shared loss, their ways of grieving were worlds apart. Contrary to gender stereotypes, Raman grieved openly and bitterly. He blamed Sheeba for Aryan's organ and cornea donation, which was widely covered by the media, as an inspiring story. He held it against her, suspecting her to be fame-hungry. He also felt that she was a stone-hearted woman with no sorrow, and had forgotten their only son so quickly. With time, his bitterness only got worse.

Sheeba, in contrast, was a private and quiet griever. She hid her emotions behind a stoic mask of strength that no mother should have to wear. She went about attending to her domestic responsibilities, and caring for her old mother-in-law and Raman, quietly enduring their laments and insensitive comments. Beneath her silence, she was slowly slipping into chronic grief, which no one except Sana could notice. Disturbed by their condition, Sana feared for her parents' mental well-being, and persuaded them to seek professional help.

The bereaved parents slowly returned to life, restoring a sense of well-being, albeit with some medical issues. Their loss still aches, may always do. But Raman has accepted it without bitterness. He no longer holds anything against Sheeba. If anything, he is proud of her courage and strength, and regrets his insensitive conduct. Having faced and embraced her pain, Sheeba began expressing her feelings through painting. She now raises funds through the sale of her paintings to finance her organ and cornea donation awareness campaign. Sana and Raman actively support her. The family feels wrapped in the warmth of the thought that Aryan gifted life and light to others even as he died on his own birthday.

—◆:◆—

How did Sheeba transform her pain to purpose?

How did Raman find a way to make peace with his loss and grief?

How did Sana facilitate her parents' grief journey, and her own?

Grief affirmation is the way. It is that phase of the *GROWTH Mandala pilgrimage* that inspires and enables us to accept our loss and honour our grief. The story above reflects other phases of the pilgrimage as well, which we will learn about in later chapters. For now, let us focus on grief affirmation.

GROWTH Mandala
Created by Neena Verma

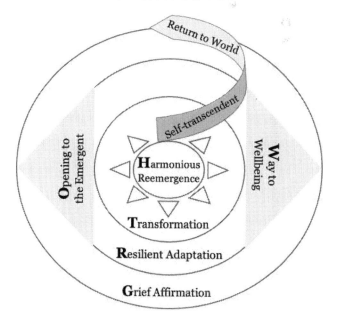

Hope you remember the outermost circle (aka ring of fire) of the GROWTH Mandala that we talked about in the last chapter. This circle represents the *grief affirmation* phase which has five broad facets that one can traverse simultaneously or separately. I have woven these facets together as a framework named **ALIVE—**

- Accepting the reality
- Living with grief
- Invoking faith
- Virtuous integration
- Engaging anew

While I would delve into the ALIVE framework in the order as listed above, please think of it only as a creative and coherent order of appearance, rather than a normative or prescriptive order that you must follow. Once you have read it all, it is for you to decide which of the above aspects calls out to you the first or the strongest, and where you want to begin your grief affirmation journey.

ACCEPTING THE REALITY

Like the ring of fire, grief affirmation too, symbolizes a journey through the dark night of the soul, where the first thing that we are called to do, is to acknowledge and accept the reality. Unacknowledged grief doesn't go anywhere. It just piles up in hidden layers. It is likely that this pile turns growingly painful, if left unaddressed. Accepting reality is a good point to start for an affirmative and healthy grief journey.

Acceptance is an organic process. Approach it in a gentle and patient way. We need to allow the experience and the process of acceptance to unfold in a natural way. It is wholesome when it happens at all levels—body, mind, heart and spirit. Acceptance is not a one-time event. It doesn't happen in one go. It happens in spurts. We tremble. Yet stride on. We fall. Yet gather ourselves again. We feel miserable. Yet stay hopeful. We shouldn't be surprised or disheartened if we find ourselves moving one step forward and two steps backwards. It is like playing a board game where the opponent-dice (aka our grief reactions) can knock us off any time. Like a good player though, we choose to gather ourselves up and start playing again. We choose to flow.

Acceptance can be in parts. Some aspects of our story we might accept more readily, and there are some that we resist, or even resent. In my case, while I could slowly acknowledge the reality of my loss, it took me long to believe that a young healthy person could die of a silent heart attack without a sign or symptom. And it took me forever to come to terms with my son's physical absence. I still find it hard. I still long to see him, touch him, talk to him, feel him in person. Yet in no way does my yearning negate or minimize my acceptance of my loss.

It is OK if acceptance is slow, fragmented or not meeting the social expectations. It takes time. Sometimes an entire lifetime. More importantly it takes patience, faith, compassion and a heart full of courage. Please don't let yourself be overwhelmed by pressure of expectations or advice from others, however well meaning. And please don't torture yourself to 'do' the acceptance faster than your system is naturally coping. Acceptance is not 'done'. In most cases it happens naturally and organically. We have to respect our rhythm and pace. Allow and acknowledge your feelings, laments and questions. Sometimes just acknowledging our inner reality creates a way for its healthy resolution, even transformation. Talking of questions, it is normal to be tormented by the brutal WHY.

And it is very much possible to navigate our way around it in a harmonious manner.

WHY O WHY

Many of us are haunted by the agonizing WHYs, especially when the loss is sudden, untimely, unexpected, stigmatized, by violence, traumatizing, or out of order in any way. Losses like these can understandably rock our faith and core life-view, triggering a flurry of angry WHYs. With my young, healthy, bright son passing on suddenly, for quite some time I remained in the grip of the painful WHYs—Why did my son die? Why did he have to go so young? Why a silent heart attack at 22 years of age? Why were there no signs or symptoms? Why didn't he get timely attention? Why on one of the happiest days of his life? Why before me? Why am I chosen to outlive him? Why? Why?

In most cases, as we acknowledge and let them be, our WHYs tend to soften and fade, unless when grief has turned complicated. With harmonious acknowledgment, our WHYs may even undergo transformation like it happened with me. My agonized mind was swamped by a thousand WHYs—fierce and unrelenting. The grief-struck mother in me needed solace, and answer. But God was silent. It is hard but I must admit that once in my anguish, I even bemoaned God. Yet, in another corner of my heart, I somehow knew that there were no answers. Acknowledging them not just helped me walk through the dark tunnel of my WHYs, but actually transformed my feelings. From thinking of God as the supreme puppeteer, I began to see Her/Him as the *supreme parent* who sent me all the compassion, faith, patience and courage that I needed to face and endure my WHYs without being devoured by them.

It is OK to feel beset by our WHYs. But not-OK to feed them. When deluged by WHYs, we need to hold ourselves warm and compassionate. I did just that. I held myself in compassion. I let my faith and love take care of my anger. Remember it is about attending to and taking care of your anger, not ignoring, suppressing or controlling it. It calls for emotional and spiritual courage to face our demons. And we all are endowed with that. Being able to acknowledge and witness our WHYs actually frees us. By the grace of God, I didn't remain captive for long. As much as one wounded part of me was gripped by the WHYs, another wise part of me gently held the space for my grief-struck mind and heart to vent. Both my wounded part and my wise part belong to me. It is true for each one of us. Together, our wounded and wise parts make us whole. In the end, the wise parts find a way to heal the wounded parts. All that we need to do is to—

- Be kind to ourselves, and not shame ourselves for our WHYs, however improper they sound to ourselves or others.
- Not fight for answers. The more we hold our WHY tightly, the more we intensify our inner turmoil.
- Understand that some questions have no answer. They are best resolved by being in humble contemplation. If at all there is an answer, it will emerge only from within ourselves.
- Accept that sometimes it is OK to not know, and that sometimes not knowing is the only way to supreme knowing.
- Trust that nature will reveal what we are meant to know, when we are ready to absorb and appreciate the deeper-knowing.
- Remember that sometimes, '*WHY is meaningless. But life is meaningful*'. I received this gift of insight from

my younger son. Read more about it in my story under the 'Invoking Faith' section.

LETTING

Yes, you read it right. I have purposefully used the word '*letting*' alone, not '*letting go*'—the cliched advice that bereaved people commonly have to put up with. In grief affirmation, first and foremost, letting is about *letting the reality sink in*. It is about being in humble and patient witness as nature's wisdom reveals what wants to happen. When we are willing, ready and able, the knowing that we need, shows up. We have to let that *knowing* unfold in a natural way.

Indeed, letting is about letting go as well. The question though is what does *letting go* mean for a person in grief? There is no absolute answer to this question. Quite often the way grievers are advised to '*let go*' tends to imply that they are clutching on to their deceased loved one. Of course, it could be true in exceptional or complicated grief cases. But in most situations, it is not. In the immediacy of the loss when pain looms large, the repeated mention of '*let go*' may actually make the bereaved withdraw and close themselves. Good intention of carers and well-wishers notwithstanding, sometimes the '*let go*' sermon can hurt more than help. When interspersed in a sensitive conversation and implying '*release of suffering without denying pain*', it is likely to have an affirmative impact.

Let us face it. We don't have to eject our loved ones from our heart and mind. The relationship doesn't die. Even after their mortal journey is complete, our loved ones continue to live in our consciousness. We all want to, lovingly, preserve the bond. We owe it to ourselves and to our deceased loved one. By all means, we should let our relationships become an eternal loving bond, albeit in a healthy way. It is the suffering that we need to let go and release, not our loved one's presence in our consciousness. So be gentle with yourself when others push you to let go. Let us hope and trust that they mean well. That said, you alone know what let go means for you, and when you are ready to do that in a harmonious way. Let your suffering be organically released, whether through yoga, meditation, expressive arts, writing or any other therapeutic medium. Trust your instinct and honour your natural rhythm.

There is another important form of letting that we don't commonly talk of—*letting come*. Both letting go and letting come complement and complete each other. For suffering to be released, we must be willing to '*let in*' a healthy way of coping and living with our grief. For him to let go of his anger and resentment, Raman had to allow his warmth and trust to be rekindled. He had to *let in* humility and compassion. He had to let-surface his inherent healing capacity to let go of his suffering, and balm his wounded heart. We all can do it. Of course, it is not easy. It is not hard either.

Transformative Tip 1

Let-Go and Let-Come

This experience involves deep-breathing and reflection. Please choose a quiet and comfortable space and time to do it.

- Breathe-in to the count (4–6) that your body feels comfortable. Hold and exhale to a similarly comfortable count. Be gentle. Repeat 8–10 times.
- Notice, without judgment, your sensations, feelings and thoughts.
- As you exhale, gradually allow your inner tensions to be released.
- Express (vocal or silent)—'*Thank you "guilt"* (or

whatever you seek to let go) *for your role in my growth. Time for us to bid good-bye.'*

- Simultaneously, keep inhaling new gifts of life from mother nature—the touch and smell of breeze, bird-song or whatever nourishes you.

- Express (vocal or silent)—*'Thank you "bird"* (or whatever stimuli you are receiving as a gift) *for your happy sound and message of living-in-the-moment (or whatever be your learning). I receive it with gratitude.'*

- When exhaling—let go without complaint. When inhaling—let in with humility and curiosity. Do both in harmony and with gratitude. Thank each for its good role in aiding your awareness and growth.

- Be kind to yourself. Stay mindful of your experience in the moment. Do what naturally feels good. Be sure not to task yourself.

- Later in the day, find a peaceful moment to journal your experience.

- Write what you let go of on a piece of paper, and trash or burn it. Taking Raman's example, he let go of his 'guilt' over hurting his wife.

- Write what you let in on a piece of paper, and pin it at a prominent place where it greets you every day. For Sheeba, it was her emergent gift of expressive arts that helped her release her pain through painting.

- Feel and express gratitude to your heart, mind and other parts of your being; and the people and elements in your environment that support your let go and let-come experiences.

—❖—

LIVING WITH GRIEF

Being able to accept our loss is a good start. It is not the end of our trial yet. Living with grief is a long journey. Painful, unnerving, angst-full. Also, cathartic, affirmative and transformative. We need to witness our grief, allow ourselves to feel not-ok, take things one moment at a time, and be fully present to our swing and sway coping.

WITNESS YOUR GRIEF

Being in grief can feel as if we have been thrown in a deep narrow gorge. It is dark. We can't see our way up or around. Every turn feels like a blind turn in this gorge. Strange creatures are frighteningly moving about us. At every step we feel more frozen than alive in our senses. We feel lost, desperate and defeated. And yet, some warm force within chooses hope over despair. How? Indeed, the gorge we have fallen into is a long blind alley. There is no sight of an opening anywhere. Yet, each ditch or thorny bush or strange creature that we encounter has a message for us. As we begin to witness our journey through the gorge, it begins to evoke more awe than fear.

Once on a coracle (basket boat) ride on the Kaveri river in the south of India, we were passing under a huge tree that had its vastly spread branches bent over a long stretch. Enjoying the soft tickles of passing branches, we suddenly noticed a snake dangling from a branch that our boat was fast approaching. Even as the rest of us nearly screamed with fear, the boatman and my transcended son (then 15) stayed calm and steady in their breath. Though frightened to the core, we somehow followed their lead and kept our breath steady. Lo and behold, we didn't just pass by safely without disturbing the snake or getting harmed by it, we even felt filled with awe at its splendid red-brown shining beauty. Never before, in my life, could I have imagined myself staying calm at the sight of a reptile, least of all a snake. And here I was, admiring its beauty. Snake—beautiful! I couldn't believe my own experience. My transcended son exclaimed—'*not every experience needs a reaction or logical explanation*'. How true! And how wise!

Sometimes an experience shows up only to reveal a lesson and we learn it best by witnessing it rather than reacting to it. Grief is one such experience. Like it or not, loss and trauma will bring along grief. There is nothing we can do to avoid it, duck it or shoo it away. It frightens us, appalls us, torments us, but only as long as we are reacting to it. Witness it unfold, and not just our pain and sorrow begin to melt, but beyond that, our sleeping strengths, virtues and resources that we were either not aware of or had forgotten, also begin to surface.

As we stay in faith and witness our journey through the (grief) gorge that we must traverse, we instinctively feel within, a surge of strength. Looking around with awe, we begin noticing tiny grass-blades quietly sprouting out of mighty stubborn rocks. We begin to find openings that hold promise of growth. Crawl, kneel, elbow or hike, we choose to tread the path. Where we couldn't find even a trail, we make a path by walking in faith. Our grief journey becomes a pilgrimage, and we a pilgrim.

IT IS OK

There could be days when you want to shut the door on others. It may feel impolite. It is ok if this is the only way to secure your quiet healing space. There could be times when others make insensitive comments. It is ok to feel wronged or hurt.

Ignore if you can. And if you can trust their maturity and objectivity, it is ok to sensitize them about the effect of their comments on you. If their insensitive ways still persist, it is ok for you to fold back.

There could be times when your mind goes for a toss. It is ok. In the face of fear, hurt, grief, anger or any other similarly upsetting state—the primitive part of our brain is more active than the more sophisticated emotional and executive (thinking and doing) parts. In such a state, our thinking and processing capacity is not fully available to us. We feel as if our mental faculties have stopped functioning. We feel blank or confused or incompetent. It is normal, and it is passing. In some odd cases, mental functioning may get severely or more permanently affected. But in most cases, it restores. Be gentle on yourself and don't strain your already stressed brain. Allow it to heal, rest and regain functionality as per its natural rhythm.

There could be times when you feel vague aches. You feel sick without a clear reason. You may not want to get out of bed, not even to bathe. It may feel untidy. It is ok. Allow your body the rest it needs. It is ok to ignore comments and suggestions to exercise, pop a pill or go for other such superficial treatments. It is ok to follow your body's lead. It is ok to rest and let your body recuperate naturally as long as you don't sense a real reason for worry; in which case you must seek medical help. Do whatever helps you release tension in a safe, healthy, non-addictive and harmonious way. Sometimes sleep may evade you. Even when you do get some, you might feel tormented by nightmares, wake up feeling thirsty, sweat profusely on a cold night, or shiver in a summer month. You might feel restless, fatigued or anxious. It is normal. That said, disturbed sleep adds to our already heavy grief stress. Please give your body due rest even if sleep remains elusive.

In grief, the not-ok effects stay for some time. It is ok to remain in not-ok-ness for some time rather than suppressing or hiding it. By all means, do fulfill your responsibilities, especially towards young kids or elderly people, if there are any that you must take care of. But even for that, it is ok not to bother with elaborate routines. Seek professional help if such not-ok-ness persists for long or some complications are evident. That said, ok or not-ok, take life one moment at a time.

ONE MOMENT AT A TIME

In grief, it is normal to feel deluged by a tsunami of emotions. Typical human instinct is to fight, take flight or freeze when threatened by adverse stimuli. It is no different in grief. Different people have different reactions. Some people get weighed down by their pain and sorrow, some resign to fate, some look for ways to suppress or escape their pain, some go numb with fear, and some lament bitterly. None of these are abnormal. But they don't help ease the pain, fear or anguish. True, we don't normally think through grief. True, our instinctive reactions are triggered by our primitive brain. Also true, as much that humans are uniquely endowed with sophisticated parts of the brain that enable us to respond in an affirmative way. All that we must do is—be mindfully present in the moment. After the initial surge of instinctive grief reactions begin to settle, it is both possible and advisable for us to slowly become more present to our feelings, thoughts and overall state, and start responding in a more conscious way.

Is it easy? No.

Is it possible? Yes.

Taking life one moment at a time is the key. In grief, the weight of our emotional turmoil is heavy. We need to go slow to be able to travel far. Living more fully in the moment helps us face and embrace our pain. We need to cultivate or enhance a Zen-like slowness, allowing each experience to unfold and each moment to reveal its true meaning. We need to become present in the moment. Famous Buddhist monk Thich Nhat Hanh avers—'Life is available only in this moment.' Living more fully in the moment helps us stay rooted. It is not about sitting in silence, becoming passive, observing or meditating. It is about becoming fully present to what is happening before and around us, what we are experiencing in the unfolding moment, what meaning we are making and how we are responding. Once we begin to see with mindful eyes, and consciously choose our response to the experience on hand, we begin to notice things beyond our pain and sorrow. We begin to face and flow, rather than fight, flee or freeze.

When Sheeba began to slow down, breathe deep and live more fully in the moment, she started to notice the myriad hues of nature which found their way into her paintings. Someone who had never handled a drawing pencil, leave alone a paint-brush, had begun to paint at 56 years of age. And how! Her paintings found ready buyers not because people wanted to patronize a vulnerable, grief-struck mother, but because they saw life coming alive in her art. Without skirting or suppressing her grief, Sheeba let her pain and her reverence for life be painted together on the same canvas. Living life one-moment-at-a-time, she started to feel fully awake and aware, and in the process embodied what Thich Nhat Hanh calls 'peace is every step'—

> Peace is present right here and now, in ourselves and in everything we do and see. Every breath we take, every step we take, can be filled with peace. We need only to be awake, alive in the present moment.

Pause and Ponder-1

*'The butterfly counts not months
but moments, and has time enough.'*

—Rabindranath Tagore

Think of what Guru Rabindranath Tagore and Thich Nhat Hanh have to say about living in the moment, and reflect on the following:

- What is your way to receive each new moment? Passive, unaware, welcoming, awake, mindful or some other way?
- How do you typically respond to different life events and experiences? Fight? Flight? Freeze? Face? Flow?
- What effects ensue from your typical response pattern? Would you like to bring a change? Why? And how?
- What new/different/better you need to do to become fully alive, awake and present in the unfolding moment?

SWING AND SWAY

Explaining their 'dual-process model of coping with bereavement', grief experts, Margaret Stroebe and Henk Schut, maintain that in grief we oscillate between loss-orientation and restoration-orientation. Their research establishes that such oscillation enables a natural balancing process between loss-oriented experiences such as pain, sorrow, angst, rumination, yearning, anxiety, despair, on one side; and restoration-oriented responses such as resilient adaptation, attending to routines and responsibilities of life, well-being restoration, returning to work, rebuilding financial or social security and more, on the other side. I like to think of restoration-orientation as fundamentally life-orientation. In that sense, the swing and sway is between healthy affirmation of loss and meaningful reconstruction of life, with both allowing respectful space for each other. This is what the wheel of life is all about—birth, growth, decay, death (and rebirth depending on your belief about the same). The Hindu Holy Trinity of Gods, Brahma (creation), Vishnu (sustenance) and Shiva (destruction and regeneration), each represent one essential aspect of the wheel of life. Together they complete the eternal cycle of life. No wonder Shiv in Hindi also means eternal-truth.

Please give yourself permission to swing in and out of loss-oriented pain. It is absolutely fine to grieve, ache, yearn and ruminate for as long as it naturally happens to you, unless the grief has turned chronic and there are secondary complications. And please allow yourself to seek restoration. There is no reason to feel guilty about the desire to rebuild a new life and enjoy its natural pleasures. In all likelihood, most people tend to swing and sway between the two states rather than being fully on one side. It actually helps to restore balance. Remember, the past is never fully gone. Much of it lives on and serves as a foundation for the present and the future. Good drivers intuitively know when to move forward, when to put on the brakes, and when to look in the rear-view mirror. Follow the cue of your inner driver and let yourself sway back and forth between rumination and restoration. Just be sure that your rumination stays more reflective than intrusive, and your restoration process keeps growing.

Transformative Tip 2

Heal and Grow

1. Think about the loss-oriented stressors (anxious rumination, anger, guilt, yearning, fear, pain) that you want to heal. Choose one that you want to begin with.

   - Start on a new page. Name it HEAL.
   - Write down your experience about the stressor you chose above. Write in as much detail as possible about which aspect of this stressor you want to heal, which aspect you want to purge altogether, and which aspect has a lesson for you.
   - Think of the internal (your virtues, strengths) and external (family, friends, work) resources that you think could help in purging what is harmful, healing what hurts, and preserving what you value.
   - Jot down in detail.

2. Simultaneously, think about the restoration-oriented life-aspects (health, relationships, social capital, career, financial security) that you want to rebuild or grow anew. Choose one at a time.

   - Start on a fresh page. Name it GROW.
   - Think of what you have chosen to restore, rebuild or grow anew.
   - Close your eyes. Take a few deep breaths. Invoke the child inside you and imagine a good genie has fulfilled your desire. Soak in the experience with child-like innocence.
   - Continuing to imagine that your dream has come true, guess what internal (your virtues, strengths) and external (family, friends, work) resources, and

specific actions might bring it to true reality.

- Jot down in detail.

1 and 2. Together

- Revisit your notes after a day or two. See if and how the HEAL and GROW section are interconnected.
- Create separate, joint or overlapping guide maps as you deem wise.
- Consult someone trusted if you feel the need. Seek their help to design your guide map, start the journey and stay on track.
- Start taking tiny actions. Keep striding, one step at a time.
- Review after a fortnight or a month. Notice and celebrate your good progress. Sustain and amplify it. Change/modify/drop what you think doesn't work.
- When you feel satisfied, move on to the next.
- Remember to honour your journey, however slow or trying it feels.

INVOKING FAITH

Krishna Gotami learnt the painful way that death cannot be fought with. She came to realize that accepting nature's law of impermanence, and affirming one's loss is the first step towards transcending grief. So did Sheeba, Sana and Raman. And thus, began their growth pilgrimage from trauma to transformation.

The grief affirmation phase of the GROWTH Mandala pilgrimage is a transcendent journey in faith. Not knowing how and whether we would be able to handle it, we choose to step on the threshold of our pain. Traversing one moment at a time, we begin the pilgrimage, honouring our grief and allowing it the sacred space that it needs in our consciousness and life. True, grief creates a gaping hole in our entire being. True, it shatters our faith and beliefs. True, at times it even feels as if we are sucked into a frightening bottomless blackhole. Yet, grief and faith do not forbid each other. What remains equally true is that the sacred void of grief and pain can't be filled with anything external, but only with our own light. True indeed, that we instinctively know how to let our inherent *helio* (life-giving light) enter the dark hole of our grief. True most certainly, that we all have the innate wisdom and strength to affirm grief and allow it the due space, time and energy it asks of us. True above all, that deep inside we know intuitively, why and how, we must stay in faith.

A barrage of condolence messages awaited me in my mailbox the day I opened it after some weeks of my loss. As much as I meant to honour the kindness of senders with a personal word of gratitude, I was also finding it difficult to read through mostly standard, and some painfully cliché messages. And then I came across this brief one—'may your faith stay strong'. I responded with gratitude, and moved to check the remaining mails. But the message stayed with me. That mail kept calling me back.

Faith! How? And why? What was there to be in faith about? I had been, suddenly and ruthlessly, robbed of my most precious belonging. The message both disturbed as well as intrigued me. The more I tried shrugging it off, the more it kept tapping on my heart and mind. I even felt somewhat angry at this nicely worded sermon. A resentful voice screamed within—*'Does he realize what it means to lose a child?'*. He did indeed. I was so caught up with my own pain that I had forgotten about his loss. He had been living with a prosthetic leg for four years ever since an accident took away his wife, two children and his leg. For long, his grief was laden with guilt, not being able to forgive himself for surviving when his loved ones had all died. Grief. Pain. Guilt. Loneliness. Fear. Angst. Who knew the dreadful combo better than him! The sense of bereft-ness and brokenness that he was living with—will I ever be able to even imagine, leave alone understand?

In that poignant moment, something within me began to thaw and melt. The following day, I called him wanting to say so much, including offering an apology for the hard feelings I had nurtured for a brief while. But I couldn't say more than a broken word of sorry, and a warm thank-you. In our long phone call, only silence, sighs and sobs spoke. Yet, we both heard and understood each other's pain. What I still needed to understand was how to stay in faith when a part of me was feeling cheated by destiny. A week later nature sent me the answer through my younger son.

MY STORY

My younger son was home for his semester-break holidays. One bright afternoon we went out to a garden. It was just the kind of winter day we used to love for our impromptu Sunday picnics when my children were small. The garden was vibrant and fragrant. There were happy sounds all around. But I resented it all! How could nature be in bloom when my life had come apart! I wanted to rush back home. But my younger son held me, as my yet-silent grief burst into a flood of tears. After what felt like an eternity, I slowly regained composure, as a tiny bird came fluttering and started to endearingly play around us. In that precious moment, I came alive as my just about 18-year-young son, himself deep in pain, wrapped me with his warm wisdom—

See Mamma, what has happened has happened. Grief has come to live with us. We have to let it in. Yes, pain is huge. But so is life, Mamma. Sun is still rising every morning and doing what it must—give light and life. Grass is still green. Birds are still singing. Moon still shows up with its milky light. Life is alive, Mamma, and so are we. 'Why' is meaningless. But life is meaningful. Let us walk with life and let our pain walk with us.

He didn't try to pacify me. He didn't sound resigned. He didn't do anything that you could expect from a person in grief. He didn't say anything preachy or cliché. He just affirmed the reality as it was.

When did my exuberant kiddo grow up and become an adult? And how? So wise and calm. On one plane, I felt filled with awe, gratitude and love. On another, I felt concerned if our loss had pushed him to mature faster than he should have. Indeed, he had become wiser, stronger and a lot more appreciative of life.

My young son had just shown me that the way to transcend our grief was to let it have its due space and course in our life. And that it is possible to say YES to life, no matter what.

SAYING YES TO LIFE

I picked up from where my younger son had closed our conversation that day. With love and gratitude, I received and celebrated his wisdom—'*Why is meaningless. But life is meaningful*'. And I chose to say '*YES*' to life, affirming both the misery and the meaning it brought along. We honoured our grief and let it walk with us, even as we chose to walk with life.

We invoked faith. And a humbling turn of events guided us to take forward my elder son's inclusive learning mission that he had started at just eight years of age. We decided to build on the library endeavour that he used to independently run for socio-economically disadvantaged children. By the grace of God, we have so far founded one mobile and eight static libraries. The ninth is delayed because of the pandemic. And we hope to keep adding.

Faith, indeed. Faith, I came to understand, is what we have when all else has been taken away.

Pause and Ponder-2

Think of a time when your deeply held values or beliefs got shaken because of a loss, trauma, bereavement or any other adversity.

- How did this affect your world-view and core faith?
- What mental and emotional churn did you go through?
- How did you cope? How did you make peace?
- It is, indeed, hard to look for the silver lining when thundering clouds have burst on your head. What nonetheless do you cherish in your story as a lesson of awakening? How has this transformed you?

VIRTUOUS INTEGRATION

'When we embrace the dark,
We become ready to welcome the light.'

—Neena Verma

Having restored our faith, accepted our reality and found a healthy way to live with it, it may seem that we are now ready to move on. Truth is there is no *'moving on'* from grief. It is not a lost or broken phone that we can forget and put behind us as soon as we have a new device in hand. Bereavement can make a permanent hole in our life. A harmonious way to live with this hole is to fill it with the life-giving helio (light) that emanates from our whole (not fragmented) being. Understanding that all our life experiences together make us whole, paves the way for virtuous integration of grief with other aspects of life, rather than fearing, avoiding, suppressing or purging it. Here the word 'virtuous' means sacred, wholesome, harmonious, earnest and adaptive. Like other experiences, our grief, too, forms the warp and weft of life. As we honour this reality, we begin to adapt and weave grief into the overall fabric of our life, rather than feeling tortured by urges to tear and destroy the fabric itself.

Talking of adaptation, there are various ways in which people cope with pain and grief. Diversion or distraction can be helpful as a temporary measure, that too, only if it is not to suppress or run away from difficult emotions. It is healthy when people get productively busy with work or volunteer for a good cause or other meaningful pursuits, but not by ignoring or disregarding their grief and pain. It can prove unhealthy if it is more an escape than a purposeful harmonious move. And it is both unsafe and unhealthy if diversion involves substance abuse or any other harmful activity.

While it is true that a highly independent person might experience or exhibit less distress, sometimes it might actually be conscious or unconscious diversion from grief because of avoidant relationship pattern. In such a case, grief may manifest in a delayed or disguised way. In contrast, those with insecure-attachment style may tend to cling and get overly preoccupied in relationships, which can trigger chronic grief and separation distress after bereavement. Unlike both these types, people who are securely attached in their relationships have a better likelihood of approaching grief in an adaptive way. That said, we all can learn to cope with grief in a healthy way. It is advisable as well as possible. Our hearts and minds intuitively know the way. Whether overwhelmed by separation distress or experiencing vague grief, we can learn to attune to our grief in a conscious and acceptant way, and affirm it as a sacred character in our life story.

Virtuous integration of grief is about honouring the wheel of life that is bound by its very nature to keep turning on its own, whether we like it or not. And if it is so, it is better to choose to participate in its sacred movement, rather than being dragged on. Virtuous integration of grief opens the path forward to move with (not move-on) life. It enables us to imprint the loss and grief into our personal history like any other significant life-event. It helps us live with our grief without becoming preoccupied with it or feeling the weight of it on our back, even when it occurs or recurs with intensity, which it does in waves and cycles. From a state of feeling '*dis-membered*', we are able to move towards '*re-membering*' memories, feelings and thoughts. We will learn some more about it in chapter nine.

Virtuous integration of grief honours the wheel of life, allowing space for both grief and will to live. It is about saying—life matters and so does grief, and the two can and do acknowledge each other.

—◆—

ENGAGING ANEW

Traversing across our grief affirmation journey, at some point, we begin to return to life and world. But we are a different river now.

'You will heal and you will rebuild yourself around the loss you have suffered. You will be whole again but you will never be the same. Nor should you be the same nor would you want to.'

—Elizabeth Kubler-Ross and David Kessler

It is said that our body cells continually die and regenerate. Without getting into the science behind this, let us focus on the underlying message—we are not the same body or person that we once were. Grief, too, is an evolving process. Our feelings and thoughts are in a constant and frantic churn. However, this churn is essentially accompanied by renewal. Such is the law of nature. Spring is sure to follow winter. The season of grief too abides by this law. But for growth to ensue, we must engage anew with life, ourselves, our deceased loved one, and others.

EMOTIONAL HEALING

Self-care, in grief, is perhaps the most important thing. And very often it takes a beating, especially for women who have to shoulder multiple responsibilities. I know this first hand, and so must many of you who read this book. We need holistic self-care when we are preparing to re-meet the world and re-engage with life. Self-care is not selfish. It takes very little—deep breathing, due rest, basic nutrition, gentle exercise, yoga, meditation or whatever else suits us. We will talk about all these and more modalities at length in chapter seven.

For now, let us focus on the often invisible, but very

important, aspect of self-care—emotional healing. The weight of emotions is heavy. And it can be harmful if we hide, suppress, or even worse, repress our emotions for far too long. It shows up in body. My unusual and excessive weight and hair loss, menopausal complications and sudden manifestation of diabetes could all be related in some way or the other to keeping my emotions buried under the weight of responsibilities and the expectation to maintain the *'strength-mask'*. I paid a heavy price. You should not.

In grief, emotions can show up in myriad hues and forms. Hope you recall the entangled ball of emotions that we talked about in chapter two. We all can learn to disentangle this ball. Let us learn one of the many ways.

Mandala Art

Heal-Thy Self

This, as you know, is a meditative arts exercise. Please do it when you can be in a quiet reflective state by yourself.

- Think of your entangled ball of emotions. Identify one emotion that you want to start with.
- Breathing deep, experience this emotion as if it is happening in this moment. Notice where in the body it shows up, and with what effect. Become aware of its presence in your heart and mind.
- Notice what, if any, wounds you feel. What healing do you seek?
- When you feel fully associated, draw a mandala representing:
  - your emotion and the pain you feel—in the outermost circle
  - the healing you seek and visualize—in the middle circle

- ◆ the specific actions you are willing to take to heal your emotions—in the innermost circle
- ◆ healed and healthy Self—at the centre
- Now reflect upon the following and write down your reflections:
  - ◆ How was the experience of drawing this mandala?
  - ◆ What emotional healing process does this mandala suggest?
  - ◆ Notice various shapes, colours, symbols of nature on your mandala. What message do they have for you?
  - ◆ What emotional healing protocol would you like to design for yourself? What would it include—inner reflection, outward expression, yoga, arts, writing, music, dance, nature, social service, meditation, therapy or something else?
- Create an action map. If you feel the need, consult someone trusted, even a professional if so required. Seek their help to create your action map, get started and stay on track.
- When it comes to taking-action, a little discipline helps. While you don't have to regiment yourself, do try to be as clear and as specific as possible.
- The day you start your healing journey, sow a plant of your liking. Give it a name that represents your *HEAL-THY Self* journey. Feel the soil and the seed, both in your hands and your heart. Take good care of the plant as it grows. And let the plant take care of you. See your growth in the plant's growth and vice versa. Ask it to remind and nudge you to keep striving forward. Celebrate your small or big leaps with it. Ask it for solace or even suggestions as if it were a confidant or a therapist.

> • The day you feel satisfied in your emotional healing journey (I promise it won't take you long to be there), start with another emotion that you want to heal.

ETERNAL BOND

Dr Robert Neimeyer, the grief researcher and the creator of *'Grief Therapy as Meaning Reconstruction',* has an altar for his mother on his bookcase where he has placed her photo and mementos, some of which are from her own childhood. I have a special corner in my children's room arranged as my son's tiny nook, something that he secretly wanted for his never-ending reading immersions, but I could not arrange in his lifetime. Apart from his picture and a few precious keepsakes, his cornea-donation appreciation certificate and his university degree, which life didn't give him opportunity to receive, sit on the altar. I have started to fiddle on my son's keyboard, though the clumsy me is not even a shade close to his effortless play. Sheeba has hand-painted her son's portrait and adorned it with a pearl necklace that he had gifted her, bought with his first salary.

Why would a renowned grief expert like Dr Neimeyer do this? Why do Sheeba and I do this? Is this clinging on to the memory of the dead? Some people would think so. But those who understand that the relationship with the dead doesn't die with them, would appreciate that what we have on the altars and in the remembrance-niches, are not just things. These are our quiet loving ways to say that we honour the special place that our deceased loved one continues to have in our hearts, our minds, our life. Dr Neimeyer, Sheeba, and I are letting our relationship become an eternal bond of love, just as many of you might have done. Things on our altars are symbols and souvenirs that help us remember, preserve and celebrate our bond. These are remembrances that transcend life and death. We will talk more about this in chapter nine.

ENGAGING WITH OTHERS

Having accepted our loss, as we begin to adapt to our new life, reengaging with the world may not be easy. Even if some people want to engage with us and care for us, they may be hesitant about connecting, out of their concern for doing it the right way. We can wait and hope that they will sooner or later connect. Or we can proactively reach out and sensitize them about our changed needs from life and relationships. However difficult or painful it feels, we can make the first move to start reengaging with such genuine well-wishers, and share our unfolding feelings, thoughts, anxieties and needs. Even if you are not yet ready to engage fully, honour your urge and their sincere availability, and start stepping out of your shell, one baby step at a time. It would be great if someone's warm hand of support comes your way on its own. But if it doesn't, it is ok to ask for it from those you hope, need and trust, instead of waiting forever.

Meanwhile a lot of people would have disappeared from your life, whether out of discomfort around engaging with a person in grief, or because of it being a superficial relationship, or simply because routines of life don't allow much time and energy to sit by those in grief and trauma. Please avoid recoiling in disappointment or resentment towards such people. Instead, try understanding their difficulties or dilemmas. Pick up the phone and make a call yourself, if you are missing some one strongly. Help them help you by letting them know your feelings and needs. Let them respond in their own way. If they remain unresponsive, let go. Be kind to yourself. There is no reason for you to judge yourself if others don't give you the care you need or want. Please avoid falling into self-pity that many of us tend to feel. Rather, seek to understand. Who knows what reasons they have to remain unavailable or unresponsive? It may feel hard. Yet forgive. It may feel harder to continue moving. Yet stride on.

'Life is both dreadful and wonderful.
Smile to your sorrow because you are more than your sorrow.'

—Thich Nhat Hanh

Indeed, we need to smile to our sorrow. It is hard but not impossible. It calls for resilience. Having affirmed grief, we need to meet life with resilience. Who can teach resilience better than children who are always true to their emotions! They fall, they feel hurt, they cry their heart out. And then they dust their bruises, gather themselves up and begin to run again, whether or not they get any help. Children don't think much of falling. But they care a lot about rising. They instinctively know that their strength is to be found right in the company of their vulnerability. They accept their fall and nudge themselves to rise again. They embody resilience. In many ways we continue to remain the child that we once were. When in grief, we must invoke our child-like resilience and adapt to the unfolding loss-altered life.

The next chapter explores the realm of *'resilient adaptation'* phase of the GROWTH Mandala pilgrimage. Before moving there, please remember to create and take-home your poetic affirmation for the grief affirmation phase.

PATH 4

Poetic Affirmation to Take Home

'Faith
The quiet call of soul.
An invocation for life,
In grief and in growth.

Stay awake to
what wants to happen.

Let go and let come.

In the darkest despair,
hope illuminates, and life calls.

Invoke faith.'

—Neena Verma

Listen to the song of your soul.
Create a harmonious way to stay in faith.

5

Resilient Adaptation

*'Out of suffering have emerged the strongest souls;
the most massive characters are seared with scars.'*

—Kahlil Gibran

*Simone and Neil were in the final year of school when
they started dating. Over the next few years their
relationship grew from teenage infatuation to mature
love and culminated in marriage 11 years later. Their
relationship was happily accepted by their families who
celebrated their marriage with fanfare, holding several
rituals and ceremonies representing both sides. Simone
was a part-time special-learning-needs educator and Neil
had a promising corporate career. An introvert and private
person, Simone preferred being at home after work. Neil
being an outdoor person was happy to shoulder all out-
worldly responsibilities. They were a happy couple—more
friends than spouses.*

*A picture-perfect story until 13 years into their
marriage when Neil got diagnosed with lung malignancy.
His cancer rapidly went into metastasis and he passed
away after seven months of painful encounter with
the dreaded disease, despite the best possible medical
treatment. Even before his family could swallow the hard
reality of his disease, especially since he was a non-smoker*

and a man with impeccable health habits, they had to absorb the shock of his untimely painful death.

Simone was devastated. For her, Neil was not just her husband. They had almost grown together. Their spousal relationship had in no ways dulled their thick friendship. And they also attracted a tinge of envy for continuing to be the love-birds that they had been at the start of their relationship some 24 years ago. Alongside this, over the years, Simone's dependence on Neil had grown to the extent that she completely avoided all out-worldly jobs. In the seven months of his treatment, Simone struggled hard to manage family errands, Neil's treatment, medical billing, insurance claims and other such things. She relied on a few of Neil's and her own friends. But after his demise, she needed to develop her own ability and confidence to manage her life affairs.

Being a simple, non-ambitious person, Simone had always been happy and content as a special-learning-needs educator. She loved basking in the glory of her husband's professional success. After Neil's demise, Simone felt that she had not just lost her husband, lover and an intimate friend, but even her social identity and financial security had come crashing. Neil's handsome salary and social stature had so far ensured a privileged life for them. Overnight, Simone's cocooned life turned gray with uncertainty. Her modest honourarium wasn't sufficient even for basic needs of life, leave alone the comforts that her family was used to. She worried for her two small children. Even as she swallowed the bitter reality and accepted her loss, Simone felt overwhelmed by multiple anxieties. She could have slid down the treacherous trail of her grief, worry and fear; or she could have somehow coped. She did more than just cope. She adapted to her loss-altered life with resilience and meaning.

The small special-learning-needs centre that Simone started with just three children from her living room 11 months after Neil's demise, has, in seven years, grown to become a much-respected institute with 48 children onboard as of this writing. She now runs her centre from a rented place near her home, and also offers custom-designed home-classes for mobility-constrained students with special-learning-needs. She has a six-member team working with her. Simone is not just able to give her children the comforts of life and the standard of education that they were used to, but has also discovered her excellent leadership, administrative and communicative ability that would have otherwise remained in hiding. Her family and friends admire the resilience with which she has taken charge of her life and rechristened it.

She does sometimes ruminate about her past life, feeling particularly sad remembering how Neil used to coax her to do more with her talent. But she turns her regret into motivation to put her talent and Neil's inspiration to productive and meaningful use. She could have fallen. She did, indeed, fall. But she chose to get up and start walking with life. She finds fulfillment and meaning in helping vulnerable special-learning-needs children gain better skill and confidence in life. Her centre is proudly called 'Neil's Nest'. Having tasted her entrepreneurial acumen, she is now thinking of expanding the range of her services. With the intent to extend psychological support to the parents and caregivers, she is now training to become a family counsellor and coach.

—◆—

What transformed a passive, dependent, grieving wife into a successful professional, who has honoured her grief with grit and grace, without letting it derail her life?

What helped Simone not just restore and adapt, but rise beyond her grief and fear?

Simone attributes her almost miraculous transformation to her ability to affirm her grief, and adapt to her loss-altered life with resilience and meaning. She has taken her journey beyond grief affirmation and transformed herself with resilient adaptation; the second phase of the GROWTH Mandala pilgrimage.

GROWTH Mandala
Created by Neena Verma

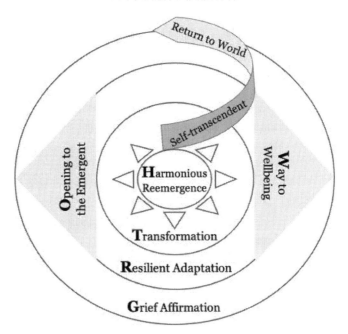

Hope you remember (chapter three) that the middle circle of the mandala, called the *ring of vajra* (thunderbolt), represents the *'resilient adaptation'* phase of the GROWTH Mandala pilgrimage. It is worth repeating that this ring represents eternal truth and power, and ushers us on the path towards the inner essential self. Simone faced and embraced the ring of vajra and invoked her sleeping inner power. This is no externally granted or derived power. We all are innately self-empowering whether or not we are conscious of its existence. And we all can discover it like Simone did. This deeply personal power sprouts from the inner fountain of strength and resilience.

The resilient adaptation phase takes us across The Great Pass of our adaptation to the mighty mountains of our loss and grief. This journey is weary and scary. We make our way through the gorge of our grief with hardy mountains of our pain looming over us. We need to watch each step. We need to face each feeling and thought. We need support to keep our balance, but there is nothing to hold on to except the rough surface of our pain. We feel tempted to give up. But there is nowhere to return. More importantly, something called *hope* remains more steadfast and indomitable than our pain and fear. We see our own light within, and walk on, hoping to see the light on the other side of The Great Pass of our pain. Even as we feel weak and fearful, we choose to face and honour our vulnerability. We choose to gift resilience and strength to our vulnerability. Welcome to the resilient adaptation phase, where you hold on to yourself with faith, hope, poise, grit and meaning; find or kindle courage within, and pick yourself up with all the strength at your command.

A popular parable goes like this—

Three bricklayers are asked: 'What are you doing?' The first says, 'I am laying bricks'. The second says, 'I am constructing a building'. And the third says, 'I am building a cathedral'.

Adapting it to grief context, let us rephrase the parable—

> Three grievers are asked: 'How are you doing?' The first
> says, 'I am suffering'. The second says, 'I am coping'. And
> the third says, 'I am adapting'.

There could be an endless list of what different grievers would
feel and say. To each their own. Let us return to the three
grievers from the parable. None of them should be judged for
how they feel. Their different grief responses do not deserve to
be compared, but held in contrast, for the sake of perspective
taking. We all know that grief and pain are unique to each
individual. Let us assume all three have come to terms with
and accepted their loss. For the sake of our learning, let us talk
about what makes their grief journeys different. It is their way
of being with their grief. While grief, as a reaction to loss, can
remain a passive experience-state, grieving is an active process
whereby the griever makes a conscious choice about what to do
with their pain and loss-altered reality rather than remaining
a passive subject of the same. The third is an active griever
who has made a conscious choice to adapt to loss-altered life.
This griever knows that a storm-beaten tree might bend, but
intuitively knows how to restore and grow again. This griever,
like Simone, invokes the essential human virtue called *resilience*,
and chooses to restore, adapt and rebuild a loss-shattered life.

> *'To everything there is a season, a time to every purpose:*
> *A time to be born... a time to die;*
> *A time to break down... a time to build up;*
> *A time to mourn... a time to dance.'*

—The Old Testament of Wisdom

The third griever recognizes that the time of death is just as
real as time of birth. It needs to be affirmed. This griever

understands that break-down doesn't forbid rebuilding. This griever knows that 'time of grief' actually has a sacred meaning in the 'time for life', and heralds 'time for growth'.

MY STORY

In 2004, I learnt a new perspective on resilience from my then 12 years young, now-transcended son, Utkarsh. As part of his summer holidays assignment, he was to write an essay using 10 meaningful words starting with 'R'. And he chose 'resilience' among others.

I was astonished by his observation that the popular yo-yo example was an incomplete expression of resilience. He held that in its return, the yo-yo can rise up and grow beyond its original position, if we were not to clasp it with our palm and obstruct its ascent in the process. He asserted that in recovering from the fall, it is very much possible for the yo-yo to discover its buoyancy and power to rise beyond its previously known limits. This is what resilience is all about—discovering our strength in our vulnerability, and choosing new horizons as we rise up (not just bounce back) and grow beyond.

Utkarsh taught me that resilience is more than just getting up and recovering. That resilience is taking a leap, and rising up and growing beyond. That resilience is about being expansive as much as it is about being restorative. It was a fresh and deep perspective, coming from a young child. I found it to be of meaning and substance whether in dealing with my own adversities, or in helping my clients deal with theirs.

That said, resilience assumed new meaning for me when, 10 years later, in 2014, I lost my profoundly wise son.

> *My understanding and embodiment of resilience found new depths with my own encounter with grief. And my work as a grief practitioner got deeply transformed as I recognized the true meaning and role of resilience in adapting to the loss-altered life.*

—◆—

RESILIENCE
RISING UP AND BEYOND

Whether it was the plague at the turn of the twentieth century or COVID-19 a century later, or several other traumatic events, humankind's history is testimony to human resilience. The life-story of Joe Biden, the current US President, is a classic case in point. From conquering a speech impediment of stuttering, and becoming the second-youngest senator at 29 years of age, to losing his wife and daughter in a road accident just six weeks later and being told that his sons had a poor chance at survival from critical injuries, to raising his sons with such devotion that he commuted everyday between Delaware and Washington DC, to pioneering the climate protection movement, to serving an entire lifetime as a US senator surviving several controversies and setbacks, to losing his beloved son to brain cancer in 2015, to just five years later successfully leading a tough election in the midst of a pandemic and becoming the 46th president of the USA at the unlikely age of 77 years—Joe Biden is resilience personified in every sense of the word. In a 2015 speech, he shared what his mother once said to him—'Joey, out of everything terrible that happens to you, something good will come if you look hard enough for it'. Can there be a better way to explain what hope, resilience and meaning are all about?

Resilience leads us through the journey of adapting to life after loss and trauma, with fortitude and meaning. Though grief brings along multiple difficult emotions, fear can be particularly engulfing. Worries and anxieties of all kind take over. It is not uncommon for bereaved people to feel weary, scared, lonely and consumed by their sense of insecurity. But oftentimes circumstances and basic needs of life put practical pressures on us to quickly adapt and reconfigure life even as we might still be struggling to come to terms with our loss. Most of us are able to cope and adapt because humans are naturally hardwired for resilience, however beaten or weak we might be feeling in the face of loss, trauma or adversity. Simone had to suddenly step out of her sheltered cocoon and start figuring out even basic matters of life. And she did rise to the occasion, discovering her hitherto hidden resilience and strength. She could have continued her part-time engagement, or at best tried getting a full-time employment. This would have sufficed in some way to ease her financial tensions. But she chose to think more expansively than restoration alone.

Simone chose to stretch and explore beyond her self-set confines. Instead of drowning in pain and fear, she faced and embraced her vulnerability. She took ownership of her response to her pain, shifting gears from the primitive parts of the brain that trigger fight, flight or freeze reactions, to the more sophisticated parts of the brain that prepare us to face our circumstances, make sense of our experience and enable advanced mental functioning. She chose the path of strength without fighting with or being in denial of her vulnerability. She acknowledged her vulnerability, and looked for strength and hope right where her despair was throbbing. She would have easily succumbed to her fear and worries if not for her *will to restore*, growth wisdom, openness to adapt, and courage to carve out a new life larger than her pain, sadness and fear.

She decided to adapt to her grief-altered life by choosing active response over passive suffering, and moved forward with life, gracefully affirming and adapting to her grief, but not letting it sit on her back.

Simply put, resilience is the ability to restore from loss, trauma, adversity, or even life-threatening events, and maintain stable physiological and psychological functioning. It is commonly understood as the will and the ability to bounce back from the adversities of life. But to fully honour its true essence, we should think of resilience in terms of not just its restorative capacity but also its expansive power that Utkarsh taught me about. Resilience doesn't mean we control tears, deny or disregard our vulnerability, or maintain a forced or masked stoicism. Rather, it involves a humble acknowledgment of one's vulnerability, gentle and firm self-nudging, openness to learn and seek help, psychological suppleness to adapt and re-align in the wake of loss, trauma or adversity, and the will to make restorative and expansive efforts.

There are no easy answers as to why different people show up differently on the resilience spectrum. While some are torn apart by their loss, some restore well, and some emerge stronger. One thing though is certain that we all have a resilience muscle innately present within. All that we need to do is what Joe Biden's mother (I assume all mothers of the world do something similar) advised him—'look hard enough for the good'—no matter how horrible our circumstances may feel. I would humbly add to that, hold yourself gently and firmly, and nudge yourself to keep moving.

All through our life we collect a lot of wisdom that becomes part of our DNA and gets activated on its own whenever we are in trouble. This supple *growth wisdom*, called sagacity, lives quietly and deeply in our reflex mechanisms. *Sagacity* is the wisdom and insight that we hold onto, consciously or unconsciously, through all the life experiences that we encounter. It can be something we have learnt and cultivated through formal learning and conditioning processes. It can also come from myriad other sources like poetry, literature, mythology, cinema, song lyrics, scriptures, spiritual sermons, quotable quotes, great sayings, life lessons, or what a guide-figure might have told us, like what Biden's mother told him. Our sagaciousness is an important ingredient of our resilience. Stay in constant contact with your sagacity, and honour it by drinking from its deep sacred well.

Pause and Ponder-1

Make a conscious contact with your sagacity and reflect on the following:

- What precious insights and life-lessons does your sagacity hold?
- What growth wisdom enables you to bounce back from adversity, and rise up and grow beyond your previous limits? How?
- What is your resilience mantra—a song-lyrics, a jingle, a poem, a couplet, a scripture verse, an adage, a precious sermon, or what?
- In what way has this resilience mantra been helping you adapt to loss or trauma shattered life? What else do you wish to add to this mantra?
- If you were to contribute a resilience-specific wisdom-pearl to others' sagacity, what would that be?

SHEPHERD YOURSELF

It is not surprising for grievers to find that many people they hoped to receive help from, either just disappear or are not able to extend much help. Be generous to forgive. Most people are not individually attuned or socially groomed to be with another person's grief or pain. Grief is a lonely journey down a slippery slope. Yet, we are not alone. An amazing shepherd whom we can most consistently rely on, has our back. This shepherd is yourself. It is likely that in grief your human need for connection might remain unfulfilled in parts or full. No complaints. When you don't have anyone else to connect with, you still have yourself. Hold yourself dearly under all circumstances, even more so when no one else is willing or able to hold you. Hold yourself with compassion, care, calm, courage and confidence. Let your heart, mind and soul stand beside each other, and join hands to carve a new path ahead of you when all known paths have disappeared. Whether or not you get the benefit of external scaffolds, hold on to your inner anchors. Be gentle and patient with all things, but most of all with yourself.

If you haven't yet watched the movie *Cast Away*, please do. Apart from being one of the many stellar performances by Tom Hanks, the movie is a poignant story and profound lesson in resilience in a very real and earthy sense. The protagonist, called Chuck Noland, is a FedEx executive who is forever on the move, troubleshooting problems around the globe, and working with the precision of a clock. And here he is—stranded on a desolate island after the flight that he was on board, crashes on the Pacific Ocean. No clue as to where in the world he is stranded. No idea if he will be able to see his beloved fiancée ever again. No clock, no beeper—all his steadfast identity anchors gone. No sight of edible food or any other survival mechanism. No problem to fix, except his existential despair to survive and keep his *will to return* alive. No human presence, except for a companion he creates out of a ball that he finds in one of the FedEx packages that have washed up with him after the crash. He names this companion Wilson after the brand name displayed on the package. If you really want to watch one of the most moving screen depictions ever, of someone grieving, you must watch the two scenes—first, when Noland loses Wilson (the ball companion) but finds it after some struggle, and second when he eventually loses it for good.

Why would the protagonist create a make-believe human companion out of a ball? Why does he keep talking to it? Why does he break into grief after losing Wilson? What does this companion represent after all? What does Noland get from it? Wilson, the companion, is none other than Noland's inner shepherd that affirms his existence even on that lost uninhabited island. It nurtures Noland's will to live, fills him with hope, and makes him continue to engage with life no matter what. In a touching scene, when he eventually returns home after surviving the harsh life-defying circumstances, the protagonist Chuck Noland hauntingly remarks:

> And that's when this feeling came over me like a warm blanket. I knew, somehow, that I had to stay alive. Somehow. I had to keep breathing. Even though there was no reason to hope ... So that's what I did. I stayed alive. I kept breathing. And one day ... the tide came in, and gave me a sail.

Resilience is precisely that—the warm blanket of will to live and will to restore that surfaces tenderly from within when we seem to have lost all our anchors. It is that loving nudge to stay hopeful even when there is no reason for hope. It is the gentle reminder to keep breathing until the tide that would give us a sail comes along, which it will most definitely. And all of this is a gift from the wise and warm shepherd that lives inside ourselves. If there is only one thing you could do to stay resilient in the face of dark, just keep yourself in the guidance of your inner shepherd and wrap yourself with the warm blanket of self-care.

Pause and Ponder-2

Think of an old or present trauma, loss or adversity, that has left you feeling low on hope and strength. Fill up the blanks in the following sentences. Feel free to write as few or as many words as naturally come to you. Be sure to give an honest voice to your feelings.

- I am...
- I am breathing...
- I feel...
- I think...
- I hope to...
- I want to...
- I value...
- I believe...
- I love...
- I care for...
- I care for myself...
- It is OK that I...
- I seek...
- I choose...
- I pursue...
- I cherish...
- ... ... (any other that you deem important)

RISE
A PATHWAY TO RESILIENT ADAPTATION

Most people cope with and survive grief. But some turn it around completely, taking growth and transformation to a new level. Resilience is common to both, even as their pursuit and fruit may seem different. For most people, resilience means being able to endure and bounce back. But, for some people, it does not stop at just being able to restore. These people discover, in their fall, their hidden (or buried) buoyancy and capacity to rise and grow beyond their known or past limits. Simone did just that. Career and professional success had never meant anything to her. Had resilience meant only restoration for her, she would have restricted her work to only as many students as she needed to meet her life expenses. But she discovered her potential and let it flourish. There was no magic. Simone made a conscious effort to make it happen.

The MacArthur Fellow and Positive Psychologist, Angela Duckworth, who has done extensive research on the phenomenon of 'grit', insists that 'effort counts twice'. Applied to grief context, this asks us to actively own our grieving process. Our grief belongs to us and there is no way we can, or should, deny the reality of our experience. That said, we should not remain in passive suffering. It is very much possible to tap into the inner reservoir of our abundant strength and growth wisdom. We can and should choose to transcend our pain and fear, rise beyond, and mindfully choose our response to our grief-altered reality.

Honouring the perspective that resilience signifies not just restoration but also expansive rise, and putting together the distilled wisdom gained from my professional and personal experience, I have conceptualized a four-aspect framework of resilient adaptation called **RISE—**

R—Restorative will
I—Imaginal wisdom
S—Supple strength
E—Expansive emergence

Each of these aspects is a sovereign phenomenon, yet interwoven with others. You can work through all, or focus on the one that seems specifically important in your journey of resilient adaptation. I invite you to please read all, and then decide where you want to put your energy.

RESTORATIVE WILL

Do you recall the tree analogy from chapter three, that PTG researcher Dr Stephen Joseph talks about? Some trees get totally uprooted by the storm. Some bend, and recover as the storm withers away. And then there are those that not just regrow the storm-beaten stems and branches, but actually have new greens blooming at places which were bare before. To each their own resurgent spirit, muscle for recovery, and span of spread. Yet each is essentially similar in a very basic way. Whatever be the level to which each tree restores or grows, will to restore remains centrally important in each one's quest for resilient adaptation. Same is true of humans. Life has a great gravitational impact on us. Even in its worst phase, life nudges us towards restoration, movement, growth and meaning. I must pause here to clarify that 'restore' in this context doesn't mean restoration of pre-loss reality. That we know is irrevocable. 'Restore' here means rekindling will to live and *will to sustain*. Will to live and restore is as basic as breathing. It comes before and stays above all other profound pursuits of life. At the same time, will to restore also involves something as expansive as wanting to grow beyond our loss.

Tom Hanks, who had played Chuck Noland in *Cast Away*, heart-warmingly quipped in an interview—'at the end... it's going to be okay... as long as you keep breathing and have a certain kind of perspective and proportion to your life.' What a simple, yet profound, take on living with loss and trauma, realizing that the first simple yet brave step to restoration is to keep breathing, and keep our sense of perspective alive. Here, breathing is more symbolic than literal. It represents the fundamental human spirit that chooses to return to life even if it means a new normal that we adapt to or create out of our resilience.

In adapting to grief-altered life, it is essential that we sustain our will to restore our well-being to whatever extent and in whatever manner possible, and to rebuild life. In most cases, our restorative-will stays alive, even if buried for some time under heaps of pain, sadness, fear and other emotions. But in some complicated cases, it is not surprising for people to lose their will to restore. Even as I underline the critical importance of professional care and intervention, if it is so needed in such cases, I also wish to highlight that it is very much possible for us to help ourselves in recovering our will to live and restore. Have you ever noticed a tiny green shoot determinedly sprouting from cracks and crevices in concrete surfaces? So commonplace and yet unrecognized for the phenomenal resilience lesson it holds, something that is evocatively captured by Gwendolyn Brook as—'Wherever life can grow, it will. It will sprout out, and do the best it can.' This is what restorative will is all about. Howsoever high and far our pursuit of resilience takes us, we essentially begin with will to restore. And it is the magic kernels of faith, affirmation, hope and meaning that guide us on the path to creating a meaningful life out of our loss-altered reality.

The age-old Japanese art of 'kintsugi' fixes broken pottery by using a special tree sap lacquer seasoned with powdered gold or silver.

The famous art whose name (kintsukuroi or kintsugi) means 'golden joinery' in Japanese, not just repairs the broken piece, but transforms it—giving it a beautiful new look, while preserving its original form and honouring the crack as part of the unique history of the broken piece. Such a profound and creative way to restore and honour beauty in brokenness.

Mandala Art

Grief Kintsugi

This, as you know, is a meditative arts exercise. Please do it when you can be in a quiet reflective state by yourself.

- Think of a loss, adversity or trauma that has left you feeling broken. Associate fully with your sense of brokenness.

- Imagine yourself to be a piece of pottery and your brokenness as the crack in the pottery that needs to be mended and restored.
- Draw the broken pottery depicting your grief as clearly as possible.
  - Let the broken part tell its story through your drawing.
  - Also highlight the parts that still stand whole, strong and beautiful.
  - If you feel more creative, draw it like a mandala.
- Now start again on a different page/sheet:
  - This time draw the broken parts with a golden, silver, or any other shimmery colour you like.
  - Visualize expansively. Let your imagination guide the depiction of the broken and the whole parts, and the piece of pottery itself.
  - Allow yourself to fully associate with your emergent feelings.
- Now reflect about the following and write down your musings:
  - How do the two drawing experiences contrast?
  - Notice what shapes, elements of nature, and colours emerged in the second drawing. What do they represent?
  - What would someone looking at your second drawing learn from you as far as will to restore, grow and renew is concerned?
  - What do you intend to do with the new awareness or insight that this Grief-Kintsugi experience has left you with?

IMAGINAL WISDOM

'Between stimulus and response there is a space.
In that space is our power to choose our response.
In our response lies our growth and our freedom.'

—Viktor E. Frankl

In grief, it is common for our mind to keep swaying back and forth between loss-oriented ruminative and restoration-oriented reflective thinking. The way we frame the narrative of our loss impacts our coping mechanism and restorative muscle. When we are deluged by intrusive feelings and thoughts, we tend to unconsciously weave self-limiting narratives like 'this is the end' or 'my life has no meaning now'. In contrast, the more affirmative our narrative, the better the prospect of our restoration and growth. In no way do I mean to suggest that we should force ourselves to see our pain as any less terrible than it is. My intention, instead, is to highlight the importance of staying aware of how the narrative of our pain is helping or harming our restorative journey. The good news is that by invoking our imaginal wisdom we can impact our narratives in a positive way, thereby enabling our healing, resilient adaptation and growth.

The human brain is constantly wiring and rewiring itself. It is adaptive, and keeps learning and growing till our very end. What was always known to Vedic, Buddhist, Sufi and other oriental philosophy practitioners, is now endorsed by science as something called *neuroplasticity*. This simply means that as we learn and practice new things, we create new neural connections and maps in our brain. This neural (re)wiring is happening all the time inside our brain without our awareness. But it is very much possible to influence our neural activity by consciously engaging in such experiences that shape our thoughts and feelings in a desired way. How relieving to know that we have the power to influence our brain behavior. Imaginal wisdom is the way. Deliberate visualization and thinking about resilience and growth help us recover and renew our will to sustain, *will to grow* and will to meaning. As we mindfully feed our brain with optimistic thoughts and growth-oriented imagery that evoke healing, calming, centering and strengthening effects, new restorative neural pathways begin to form in our brain.

True, indeed, that in grief even coping can feel painfully difficult; growth is certainly a far cry. Yet it is so strong a human urge that we cannot ignore it for long. While rumination is normal, it is important for us to recognize and transform it. Richard Tedeschi, the post-traumatic growth pioneer advocates '*reflective rumination*' which involves paying deliberate attention to what we think and say to ourselves. Bring in the constructionist principle of '*appreciative inquiry*', a strength-based positive change approach, which goes with the popular tagline '*words create worlds*' and maintains that we influence our reality through our thoughts, language and metaphors. Indeed, words do create worlds as you may recall from the story of Tanya and Tisha (chapter two) who, even in their shared losses, held totally different narratives. As Tanya began to reframe her loss, it transformed from feeling like an earthquake to being a hot water spring. Her reframed self-narrative played a significant role in helping her heal, and rekindle her resilience and will to meaning.

Combine the power of '*reflective rumination*' and '*appreciative inquiry*', and we get a creative way to activate our imaginal wisdom and construct a restorative and growth-oriented narrative. I pause here to emphasize that imagining and weaving a growth narrative does not mean that we whitewash our pain with made-up positivity. On the contrary, we can invoke and activate our imaginal growth wisdom only when we recognize and own our grief and pain. In the process ensues a profound transformation that is best explained by the caterpillar to butterfly metamorphoses process. When the caterpillar begins to decay and dissolve into a gooey matter, the hitherto dormant primordial cells, called the *'imaginal cells'* begin to activate themselves. Initially, the imaginal cells operate as a single-cell organism, thereby attracting attack by the immune system of the decaying caterpillar. As they continue to strive, eventually the imaginal cells connect with each other, cluster together, and emerge as a multi-cell single organism that we call butterfly. Isn't that amazing! So is the process of resilient adaptation, whereby our imaginal wisdom unfolds in the face of grief and trauma, renews our will to grow, helps us transform like a butterfly, and nudges us forward towards a meaningful future.

—◆—

SUPPLE STRENGTH

*'The oak fought the wind and was broken,
the willow bent when it must and survived.'*

—Robert Jordan

Strength in the context of grief is subtle, and supple. It lives in the company of its shadow-twin called vulnerability. Like an adaptive willow, it knows when and how to bend, and when and how to resurge. During a recent cyclonic storm that hit the west coast of India, a video went viral where the lashing cyclonic winds and rainstorm were beating a palm tree down. It was an awe-inspiring sight, to see the grit and grace with which the tree swayed from side to side, neither fighting the brutal storm, nor letting the storm rip it apart. Resilient adaptation in the face of grief is just so. It is not fighting with your pain and grief. It is also not letting yourself be robbed of your will and ability to stay strong, adapt and resurge. It is about supple strength—acceptant, self-assured, responsive, adaptive and transformative. Supple strength is not about defying or demonizing the dark, but honouring it and responding with purpose and poise.

Resilient adaptation is about staying aware of your vulnerability, and staying awake to your strength. This state of being simultaneously aware and awake doesn't happen in a neat clear way. It can be frustratingly haphazard, like one step forward, two steps backward and many steps sideward, floating between painful experience of grief and pain, and purposeful efforts at rebuilding life. We can, nonetheless, turn this meandering movement into a meaningful exploration of the inner strength that stays richly alive, no matter what.

> *'So few grains of happiness, measured against all the dark,*
> *and still the scales balance.*
> *The world asks of us only*
> *the strength we have and we give it.*
> *Then it asks more, and we give it.'*

—Jane Hirshfield

Read 'grief' in place of 'world' in this poignant poetry by Jane Hirshfield. Grief does indeed ask of us all our strength, and we give it. And then it asks us for more strength, and we must give more. What is astonishing about our strength is that it is abundant, and it is abundantly supple. The more we drink from the reservoir of our deep innate strength, the fuller the reservoir becomes. All that is asked of us is humility to acknowledge our vulnerability, curiosity to understand its hidden message, a hopeful attitude, will to adapt, change and grow, optimistic thinking, mindfulness, loads of patience and deep faith. Believe me—it is possible and it is very much worth the effort.

Neuropsychologist and resilience expert, Rick Hanson, talks of four major ways—recognizing our reality; resourcing ourselves; regulating thoughts, feelings and actions; and relating skillfully—in which humans meet their three basic needs of safety, satisfaction, and connection. In the context of grief, often our need for safety assumes greater significance than the other two needs. Rick Hanson identifies compassion, grit, calm and courage as the four human strengths relevant to our need for safety. How amazing that an accomplished neuropsychology expert's research confirms what many of us grievers know first-hand in our journey of resilient adaptation to our grief-affected life. Grit and courage indeed, albeit not in a dynamic powerful sense, but in a calm, compassionate, responsive and supple way. We need to reconstruct our loss-altered life with poised courage and mindful responsiveness, while staying compassionate and respectful of our vulnerability. Let us write the story of our supple strength.

Words Create Worlds

Therapeutic Writing

Picture a rock by a riverside—ageless, solid and unyielding. It lets the river's playful surfs frolic on its indulgent surface, and also lets the river's wild rapids wreck fury on the same surface. It knows how to live joyfully and it also knows how to endure pain, forgive, heal and adapt. The more the river throws its weight on the rock, the more its edges soften and the more its surface smoothens. It lets the attacking water transform into hospitable moss. It isn't surprising to, one day, find tiny green shoots making a home around and underneath the rock.

- Now picture yourself as the rock and your grief and pain as the rough river rapids breaking on the rock.
- From this point onwards, it is your picture. Write your life-script as you like. Shape the protagonist's (yourself) character the way you want it to respond with resilience and supple strength, and reshape loss-altered life.
- Let your will to restore, will to grow and will to meaning inspire your imagination and your narrative.
- After a few hours, reflect on the following and journal your reflections:
  - How does this story-writing experience feel?
  - What do you discover about yourself and the suppleness of your strength by picturing yourself as the rock which softens, smoothens and strengthens under the pressure of river rapids, rather than stiffens or weakens?
  - What new insight has emerged?
  - What does the journey ahead look like?
- Pick your story again after a few days, and read it as if you were a detached reader—appreciate the author (yourself) for the amazing twists and transformations that s/he has woven, and advise the author (yourself) about what more/better you see is possible.

—◆:◆—

EXPANSIVE EMERGENCE

'Just beyond yourself.
It is where you need to be.
There is a road always beckoning.'

—David Whyte

Indeed. A road always beckons. Grief may last long, sometimes an entire lifetime. Yet, the tiny greens of love and life continue to sprout and bloom on the very rock of loss. Spring always returns, even if altered by a harsh winter. Season of growth is sure to follow season of grief. We need to accept the season of grief before we are given the chance to welcome the season of growth. We need to see the road that beckons us just beyond ourselves. And we need to let our will to restore and will to grow take the expansive soar that they are meant to take.

As we prepare to reengage with life and world, things seem different from how they were in times we have had to leave behind. Truth is, we have changed as much or may be more. When people and the world around seem like strangers, be willing to take this as an opportunity to discover the stranger in yourself. Your resilient reengagement with life opens the pathway to a *'new you'*—someone who knows both love and loss, someone who knows how to harmonize light and dark, and someone who is willing to find meaning even in things that make no sense.

The *'resilient adaptation'* phase had you traversing the Great Pass across your grief gorge. You are now ready to emerge in a green valley that awaits you. More importantly, an *expansive-you* awaits you on the other side. As you are poised to emerge, be willing to greet the new you with affirmation, compassion and resilience. Be willing to welcome your new life with faith, hope, supple strength, will to grow and will to meaning. Be willing to meet the world with humility and gratitude. Every event, every experience and every person in your life, however joyous or painful, has something to offer—some help, some resource, some support or some hard lesson. Receive it all with gratitude. And then get ready to spread your self-assured wings.

Your heart is sensitive, strong and spacious. It has enough room and wisdom to tenderly hold your loss alongside your abundant spirit for love. Let your love for life reemerge and take care of your pain. Give yourself permission to live, love, even laugh. Give yourself permission to heal, grow and transcend. Open yourself to the emergent and let life guide you to what wants to happen.

'Hope is the thing with feathers
That perches in the soul,
And sings the tune without the words,
And never stops at all'

–Emily Dickinson

For many, hope is a natural response in the face of adversity. But it isn't missing in those for whom hope doesn't happen as a reflex impulse. As Emily Dickinson puts it so evocatively—*hope perches in the soul*—whether or not it shows up. Being in hope helps us nudge and shepherd ourselves forward. Like strength and vulnerability, hope too has a shadow-twin called despair. Hope never leaves despair alone, no matter how deep we sink into it. Keep your in-faith curious eye open and you may spot the quiet but sure presence of hope right where despair looms large. All that you need to do is—open yourself with faith and welcome the emergent. Let us move to the next chapter to do the same. Before that, please create and take home your poetic affirmation.

PATH 5

Poetic Affirmation to Take Home

'High rests on low.
Storm or flood, river stays in flow.
The cloudburst that ravages,
is followed by magnificent rainbow.
The landslide that rips the earth open,
has the spring water on us bestow.'

—Neena Verma

Acknowledge the cloudburst
Navigate the flood
Ride the tide
Sail and soar
Be the rainbow
Dance in the skies

6

Opening to the Emergent

'To see a World in a grain of sand,
And a Heaven in a wild flower,
Hold Infinity in the palm of your hand,
And Eternity in an hour.'

—William Blake

Saba was a happy-go-lucky person. Her husband, Samir's, transferrable government job took them to different cities. Saba saw this as a privilege and thoroughly enjoyed soaking in the beauty and culture of different cities and regions, even though the frequent movement and relocation kept them on their toes. Not keen on academics or work, she was happy being a homemaker and never liked Samir's gentle prods for education or vocation. She was a very good singer, with a music diploma from a reputed institution. But she didn't give her talent due attention, leave alone putting it to professional use. Over the years she had settled well into the smug routines of life. Though, sometimes, she passingly worried about their poor savings, but the charms of Samir's secure, respectable and in some ways privileged career as a government officer did not allow such worry to last long. She was always able to shake this worry off her mind until one day when Samir did not return home. On his evening walk, in a nearby garden, he saw some hooligans harassing a young girl. While other passers-by quietly left, Samir confronted them. In the scuffle that ensued, one of the hooligans pushed him. Losing balance, he fell on a sharp garden rock and had a fatal head injury, dying on the spot of a brain hemorrhage.

In a blink, Saba and her children's lives were torn apart. No one could make sense of this shocking tragedy. Her house was filled with relatives and visitors offering condolences. But once the social buzz faded, only two colleagues of Samir maintained regular contact. They filled in for various household needs, and made sure that Samir's dues were released as quickly as possible. Their families too joined in, offering Saba and her children a sense of belonging and care. But shattered to the core, nothing brought them any solace.

Overwhelmed with trauma, grief, fear, anger and worry, Saba was slowly slipping into depression. With Samir gone and Saba herself shaken, their children felt insecure and anxious. They didn't just lose fatherly guidance and protection, but were also missing the care of their mother who otherwise kept the home and hearth happy. Maturing overnight, her small children understood and made good with whatever life offered. But Saba's father felt concerned, and decided to intervene. He persuaded Saba to take professional help, and also enrolled the children in an art course, hoping it would offer some therapeutic support to the kids. It took her a good two years before Saba started to respond positively to therapy.

As she began restoring a bit, Saba felt deeply disturbed by the gloom writ large over her children's personality, even though they had been keeping themselves meaningfully engaged with their school work and art lessons. The second thing to hit her was the financial worries. They couldn't forever live off Samir's service dues and Saba's father's care and support. Saba needed to do something. But she decided not to act in haste. She allowed herself time and space to recognize, understand and absorb her new reality. Slowly and gradually, she started making sense of how her new life was unfolding. Stepping out of her shell, she started to reengage with people—her children's teachers, friends and their parents, and genuinely concerned neighbours, friends and relatives. She welcomed suggestions from all, even if much of it was cliché. But it was only with due discussion with her father and Samir's steadily supportive friends that she began taking baby steps. Given her modest educational background and lack of work experience, she needed to equip herself with some job-ready skills. So, she began researching various options.

Meanwhile, acting on her therapist's suggestion, Saba had resumed her music practice, tuning her harmonium after two long decades. On one of their visits, Samir's colleague Amit and his wife were astounded to hear Saba's soulfulness rendition. They prevailed upon her to start giving music classes to their daughter. It didn't take long before word spread and more people started asking her to teach music to their children. Slowly but surely meaningful vocational opportunity emerged from her nearly forgotten talent. Over time, she began earning enough to start her own advanced training in music, hoping to become a vocalist. It was a deeply moving moment when she earned her Visharad (Indian classical music degree). She chose to dedicate it to Samir.

Saba had many people to thank—her children, Samir's loving spirit, his friends, her father, her therapist and so many others. But none more than her own patient, humble, open-minded, gritty and receptive self. Her willingness and ability to tune into her emergent reality, enabled her healing, growth and transformation. Saba truly saw 'infinity in her palm' and rebuilt her world from the grain of her grief.

—◆—

Is it easy to walk on the fiery embers of traumatic grief the way Saba did? What enabled her to transcend her grief, and not just find her feet but actually carve a new pathway?

Having traversed affirmatively across the gorge of grief and having strode through the Great Pass of resilient adaptation, we may find ourselves in the midst of inviting green meadows of life. But we may not yet feel ready to take the invite. It is normal and understandable. Our wound may still be hurting even though it has begun healing. How to contemplate eternity in a moment, and behold heaven in a wildflower, when one is struggling to manage even the most basic needs in the post-loss life? To see the world anew from the still sore, teary eyes isn't easy. Indeed, we shouldn't hurry ourselves. But stride we must, opening ourselves to the quest unfolding in front of us. A difficult task, indeed, with no clear way about it. One part of us may feel that we can't do it. But another part knows that we can, and should, open ourselves to the emergent.

GROWTH Mandala
Created by Neena Verma

The 'opening to the emergent' phase is represented by a consciousness triangle in the GROWTH Mandala that holds the wisdom we need, to seek, find and create what is still possible, despite and beyond our loss. Its three vertices of hope, light, and mindfulness, prepare us to open ourselves to our loss-altered reality and reengage with life and the world. As we spread our horizon of hope, harmonize our dark and light with grace, and engage mindfully with our loss-altered reality, we start noticing possibilities of growth along-side pain of grief. How?—is unique to each one of us. We all need to find or evolve what best works for us. A good point to start is to open up to the emergent reality, attune to it, flow with it, and create a new life-narrative. That is what Saba did. She looked at her unfolding life with acceptant and awake eyes, and allowed her circumstances and supportive elements, and people in her life to guide and mould her. When pain was closing in on her, she unfurled the petals of her open and receptive self. She invited hope home, and served all of her resilience, openness and adaptiveness on the altar.

HORIZON OF HOPE

'Where there is ruin, there is hope for a treasure.'

—Rumi

The horizon of hope is expansive. Hope can be a virtue, an innate strength or natural disposition. It can also show up as a feeling or thought. The realm of hope is essentially one of faith. All that is broken holds the promise of restoration, transformation and renewal. That said, for hope to take us to the other shore, it must live in our action. For hope to manifest desired effect, it needs intention, resolve and effort as much as faith. Interestingly with intentional mindful action we can actually cultivate a hopeful disposition even if it is not naturally present. It is very much possible for us to uncover our deep-seated hopefulness, and consciously cultivate mindful optimism. Having an optimistic outlook doesn't imply assured positive turnarounds. It simply means that we offer more hopeful energy to our adaptive grieving process.

Hope calls for openness, suppleness and mindfulness. It may not have a clear destination or path. But on the long walk through the blazing desert, hope shows up as faith that an oasis will emerge sooner or later, if only we stay put and keep striving. Hope is not a rosy-eyed or superficial fogging of self or others. It is a deep-felt experience that either happens by itself or upon our sincere invocation. And when it happens, whether organically or through mindful contemplation, it transforms our narrative and thus our reality. Consider these—

> 'It would be good if she could get a job. But given her modest education and no work experience, chances are poor. Let us help her.'
>
> 'True, job prospects are poor. And true as much that her good music background opens up many possibilities for her. She is worthy and capable. Let us cheer and support her as she builds self-reliance.'

These are just two of the many comments that well-wishers or random people made about Saba's situation. Notice what goes before '*but*' and what follows it in the first comment. The nature of 'but' is such that it psychologically nullifies whatever has been said before it, and kills hope. My personal practice is to—*butt the but out*—to the extent possible. If we must use 'but', which we have to sometimes, let us be careful to place the unhelpful/pessimistic statement before it. It is not hogwash. It has proven neuro-psychological significance. Notice how the first statement closes doors and views Saba as incapable, dependent and helpless. In contrast, the psychology of '*and*' is such that it opens up options as we can see in the second statement that honours Saba's capability and self-efficacy, and offers support only in assistive spirit. Hope likes the company of 'and' which opens up possibilities, unlike 'but' which closes doors. The more we feed the idea of possibilities, the more we allow the state of hopefulness to flourish.

Let me reemphasize that there is no reason to be disheartened if hope is not an innate strength or reflex characteristic for you. We can all learn to cultivate and practice hopefulness, if we stay open to exploring possibilities however bleak the scenario. We need to stay mindfully grounded in hope's essential elements of faith, will, belief and effort. We need to stay in faith that what we need or want can manifest if we believe enough in our worthiness and capability, and continue making necessary efforts. Saba did just that. And she lit the lamp of growth at the doorstep of her grief.

—◆—

LIGHT THE LAMP

'We all live in a world of both darkness and light ...
all butterflies came to be in darkness ... all bees were born in
hives ... every living finger and toe was formed
in the pitch black of the womb.'

—C. JoyBell C.

As a small child, I was fascinated by a beautiful ritual that an Aunt of mine used to perform every evening while placing a tiny earthen lamp at her doorstep. One day, I couldn't hold in my curiosity and asked her about the ritual that she performed with a serene smile, as if welcoming an important guest. She warmly patted my cheeks and left without an answer. I soon forgot about it. But she didn't. Nearly two decades later, when I happened to visit her with my two-year-young first son, she asked if I was still interested to know about her lighting the lamp ritual. I was wowed by her memory despite her age, her long battle with my Uncle's sickness, his demise, and her financial difficulties. What she said is one of the best, if not the best, lessons an elder has ever gifted me. I share below her wisdom pearl (translated from Hindi) as best as I recall—

> Who revers light more than the dark. We demonize the dark as if it were a monster. But dark itself is so vulnerable. It doesn't know that light resides within itself, that light and dark complete each other. It deserves our compassion as much as light deserves our reverence and gratitude. And come to think of it, light alone is not beautiful. See with loving eyes, you would find dark captivating. Of course, I light the lamp at the doorstep for those in need of light. But it is the dark that I lovingly invite in to rest a while and illuminate itself. Dark is the harbinger of all the light we need. I just hold a tiny lamp for the dark to find its own light.

I was left speechless. For days and weeks, her profoundly wise words echoed in my heart and mind. Even as the busy grind of life overtook, her inspiring wisdom got imprinted in my consciousness, resurfacing from forgotten chambers of my mind just at the time when I needed it—at the precise moment in my grief journey when I was fighting with the dark in my life instead of opening myself to it. This timely memory transformed the caption and essence of my life-narrative from 'grief journey' to *'grief and growth pilgrimage'*. I allowed the darkness of my grief to reveal its full glory, and began to see the pre-dawn saffron of growth and meaning that it held in its embrace. As I lit the lamp at the doorstep of my grief, I began to see the light of growth in it.

Pause and Ponder-1

'When darkness emerges, the universe appears in the sky!
Remember, darkness has gifts!'

—Mehmet Murat ildan

It is only on a dark sky that we can see the dazzling stars and soothing moonlight. Indeed, dark has gifts that we would see only when we look at it with an appreciative eye, rather than holding it in unkind contrast to light.

- Think of a phase of dark, emanating from a loss, trauma or adversity.
- Open yourself to the experience of acceptant and reverent *SEEING* of this dark phase. Contemplate over its presence and impact in your life.
- Notice how this dark completes all the light in your life. How do they combine with each other and co-create a dance of insight and growth?
- Recognize and acknowledge the gifts that dark brings along.
- Think of a concrete action-map to make good of these gifts.
- Journal your reflections and plan.

'Savour the dark. Sip the light.'

—Neena Verma

MINDFUL REENGAGEMENT

Bereavement and grief try our faith and resilience in a thousand ways. Body, mind, heart, soul—all get affected. Our assumptive world gets shaken. Our life-view, beliefs, thought patterns, our very personality—all undergo change at several levels. We are not always at our functional, behavioural, emotional or relational best. Memory lapses, absentmindedness, confusion, tenderness, insensitive comments or gestures of others, are few of the many things that affect our engagement with the world. On top of it all, grief can be painfully disorienting. We need to calm our in-pain being, and stay centred, so as to reengage with life and people in a functional and meaningful way. We need to keep re-grounding ourselves. A healthy and harmonious way is mindfulness. It facilitates deeper awareness, understanding and acceptance of our emergent reality. It helps us make meaning in the moment.

Mindfulness is both a state of being, as also a meditative practice. It enables a sense of healthy grounding on a moment-to-moment basis. We are able to embrace and flow with the emergent reality. We feel more fully awake, present and acceptant. Even when the unfolding events are distressing, we are able to receive, observe and attune to them with acceptance and a sense of openness. We notice things as they are without being affected by our emotions while still acknowledging the same. We are able to respond with clarity, consideration, compassion and connection, thereby creating a more firm and healthy ground for life ahead. Mindfulness helps us create our own image and path of restoration, adaptation, healing, transformation and reemergence, rather than feeling pressured to act as per the social stereotypes of 'recovery' or 'moving on.'

MY STORY

There is no greater joy for parents than to receive their child's birth certificate. And there is no greater pain than to receive their child's death certificate. A month after my son's demise, my husband went to collect the death certificate. He returned home understandably distressed, and asked me to handle all other closure processes. It took me forever to get ready to attend to this unbearably painful task.

I made three trips to the bank before I could withstand the pain of the repeated mention of 'death' and 'dead' by the dealing staff while explaining the process. Even on the fourth trip, unable to hold back the flood of my tears, I rushed outside, only to be followed by the bank manager who, while passing by, had noticed something on my face that prompted him to check on me. Numb with pain, I couldn't speak. I just showed him the death certificate and managed to mutter, 'My son... please close his account'. The kind man took me straight to his cabin, and personally supervised the process completion, filling me with deep gratitude. Though he was extra sensitive and helpful, the dealing staff too had been professional and helpful in his own way. It was I, who in a vulnerable and tender state, was unable to handle the repeated mention of the word 'death' in reference to my son. I wasn't yet open to my emergent reality, and therefore felt pained even though the bank staff didn't do anything hurtful. Maybe it was too early in the day but my distress in such engagements continued. I experienced a similar feeling when I wrote to LinkedIn for the closure of my son's account. The responding executive's discomfort with the 'odd service request' was too evident in her communication, nothing insensitive though. Here, too, I felt a piercing pain at the mention of the word 'death'. I wasn't yet attuned to my oddly painful emergent reality.

The experience that disturbed me the most was over an insurance claim settlement. A couple of years before my son's demise we had gotten him to apply for a small single-premium insurance policy, only as part of his life-skill training. After months of unclear delay, the concerned officer, rather rudely, conveyed his suspicion that the policy had been taken in anticipation of death. The insured value was a paltry ₹150,000/-, less than my monthly income at that point in time. That is perhaps the only time in my loss-altered life that I reacted angrily. I wrote straight to the insurance company chairman, not asking for my claim settlement but suggesting the need for sensitivity training of the officer concerned. Few weeks later, I received the claim settlement directly from the Chairman's office. But my justifiably upset grieving mind wanted an apology. It took me a long time to understand that the concerned officer was only being diligent. He was under no obligation to be sensitive to a bereaved mother struggling to make sense of the inexplicable cardiac arrest that took her young, healthy bright son away.

These incidents, and some more, left me feeling fatigued and sick. Every single engagement would trigger bouts of nausea and vague body-ache. I was unconsciously closing myself to the world, and in the process losing the will to sustain, restore, explore, adapt and find a way to go with the flow of life. I was slowly losing peace and poise. Yet, a part of me stayed awake to my inner churn and helped me realize that withdrawal from the world and life had taken me away from myself too. I had even forgotten about my all-time trusted book that I always turned to whenever I was in difficulty. Desperately opening David Richo's 'Power

of Coincidence,' a profound book on synchronicity, I found
the very guidance I needed at that time in life on the first
page that I randomly opened, page 95—

> Choices continue to arise and paths continue to
> appear even until the eleventh hour of a lifetime.
> Even if the path is to grieve an ending, the next
> step is to go on ... salute the sunset with dignity,
> equanimity, and deeply contended serenity.

I returned to reading, my most loved pursuit, even though
grief had badly affected my attention and absorption. I
also sought refuge in writing, another secret passion of
mine that I had forgotten about. In the beginning it was
random and irregular. Over time, words began to flow
with ease and coherence, facilitating my cathartic release.
Eventually my stream-of-consciousness writing took
shape as my grief memoir, A Mother's Cry .. A Mother's
Celebration. Alongside, my casual doodling grew to become
deep meditative arts practice. Before I realized, my hand,
that could barely draw a kindergarten version of a fish,
was now creating intricate patterns, even mandalas and
zentangles.

A year later, I attended my first Vipassana camp and
that changed my life. I was able to see and acknowledge
my hitherto unconscious troubling feelings and thoughts.
I came face to face with my anger and bitterness in the
wake of my loss. Vipassana has helped me heal at a deeper
level. It has taught me to be present and mindful in the
moment. I now have greater willingness, openness, ability,
patience and stamina to wait without expectation, in the
unknown zone between 'no longer' and 'not yet'. I am able
to meet life more awake and acceptant. I feel humbler,
calmer, warmer, and better attuned to my emergent life.

I pause to clarify that my intent here is to only explain the positive effects of mindfully opening to and reengaging with our grief-altered emergent reality. If you are interested in learning the art of meditation, I encourage you to learn from a sincere meditation forum or teacher of your liking. Please satisfy yourself before you take the plunge. Meanwhile you can self-learn and practice mindfulness through breath awareness, and activities such as mindful eating, mindful walking, mindful reading, mindful writing or mindful drawing/painting. The idea is to learn to be fully awake, aware and present to the unfolding experience on a moment-to-moment basis. And you can do that by formally learning and practicing meditation, and/or by self-cultivating a mindful way to breathe and perform other life activities. Mindfulness is precisely what you need for a meaningful experience in the liminal phase on the Great Passage of your *'grief and growth pilgrimage'.*

—◆—

LIMINAL WISDOM

'Become totally empty.
Quiet the restlessness of the mind.
Only then will you witness everything
unfolding from emptiness.'

—Lao Tzu

The word liminal has origin in the Latin word 'limen' which means *threshold.* Liminal space is the transitioning phase in between what is *no longer* true and what has *not yet* come to life. Liminal space represents the second phase in a rite of passage, preceded by separation or loss (no longer), and followed by re-integration or reemergence (not yet). Of the various rites of passage, such as birth, initiation, marriage, death, that we go through in life, death is arguably the most painful. In bereavement, the separation is permanent. Often our identities, not just our lives, are in some way entwined with those of our loved ones. And losing them to death means losing a part of ourselves permanently. The pain, thus triggered, is unimaginably piercing. That said, this very pain and turmoil can usher profound transformation and growth, if we are willing to sit in '*sacred wait*' in the space between no-longer (loss) and not-yet (reemergence).

> '*Trust the wait. Embrace the uncertainty.*
> *Enjoy the beauty of becoming.*
> *When nothing is certain, anything is possible.*'
>
> —Mandy Hale

The liminal space is that *betwixt and between* sacred space, when we are on the verge of a new emergence. It is an abstract space between two existential states of being, where we experience a strange tension between seemingly paradoxical feelings and thoughts. Something is falling apart, and something new is taking form. We don't know what. Something precious for sure. We need to wait, stay present and be willing to witness and receive what emerges. It may feel discomforting, even disorienting to be there. This may frighten or freeze us. We may encounter a face of ourselves that questions or shatters our self-image. We may feel the urge to avoid or escape. But liminal wait is inevitable when we are going through an existential transition in life.

The seeming darkness of the liminal space may feel like the one inside the womb. We need to remember that womb is where life takes form. However difficult, this is where we must sit, waiting for unconscious wisdom to surface, and something profound to be revealed. The caterpillar must weave the cocoon out of its own decaying matter for the butterfly to emerge. Like the caterpillar we may not know, how we are to be in this liminal state. Yet we must face it, flow with it, maintain hopefulness, and allow ourselves to sit in existential wait. Alexander Dumas wisely avers,

> All human wisdom is contained in these two words—Wait and Hope.

Hope and wait indeed. Have the will to surrender-in-faith, heart to be in silence, patience to wait, and courage to witness—and you will receive growth wisdom that has been waiting to be revealed.

Mandala Art

Liminal Mural

'In the universe, there are things that are known, and things that are unknown, and in between them, there are doors.'

—William Blake

This, as you know, is a meditative arts exercise. Please do it when you can be in a quiet reflective state by yourself. This is not necessarily meditation, but may turn out to be a meditative experience. Take time to know when you are willing, ready and able to start practicing being in a mindful wait and witness state. You don't need to stop/ discontinue any routine activity unless it is too disruptive and/or you can afford to park it for a while. True art of life is to be able to simultaneously attend to the business of life, and yet stay present to what is emerging in the deeper layers of our core being.

- Find a time in the day when you can sit in silence of 'wait' (of what—you don't know yet), and feel willing and ready to maintain 'witness' (no judgement or question) state. Avoid setting yourself up for an outcome or becoming overly effortful.
- It may take some time (hours, days, months or even longer) before you start feeling a sense of silence that is both empty and full. Just set an intention to be there, and offer yourself to the experience.
- Be present and witness what unfolds naturally—sensations, feelings, thoughts, insights. Be in no hurry to make meaning of the emergent experience. If you feel doubt, or some questions/judgments arise in your mind—acknowledge them and return to your 'witness' experience.
- Give yourself and the experience all the time and patience it needs.
- Be present to what is emerging within, and outside.
- Allow the silence and the emergent happenings to reveal their meaning and message, at their own pace and in their own way.
- Be willing to 'wait' however long it takes. Maintain faith and hope.
- What 'new reality' are you being nudged towards? What 'not yet' is waiting to come true? What are you being called to change or create?
- Between the known and unknown, what new doors are showing up?
- Note down the emergent insights, and offer gratitude for the same.
- Create an expressive arts mural of your liminal wisdom.
- Allow your emergent insights to be expressed through art in a way that makes you feel calm, centred, and

sets you in creative movement.

- Sketching, painting, zentangle, mandala, collage, doodle, pottery, sculpture—pick any one or more media that you feel most drawn to.
- Notice what colours, shapes, symbols emerge in your mural. What meaning does your mural hold for you? How do you intend to bring this to reality?
- Journal your experience and reflections.

LET THE DOUGH RISE

As for time to begin anew, well, the best time is always 'now'— 'this moment'. Yet, there is something about time and timeliness that is in the realm of grace. Returning to David Richo, I felt awakened to the phenomenon of grace and providential timing as I reconnected with his wise words that 'we achieve by effort, but we receive by grace'. I knew my dharma (duty) was to stay in faith and sacred movement of life, knowing things would happen in their own time. Things remain in gestation, quietly evolving and maturing away from our gaze or knowing, manifesting and showing up just when the time is right. It is a deep, subtle and quiet process, and calls for all our faith, patience, and resilient striving. Grace is timely and that precisely is its gift. David Richo evocatively explains the complementary relationship of the two sides (active—will, hope, effort; and receptive—faith, wait, acceptance) of timeliness—

> There is a time to knead the dough,
> and there is a time to let it rise.

Those who cook know that we need to let the dough rest no matter how well it has been kneaded. Even the most expert cook invokes nature to bless the food after all that needed to be done has been done. Indeed, it is for nature to bestow, create and show us an opening when we are truly ready to transition and transcend. You have kneaded your pain with affirmation, resilience, hope, light and mindfulness, it is time now for you to let the dough of your transformation, growth and renewal to rise in its own time and way. Meanwhile, rest a while, and heal your body, mind, heart and spirit that have been in pain and stress. It is time for you to create a harmonious way to rebuild your well-being. The next chapter is your guide in that direction. Before that, please remember to create and take home your poetic affirmation.

PATH 6

Poetic Affirmation to Take Home

'Hope ...
The shy smile of a new bride.
The sweet-fatigue smile of a new mother.
The crinkled smile of a dying patient.

Hope ...
The dazzling lone star
on a dark cloudy night.

Hope ...
The balm, the nectar,
that we offer to our despair.'

—Neena Verma

Compose your hymn of hope
And strive on the way to well-being

7

Way to Well-being

'When the seasons shift, even the subtle beginning,
the scent of a promised change,
I feel something stir inside me.
Hopefulness? Gratitude? Openness?
Whatever it is, it's welcome.'

—Kristin Armstrong

Amal was 68 years old when his wife Uma suddenly passed away after a brief illness. Their 39-year-long married life saw Amal keeping busy with his career as an acclaimed marketing research professor and consultant, while Uma single-handedly managed all family responsibilities and trials of life. A disciplinarian, and a conservative and reserved person, Amal's nature did not allow much emotional intimacy. It was Uma who kept the family anchored, quietly filling up for Amal and acting as his bridge with their sons as well as his own kin.

Uma's death left Amal feeling lost and lonely. Both their sons were married and lived in different cities. Though they stayed with Amal for some time, they had responsibilities towards their families. Amal didn't quite like their suggestion to move in with either of them, even though the thought of living alone made him anxious. Maintaining an outwardly stoic appearance, he assured them of his well-being and asked them to return to their lives. Finding it difficult to share his feelings, even with his trusted friends, Amal was left alone with their long-standing home-help who, too, felt intimidated by his persona and maintained minimum interaction.

Amal's loneliness unnerved him. What he had not acknowledged for 39 years was suddenly before him. It was Uma's gracious personality and tireless toiling that had kept his life in order and had given him all the freedom he had wanted, to focus on his career. His grief had more fear and guilt than sorrow. He realized how invisibly vital Uma was to his comfortable personal and accomplished professional life. But having taken her for granted, he had never valued her selfless care and support. This realization filled him with shame and guilt, but he felt embarrassed talking about his feelings.

His children had each other to share their grief and lean on to. But Amal didn't seek or allow any emotional intimacy. Staying self-isolated, he struggled to cope with his grief, and ended up harming his well-being. It wasn't long before he fell sick with hypertension, cardiac stress and some other medical issues. This is when his elder son and daughter-in-law took a few months off and moved in to live with him. They somehow convinced him to take therapy. No mean task, given Amal's peculiar nature. It took them, the therapist, but most of all Amal himself, immense patience and a long time to acknowledge and address his emotions, and understand the need to take ownership for his health and well-being.

Affirming his grief, allowing expression to his feelings, adapting to his new reality, and making peace with his loss, he shifted focus from his guilt towards Uma to his gratitude for her. Honouring her caring and happy personality, he *decided to adopt a self-reliant, healthy life-style, and warm relationship approach. He began to engage, talk and care for others, albeit with some awkwardness which is understandable since it isn't easy to change oneself so radically at any age, even more so at Amal's age and life stage. He began engaging with his sons emotionally, giving them the sense of a secure parent base that they had nearly lost after Uma's demise.*

Taking responsibility for his self-care and well-being, he began yoga practice and started going for nature walks, resumed writing, and joined a chess club. He even began tending to Uma's small terrace garden that she had lovingly nurtured. Inspired by her absolute commitment to serve her family nutritious food, Amal promised himself to eat well. The surprise of all surprises was when he requested his home-help to teach him basic cooking. Stunned and delighted at Amal's turnaround, the home-help is back to being his usual chatty self.

As Amal understood the importance of health and well-being in loss-altered life, and practiced self-care, he could actually rebuild his life with a sense of peace and health, and live with his grief, with poise. Realizing the best way to honour Uma was by assuming her role, he began caring for his sons, their families, himself, and his home-help just the way she did.

—◆:◆—

How many of us can attempt or even imagine the kind of radical transformation that Amal went through? It isn't easy by any means even under normal circumstances, let alone in the face of grief, guilt and fear that Amal learnt to face, affirm and transcend.

What thawed his aloofness? What inspired him to take ownership for his grief journey? How did he create a way to well-being, affirming his grief and adapting resiliently?

As he recognized the need for health and well-being, Amal became open to taking professional help, and changed his view and way of life. Although, initially, this change in his approach was triggered out of anxiety, he soon understood the value of holistic living and the role of self-care, particularly in the context of grief-affected life. Interestingly his self-responsible well-being and health restoration is what helped Amal affirm his grief and adapt resiliently to his loss-altered life.

GROWTH Mandala
Created by Neena Verma

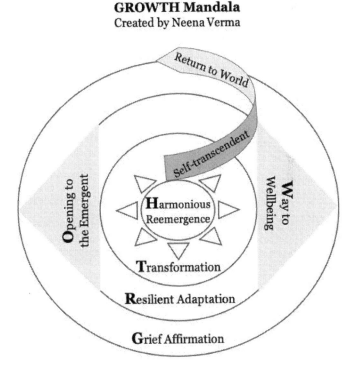

The '*way to well-being*' phase enables restorative and holistic well-being. This phase is represented by the affirmative triangle in the GROWTH Mandala that holds the nourishing energy to heal and restore wholesome well-being at bio-psycho-social-relational and spiritual levels. The motto of this phase is self-care. Of course, self-care cannot substitute professional therapy or medical intervention, if and how it is needed. That said, most people restore well on their own. Honouring this human capacity, the *'way to well-being'* phase would help you value the need for holistic self-care and well-being restoration, and learn various therapeutic ways to do the same.

SELF CARE

'Rest and self-care are so important.
When you take time to replenish your spirit,
it allows you to serve others from the overflow.
You cannot serve from an empty vessel.'

—Eleanor Brownn

Grief affects one at all levels. But we generally don't notice its subtle effects, especially those on the body. Busy attending to my life responsibilities, for close to three years after my son's demise I lived in self-neglect until my body caved under the weight of unattended grief and silently accumulating stress. It took me long to acknowledge the need for self-care, that too when an old client called to share how my 'own safety mask first' analogy had helped him make a lifestyle change and prevent a medical complication. It was time for me to practice it myself.

I decided to look after myself for my own sake, and of course, to continue attending to my various responsibilities. Though a medical issue had already turned bad, I could, still, make a timely self-intervention and prevent further deterioration. I began attending to my health needs, and got initiated into Vipassana meditation. I felt stronger and better prepared to nurture and grow my transcended son's legacy mission, and support my younger son to accomplish an important endeavour. Perhaps the most surprising change for me was to learn to say 'no' without feeling guilty. People who know me find this a long overdue healthy change in my personality. Just as people who knew Amal find his openness to emotionally engage absolutely astounding. All this begins for Amal and me, and for many people I know of, with the simple realization that health and overall well-being are even more important in grief journey than they would be in normal circumstances.

Self-care begins with recognizing, understanding and honouring our most basic needs and feelings. It enables restorative well-being. We are able to influence our deeper thoughts, feelings, mood and state of mind, thereby organizing our new life with enhanced self-responsibility. Looking after and nourishing ourselves doesn't ask for a lot. As I began respecting the needs of my body, heart, mind and soul, I learnt to value holistic well-being, and inculcated new life-habits so as to heal and strengthen myself at various levels. You can begin with simple life practices, that you already may be aware of but might have lost sight of while coping with grief. I share below a few, and encourage you to create your own repertoire that best suits your needs and life context.

Above all, hold yourself with compassion, tenderness and love. Wrap yourself in your own caring embrace.

—◆◆—

BEGIN WITH THE TEMPLE CALLED BODY

'Your relationship with your body is one of the
most important relationships you'll ever have.
It pays to make that relationship good.'

—Steve Goodier

Nothing is more restorative for a grief-sore body than deep calm gentle *breathing*. Learn pranayama (yogic breathing exercise) if you can. Combine it with elementary yoga if you like. Please learn from a credible source. Remember to apprise the teacher of your state of grief and medical challenges, if any. Even if you can't or don't want to learn in a structured way, you can still practice healthy breathing on your own. Start with gentle deep inhaling to the count of four, hold it to a similar count without putting yourself under stress, and gently allow yourself to exhale at a slightly longer count, of say, six. You can adjust the count and duration in tune with your body. Please remember the idea of deep gentle breathing is to allow relaxation, centering and enhanced awareness in the moment. This is not a test. Please avoid pressure, force or perfectionism.

Grief hits the body hard. It takes the brunt of all the stress that our mind and heart go through. We need to allow ourselves recuperative rest. Sleep is the body's way of reenergizing us. Give yourself due *rest and sleep*. Practice sleep hygiene. Avoid reading, TV, gadgets, conversations before sleep time. Play calming music. Chant. Massage with stress-relieving essential oils. Light aromatic incense. If you burst into tears while trying to sleep, please know it is normal, even helpful. Shakespeare was right when he said, 'To weep is to make less the depth of grief'. Allow your tears a healthy release. Sip some water. Ease yourself. Gently wash your face. Have some more water. Return to bed. Softly lull yourself to sleep, without making it a task. Take short naps if full sleep stays elusive. Do whatever helps you give your body due rest.

This note is particularly for bereaved parents, though many others may find it relevant or useful. It is normal for bereaved parents to feel distant in the aftermath of child loss. To some, intimacy may seem like a good de-stressor, or even an antidote to counter such feelings of distance, while some others may feel appalled by the very idea. Be sure whether you are really willing or ready yet. Feel and follow your body's and heart's cues. Say a dignified and firm NO to your partner if you do not yet feel ready for intimate contact. It is not easy. Definitely wasn't so for me. Please be true to yourself. Do what feels right to you, without pressure of expectation or advice.

It is normal and common to lose appetite or desire to eat. But we need to stay duly *nourished and hydrated*. Take what your body can absorb and digest easily. Eat light, like we do when we are sick. Consume semi-solid, healthily cooked food, fruits, salads, soup, porridge or whatever else suits your body and taste. Drink sufficient water in frequent small gentle sips. Avoid aerated beverages and alcohol. Keep your body well hydrated in a healthy way.

Movement is essential when our body is suffering so much emotional pain. We all know that body and mind affect each other. By keeping our body in healthy movement, we send a signal to our brain to prepare our system for restoration and action. Keep your body in movement, whether by way of walk, simple yoga, or any other gentle exercise that your body likes. Nature walks help us feel calmer and more grounded. Some people find a release in more active sports. Born in 1911, Indian-Brit Fauja Singh, took to running at the age of 81 years as a way to cope with his grief, having lost his wife and daughter, even though he had extreme difficulty even walking till the age of five years and supposedly had weak legs. Soon, thereafter, one of his sons also died. At 89 years of age, he immersed himself fully into running. Soon he was running full marathons. At 100 years of age, he accomplished eight world age records all on the same day. And recently at 109 years of age, the world's oldest marathoner was featured as a superhero in a children's book. All his records and accomplishments aside, the soft-spoken Sikh once told an interviewer that running just happens while he remains absorbed in talking to '*mera Rabb*' (my God). His incredible story notwithstanding, I would advise you to avoid hard or rigorous exercise for some time, unless you are a sportsperson, or inspired by Fauja Singh.

A healthy mind lives in a healthy and clean body. It is okay to skip bathing, once in a while, if you don't feel up to it. But please try bathing daily, not just for maintaining your *hygiene*, but also for deep *muscle relaxation*. Talking of the latter, grief can cause our muscles to go sore. But we may not notice that. Find or create a healthy way to keep your muscles relaxed. It could be by way of deep breathing, yoga, massage, bathing with healing oils or salts. If you so like or need, you can get physiotherapy or spa therapy. Most people, though, are able to look after themselves on their own.

We have already talked in previous chapters about the general human tendency to distract ourselves from our pain by taking refuge in work. While it may give temporary solace, we might unconsciously end up adding extra stress. Often our grief-affected body needs time and recuperative care to be ready even for simple fatigue, leave alone extra strain. Please avoid putting yourself under pressures of work, at least not so soon. *Take it easy*. Life is no mighty mountain to be climbed in one go. Go low, go slow. Respect your body's wisdom and follow its cues.

Let me underline the importance of a *medical check-up* in the aftermath of grief. While grief is not an illness itself, it can trigger some medical conditions. Our immune system may turn weak, even if temporarily. I know the ill-effects of medical neglect first-hand. There is no harm in getting a pre-emptive medical check-up done even if there are no outward signs or symptoms.

—◆:◆—

MIND MATTERS

*'Calm mind brings inner strength and self-confidence ...
very important for good health.'*

—Dalai Lama

In chapter two we talked at length about how grief affects our mental functioning. It is time to focus on rebuilding the same. Begin by slowly reengaging with work. Not professional work alone, but any and all work you do as part of your daily routine, whether professional, personal, domestic or any other. Go slow. Take time to regain your rhythm, pace and productivity. It has only waned a bit, not faded away permanently. Stay patient. Keep working but please avoid getting bound by any performance target, standard or deadline. Adopt the *one-task-at-a-time* motto. I know people who have actually surpassed their pre-loss effectiveness and re-generated themselves all anew. A slow, steady and patient stride is the key that most of these people affirm as their mantra. All said, I reiterate my request—approach work for its own sake and for good reasons, not as an escape from pain. Let your work reenergise your mental functioning in an organic way. Please don't (re)design your work as if it were a mental gym.

For *mental muscle strengthening* you can play games such as sudoku, crossword, chess, jigsaw puzzles, building blocks or any other such activities. There is nothing childish about these. Many adults regularly play such games to keep their brain active and agile. Reading and writing are also excellent exercises for our brain. Take to them if you like. Rekindle, if you were already into them.

MY STORY

I was always an avid reader and loved writing as much. But as is understandable, immersed in my pain I had completely forgotten about everything. A well-wisher sent me a copy of C.S. Lewis' famous grief memoir 'A Grief Observed.' I had already read this poignant book some years ago. But reading it again as a mother in grief, the book sang to my soul. It didn't just balm my sore heart, but also helped rekindle my much loved pursuit of reading.

I have already shared in the previous chapter how reconnecting with my treasured book 'Power of Coincidence' didn't just help me embrace the emergent, but also soothed my agonized mind and inspired me to put pen to paper. Soon my writing too resurfaced, eventually culminating in my grief memoir. I read others' grief memoirs as well, especially those of bereaved parents. Each made a precious gift of wisdom. Reading and writing facilitated my deep healing and renewal. Let me add that these activities also played a big role in helping me calm my dazed and stressed mind, and reenergize and prepare it for my loss-altered life.

Wonder how many of us know about the concept of shabbāth (or sabbath). It is the Hebrew root word for more common sabbatical. It literally means 'rest.' In ancient biblical tradition, sabbath (the seventh day) meant time for rest and worship.

> *Withstanding several personal and professional pressures, it took me a long time and a lot of emotional strength to seek sabbath for myself. My grief-stressed mind needed a respite and I decided to give it a sabbath from some non-essential things. Not just professional work, I sought leave from some stressful life expectations as well which I had quietly fulfilled before. It was hard. I had to put up with grouses and sermons. But I needed to allow my mind the recuperative rest it needed. And I am glad I did. It made a huge positive difference.*
>
> *Having experienced it first hand, I think of sabbath as the time to **pause, purge, pray, ponder and prepare.***

Sabbath is time for conscious in-faith suspension of activity. During this time we attend to basic sustenance needs, but don't drive ourselves to any goal-bound task or activity. Prayerful pause lays the path to our deeper self. If you can afford it, I would encourage you to *take a break* or long leave from active professional work, if that is what your mind needs to restore and restrengthen itself. There are a thousand ways to give your mind rest. Fill it with fresh energy, rejuvenate it, and prepare it for action in sync with your new reality. I will be talking about some of these ways later in this chapter. Explore any of those. Find or create any of your own, and practice what suits you best.

—❖—

LET THE HEART HEAL

'And now here is my secret, a very simple secret:
It is only with the heart that one can see rightly;
what is essential is invisible to the eye.'

—Antoine de Saint-Exupéry

Heart knows.

Yes, the heart knows how to heal us out of fear, sadness, anger or any other painful emotion. But what should we do when the heart itself is in pain? We should allow it space and time to heal itself. It is easy to trip over your pain. It is hard to let your heart transcend the pain. For that you need to first allow yourself to face, acknowledge and feel your emotions. Shauna Hoey wisely affirms, 'Heartache purged layers of baggage I didn't know I carried.' Embrace the heartache. It purges what we need to let go of. And it eventually makes way for something new and healthy.

☙

'Heart is where love lives
...and pain heals itself.
Beautiful memories and loving bonds
lay warm and strong beneath the pain.
The mud of pain in the pond of your heart is sacred.
Grow the lotus of love on it.'

—Neena Verma

☙

The heart is the most beautiful part of our being. We are all bestowed with a naturally forgiving, emotionally supple and self-restorative heart that knows how to shepherd itself and us from pain to peace. Let your heart lament the loss. Let it choose love nonetheless. Let your broken heart regenerate its beauty.

Nature, expressive arts, music, dance, meditation, altruism, social service and other similar pursuits bring immense healing for a sorrowful heart. And so do tears. Contrary to stereotypical perception, tears are not a sign of weakness. They are, instead, the nectar of a grief-transformed soul. Inspired by many people I have had the privilege to work with or learn from, and based on my own experience, I have come to believe in the healing power of what I call *tear therapy*.

> 'As your tears fall over that wounded place,
> May they wash away your hurt and free your heart.'
>
> —John O'Donohue

It is normal for the heart in grief to burst into tears at the slightest spur. Allow your grief-sore heart to wash its pain with tears. Instead of feeling fearful of tears or being possessed by them, they should be received with affirmation and love. They cleanse and heal our heart. Of course, you should be willing to take professional help if you experience frequent bouts of chronic tearful breakdowns. In most cases though, tears provide a natural release for our pain. Allow them a healthy expression.

—◆—

RELATIONSHIP RESONANCE

'The essence of a therapeutic relationship ...
being able to share your deepest pain
and deepest feelings with another human being.'

—Bessel A. van der Kolk

Human beings are essentially social beings. We need warm relational connect at all times in life, even more so in grief. But oddly, it often goes missing in grief, whether because people around us feel unsure about how to express their support and extend care, or because our dazed reactions give wrong messages about our feelings and needs. We might land ourselves in lonely isolation even though we may actually be wanting others to stay around, like how it was with Amal who was scared to be left alone but ended up conveying just the opposite. Or we might end up being crowded when all we want is solitude. There is something strange about grief's impact on how we, and people in our life, handle relationships. Sometimes, an invisible frozen wall comes up, which is hard to notice, even harder to thaw.

We need to learn to melt this wall and invite or receive people in our sorrowful but sacred grief space. Most people feel a strange anxiety and awkwardness in engaging with someone in grief. It may not always help if we keep waiting for others to make the right move. Be willing to initiate contact yourself, especially if it is someone particular whose support and care you need, but find them hesitant and anxious about how to approach you. Indeed, it is unimaginably hard. I would encourage you to do so nonetheless, if you are missing human connect. Sometimes all that we need is a warm quiet hug. Go seek that hug of warmth and support that you so need. Even more, offer that hug of warmth and support that others around you need. Remember there is no greater therapy for a grief-sore heart than a warm human embrace. There is no harm in making the first move yourself. Amal felt comforted when his children checked on him. He felt even better when he himself reached out to them and offered them a relationship embrace, symbolic though. His reaching out didn't just do wonders for their relationship, it also made him feel warm and secure even while living alone.

Sometimes the surviving family members may unconsciously take each other for granted, or neglect each other's relationship needs. It may get particularly difficult for them to engage each other if the deceased had been their relationship anchor, like it was with Amal and his children, for whom Uma had been the bridge. In some peculiar cases, where the surviving members already had a strained relationship with each other, their loss, even though shared, may end up further widening the gap between them. Whatever be the case, extend your hand of care and support, as also seek and accept others'. Remember the best relationships are those where people face the storms together.

Step out of your grief shell and meet people who give you a sense of comfort in your state of grief. If you feel up to it, plan an outing, especially in nature, with someone you can trust for sensitivity, support and just the kind of company you need at that time. You may consider joining a self-help peer support group that may offer you a safe, trustful and compassionate climate to express your feelings. If you aren't able to find or trust anyone in your life for a deep compassionate connect, there is absolutely no harm in seeing a grief counsellor just to express your feelings and revive a sense of human connect for yourself, even if you have no need for therapy.

Please be sure to create and maintain relationship boundaries, especially with those who emit toxic energy or cause harm in any way. I wasn't able to do that. And I ended up letting myself be harmed in a serious way. It is great to be a gracious and warm human being towards one and all. That said, be careful to stay clear of those who threaten your safety, peace and well-being.

Finally, what if your relationship with your deceased loved one was going through a rocky phase? The answer awaits you in chapter nine.

—◆—

SACRED WELL OF SPIRIT

'And so, upon this wise I prayed,—
Great Spirit, give to me
A heaven not so large as yours,
But large enough for me.'

—Emily Dickinson

Loss and trauma can shake one's faith and assumptive world. Though the shock may be more pronounced in case of traumatic, untimely or unexpected bereavement, but even in normal bereavement our life-view may get torn apart. There is no reason to feel guilty or worried if you find yourself questioning God, or feel a sense of spiritual disillusionment. In most cases such feelings are transitory. They pass. There are many ways to rekindle or restrengthen faith—meditation, chanting, scripture reading or any other spiritual practice that you feel good about. In my personal experience, the simplest and the purest way to stay aware and awake is what Saint Kabir guides us to—seek earnestly within.

'Where all do you look for me,
I am right where you are, ever'

—Saint Kabir

All the external props fall off as soon as we learn to seek within. Meditation is one route in that direction. It helps us feel calm, centred, and more fully present. Anu (Arnavaz) Aga, the famous social reformer, philanthropist, co-founder of 'Teach for India', and former chairperson of Thermax Global (a large engineering company), acknowledges the role of Vipassana meditation in helping her stay grounded and to live with equanimity. She knows loss and grief up close and personal, having lost her second daughter early in her childhood, and her husband to a fatal stroke when he was 60. Within 48 hours of his death, Anu Aga was nominated executive chair of the much-respected Thermax Group, which, at that time was facing economic downturn challenges. While she was still coming to grips with her loss-altered reality, she lost her mother-in-law, and 14 months later her young son died in a road accident. How does one cope with such engulfing grief, and yet lead the organization to greater glory? Even more, how does one transcend such immense pain, and self-facilitate a deeper transformation of oneself? Anu Aga attributes her peace, poise and enhanced self-awareness to Vipassana meditation. Yet, she is quick to advise that one shouldn't put meditation on a pedestal. And I agree. Meditation does open a path towards spirituality, not necessarily so for every one and in every situation.

An awake and harmonious self is meditative in her/his entire being, and there are many way to reach there. We do not necessarily need to be in a contemplative sitting. Kabir avers, 'Wherever you are is the entry point.' Every moment has deeper meaning and truth to unravel. Zen Buddhism maintains that we can make every experience a meditative experience, and suggests ways such as tea-meditation, walking-meditation, cooking-meditation, gardening-meditation and more. The idea is to connect with meditative energy and deeper wisdom within. I would reiterate my suggestion that you learn meditation from a credible forum/teacher. Explore as many practices or streams as you wish. Pick one that feels the best, and practice it earnestly.

Various other pursuits are also meditative in effect. I have heard many people say that activities such as nature walks, expressive arts, writing, music evoke a meditative feeling for them. I myself practice Vipassana. And poetry, music, nature walks, sketching, sitting under the star-lit mid-night or pre-dawn sky, and community service also fill me with peace and meditative energy. Find out what helps you best, and refill your sacred well of spirit with faith, serenity and love.

Sometimes, just giving an outward expression to our feelings and thoughts begins to heal our pain, and opens pathways to deeper wisdom and growth. But it is not always possible for us to find someone we can trust to hold a safe and empathetic space for us to tell our story. Even when there is someone trustworthy, some people find it difficult to bare their vulnerabilities. Amal wanted to give vent to his troubling emotions, but could not bring himself to talk about it, even though he had some trusted friends and his children whom he could talk to. But when he resumed writing and took to gardening, he found a safe and healthy space to express and heal himself. There are a thousand ways we can offer ourselves a therapeutic experience, and self-facilitate our grief and growth journey. You might already be familiar with and practising some. Let us explore at length self-therapy practices of expressive writing and expressive arts.

THE WRITE WAY

'I can shake off everything as I write;
my sorrows disappear, my courage is reborn.'

—Anne Frank

In grief, a horde of feelings swarm and choke us. If we let them remain unexpressed for long, they can create psychological burdens or medical issues. We need to find a way to give vent to our feelings even if we can't share them with another person. Writing provides a safe, therapeutic and immensely facilitative way.

Dr James Pennebaker, the originator of expressive writing, brought to fore the therapeutic effects of writing. His award-winning research established that when people in trauma, loss or other difficult situations write about their raw feelings, it helps them release tense energy, heal emotional wounds, and create health benefits. Expressive writing involves writing about an upsetting experience for 15-20 minutes a day for four days. Sounds simple. It is indeed. Yet, immensely therapeutic and transformative, as Dr Pennebaker's research suggests. It is an amazing self-therapy that helps us face, acknowledge and heal our deeper feelings and thoughts.

Sometimes grief-stories get entwined. It is amazing how one bereaved person's narrative sharing or writing can heal and support even those she/he shares loss with, through a process of interactive affirmation, adaptation and meaning-making. Hope you remember from chapter one, the story of a young mother who affirmed the grief of her still-born premature baby, and gave new meaning to her baby's presence calling her *'born still'*, rather than still-born. In her continued story, the young mother's pain was later joined by her sister's in *'finding an island of meaning in a sea of meaninglessness'* through penning down the feelings of the bereaved mother. I share below a part of the obituary note the mother eventually wrote for the baby, as gratefully excerpted from Dr Neimeyer's research paper,

> The record will register you as a stillborn child, but for me you lived all that time in my womb... We will carry you with us forever, my child, my love... You were born still... Mommy and Daddy.

The baby was aptly named 'Spirit' by the mother. Certainly a host of things must have helped this young mother transcend her grief. Most precious of all though is her own capacity to find meaning. Also, narrative retelling and therapeutic writing seem to have played a hugely facilitative role in helping her affirm her loss with meaning, resilience and grace.

Anaïs Nin puts it so beautifully, 'We write to taste life twice, in the moment and in retrospect.' Expressive writing helps us revisit and savour our loving memories as much as it provides a safe place to release our pain. I am a case in point myself. Though I was not new to writing, I know for sure that penning down my pain didn't just help me release it in a safe and healthy way, but also took me on several happy and meaningful remembrance trips. I mostly write in a stream of consciousness, flow of the moment way. Little did I know that my random chits and notes would eventually take shape as my grief memoir, which didn't just aid my own healing and growth, but also helped many readers, as I came to know from those who personally contacted me. I feel deeply humble and grateful about this. My writing spoke to my younger son's pain as well. He began giving expression to his troubling emotions. A month shy of 19, he made a presentation at the World Appreciative Inquiry Conference on the topic—'Transcending Grief—Deep Appreciation Way,' a subject that wasn't his, except for the deep wisdom that his own grief and grief writing granted him.

You do not have to be great at writing to express your emotions. Remember it is about releasing your pain. It is a welcome gift if your writing eventually takes shape as a book. But that is not the goal with which you begin expressing your feelings through writing. There are many ways you can write about your feelings—grief journal, remembrance, goodbye letter, gratitude journal, tribute, grief memoir, or a poetry.

> 'A poet can take all the grief from her heart and
> write it in fine black lines on starchy white paper.'
>
> —Lois Tschetter Hjelmstad

Many in grief, naturally take to poetry. It helps take the weight off our chest by allowing an honest expression of private and sometimes even unspeakable emotions. Poetry gifts courage and eloquence to our unconscious voice, and brings to the surface even those feelings that we are not yet consciously aware of. Poetry is also prayerful by nature. No wonder most prayers are poems or songs, and many scriptures are poetic recitations. Poetry can take many forms—conventional rhyme and meter, free verse, haiku, found poetry, sonnet and more. What matters is the safe and creative space that poetry offers to heal our pain, not the form it takes. That said, people in grief are often seen to write in a free-verse form, and quite understandably so.

Words Create Worlds

Pen Your Pain

- Create a grief journal. I encourage you to write-in-hand. The sensory richness adds greater meaning to the therapeutic writing experience. You can hand-bind loose sheets, or buy a special notebook for this purpose.

- Write for at least 15-20 minutes a day, at least four times a week.
- There is no topic for you to write on. The only brief is to continue writing without lifting your pen. Avoid worrying about spellings or grammar.
- Write the afterthoughts without erasing or editing the original thought. Whatever emerges is sacred and welcome.
- Take a leap of faith and let yourself go. If something feels scary, dive right in. No over thinking. No censor. No judgment. No self-loathing.
- It is okay to feel blank, fearful, awkward, or even stupid. Acknowledge and write, even about this. You can write in third-person if that helps.
- After a month or so, let yourself flip through your writings. Expect and welcome any and every feeling that the experience evokes. Allow yourself to savour the feelings of relief, lightness, warmth, tenderness and love, and affirm the feelings of sadness, fear and anger.
- What meaning, messages, insights, lessons emerge? Write them as well.
- Continue the practice for as long as you can and like—a month, a year or forever. Keep your journal handy to record sudden in-the-moment feelings or insights. If you don't have it handy, message or mail yourself and write it later in your journal.
- If you so need or desire, you can use any of the following prompts. Best if you let yourself write in a free-flowing way:
    - It is...
    - You...
    - I...
    - The time I/you...

- ◆ Our most beautiful moment/memory together...
- ◆ I should/shouldn't have...
- ◆ I let go...
- ◆ Forgive me...
- ◆ I forgive...
- ◆ Life...
- ◆ Death...
- ◆ Pain...
- ◆ Love...
- Pen your pain, and let your words create worlds of new meaning, and self-transcendent growth.

⬥

THE ART WAY

*'Art can permeate the very deepest part of us,
where no words exist.'*

—Eileen Miller

I hope you remember Guru Rabindranath Tagore's story from chapter one. He wrote, composed poetry, painted and sang his sorrow. Most dearly remembered for his Nobel winning literary creation *Gitanjali*, and his soulful genre of music called Rabindra Sangeet, his poetry and music inspired major social reforms. That said, before and beyond their outward positive impact, his expressive writing and arts were his way to cope with and transcend his grief. Gurudev, as the Nobel Laureate is fondly called, often referred to his art as *'sesh boisher priya'* (an affair in the evening of life).

Sheeba, from chapter four, also found a safe healing haven for her pain in painting. What began as random doodling for me evolved as sketches, zentangles and mandalas. Some of my earliest sketches made their way to my grief memoir. Music is another happy refuge for me. Kahlil Gibran rightly says, 'Music is the language of the spirit.' A client of mine has found solace in music although he never had any interest in it before. He has begun learning it formally at 61 years of age. Another client of mine took to theatre after discovering the healing effect of arts in the course of counselling sessions. She is finally able to express her feelings that had remained suppressed since she lost her husband at 27 years of age. She had no time or space to grieve, what with an infant daughter and ailing father-in-law to take care of. Her daughter, who is herself a mother now, feels happy and proud of her mother's creative unburdening of 30 years old emotional baggage.

Artistic expression does more than just honour and heal our pain. It transforms us. You do not have to be a trained and certified art therapist to express your pain. There are various ways you can do that through self-inspired arts—drawing, sketching, painting, collage, pottery, music, dance, theatre and more. Explore and find what your soul loves, and let your pain be painted and your sorrow be sung.

Mandala Art

Paint Your Pain

This, as you know, is a meditative arts exercise. Please do it when you can be in a quiet reflective state by yourself.

- Create a growth artbook. You can hand-bind loose art sheets, or buy a special art pad for this purpose.
- Collect whatever art material you would like to use—pencils, crayons, sketch pens, fine tip pens, colour, paint-brush and paper.

- Breathe deep. Relax. Take time to let your body, heart and mind feel calm.
- Listen to what feeling or experience your heart and soul want to express.
- Wrap a soft cloth over your eyes, and let your hand randomly doodle/draw/sketch/paint. Avoid temptation to open your eyes and see. Let your hand remain in movement for as long as it wants to.
- Become aware of how you feel after giving a blind artistic expression to your pain. Savour the feelings this experience evokes.
- Leave your artwork aside for a few minutes. Return after a while and have a gentle leisurely gaze over it for as long as you like. Avoid analysing. Let your artwork speak for itself. Soak in the emergent experience.
- Now listen to your heart and soul again. Pick up another feeling or experience that is waiting to be expressed.
- This time doodle/draw/sketch/paint with open eyes. Avoid conditioning, tutoring or censoring yourself. Let your hand remain in movement for as long as it wants to.
- Become aware of how you feel after giving an artistic expression to your pain with eyes open. Savour the emergent feelings.
- Once again leave your artwork aside for a few minutes. Return after a while and have a gentle leisurely gaze over it for as long as you like. Avoid analysing or interpreting. Just soak in the emergent experience.
- Experiment with any other way you wish to. Make a collage. Draw a mandala or a zentangle.
- Each colour, line, shape, element or living being that appears in your artwork has a unique energy and meaning for you. Notice whatever evokes a calming and

> healing energy, and/or brings to surface some insight. Consciously use more of these elements next time.
> - Visit your growth artbook as frequently as you can or like to, and immerse yourself in expressive arts.

It is important for you to release and heal your pain. If you can't talk to someone, or don't feel like expressing your pain through writing or arts, find another way. Nature is a beautiful outlet. I love listening to the subtle sound of new green leaves as well as the poignant buzz of dying leaves. And I love pouring my heart to the river. Its loving gifts of flowing-ness, resilience and generosity help me feel more alive. Consider talking to trees, sky, birds. They won't question or judge you. If anything, they will take you in their warm comforting embrace. Seek a healing space in nature and release your pain.

ABOVE ALL SMILE

'For all the loss, hurt and pain, she only has a smile of love.'

—Neena Verma

Love yourself.
Love yourself at all times.
Love yourself no matter what.
Love yourself even more when all that you feel is pain, fear or anger.
Love yourself, and the river of well-being will feel fresh, full and flowing.
Love yourself because that is the only way you can continue to love the one you lost.

Love yourself and allow your smile of love to once again come to life. Indeed, a smile is no quick-fix for shattering grief and pain. In no way can grief be wished away or fixed. That said, love is a more abiding part of our being. It was there before grief came calling, and shall stay ever beyond. Keep that eternal love alive. Let the smile of love resurface and adorn your being. No put-on of course. But when you consciously travel down the remembrance lane and fondly reminisce about your deceased loved one, the smile of love will surely light up your entire being. Just be careful to not suppress or hide it, whether out of survivor-guilt, recovery-guilt, awkwardness, fear of social judgment or any other such restrictive feeling. Acknowledge the emergent feeling by all means, and let it go. Return to what is beautiful and meaningful in the moment—the feeling and the smile of love that your precious memory kindled.

Smiling is a sensory experience. Hearing a kind word, seeing a beautiful sight, experiencing a warm feeling—our senses respond to the beautiful experience and show up as a smile, all in a tiny fraction of a second. A smile of deep meaningful serene love is like a rainbow. It fills our senses with peace, health, and all colours of life. Allow that smile of love to heal and nourish your grief-sore senses. Fill them with the beautiful moments and happy feelings that you and your deceased loved one co-created. Make a conscious choice to celebrate their abiding Presence in your life, and your shared life. Speak out your loved one's name and let your warm, happy, grateful and loving smile sparkle your being.

You are right. It isn't easy at all. If anything, it is painfully hard to keep your smile alive when engulfed in grief. That said, life keeps gifting us myriad ways to rekindle our deep and abiding capacity to appreciate and love. Just live those moments fully. Better still, consciously seek and create such moments and experiences that help rekindle your loving-ness.

That is all that your loved one needs to live forever in your heart and your life. Joseph Campbell wisely says, 'Your sacred space is where you can find yourself over and over again'. I would humbly add—that sacred sanctuary is right within us. Nurture that space with your smile, and let your smile of love blossom. Let it shepherd you on the path of grief affirmation and transcendence with inner calm and abiding beauty of life. As we move forward on that path, remember to compose and take home your poetic affirmation.

PATH 7

Poetic **A**ffirmation to **T**ake **H**ome

'A smile of love is
the most beautiful adornment of the soul.
Cup your smile,
and hold it precious in your heart.'

—Neena Verma

Let your smile of love
dance in your heart,
on your face,
and in your entire being

8

Transformation

*'Transform the grief which looks down into the grave
by showing it the grief which looks up to the stars.'*

—Victor Hugo

*Rahim was 11 when his father died a painful death,
succumbing to pancreatic cancer. Rahim grew up feeling
angry and sad that his father died in the absence of proper
medical treatment. Despite his reasonably good income
from a self-made small business, Rahim's father could
never save enough for themselves. Early on he had to drop
out of college and do odd jobs to support the family's needs
since his father had been rendered bed-ridden owing to
his TB. With grit and enterprising skills, he managed to
set up a small electrical goods shop which grew over time
and gave them decent earnings. But it was mostly spent to
pay for the education and weddings of his younger siblings.
Rahim's mother would pitch in by running a small tailoring
business from home. A naturally kind and altruistic couple,
Rahim's parents happily put their dreams and comforts
on the back burner, to the extent that they even delayed
bringing their own child (Rahim) into the world.*

*As far back as he could remember, Rahim had always
seen his parents struggling to make ends meet even though
their income was good enough for their needs. But when*

Rahim's father came down with pancreatic cancer, none of his uncles extended a hand of help. Seeing his father die without treatment, Rahim turned bitter towards his uncles, and prevailed upon his mother to disconnect with them. With bigger worries on her mind and grief in her heart, she quietly withdrew.

Time passed and seasons turned. A brilliant and hard-working student, Rahim studied on scholarships and graduated in engineering and management from prestigious institutions. He drew a handsome salary. Few years later, he quit the job to start his own enterprise to manufacture energy saving devices. He got married to Asma, a good-hearted management professional. Together they made a lovely couple, who grew their business fast and wide. With their financial condition improving, Rahim's mother converted her tiny tailoring unit into a free skill training center for women from underprivileged background. Rahim was happy for her, but did not want her to return to her old altruistic ways.

The wounds of their traumatic past and hard life had led Rahim to develop a world-view that compassion and helpfulness were burdensome virtues. His mother and wife worried for his psychological well-being. Though he sometimes helped those with genuine needs, Rahim mostly maintained a reserved and unapproachable persona, which was out of sync with his otherwise kind-hearted nature. The tipping point came when he refused help to one of his uncles, who, having fallen on bad days and battling cancer, contacted them for help. Rahim snubbed him away, calling it his karmic retribution time. His mother was dismayed to know that Rahim secretly felt happy to see his uncle in misery. Confronting him, she sought to know what Rahim was carrying in his heart. 'My father's pain,

*our helplessness, and their ingratitude and selfishness,'
Rahim responded. She asked him what did he remember
about his father. Much to his own and everyone's shock,
he could recall very little about his father.*

*With gentle strength and grace, Rahim's mother
took him down memory lane, and helped him recall
their beautiful family memories filled with fun, love and
wisdom. He broke down, realizing that his bitterness had
even subdued the memory of his parents' dearly held
motto of 'shukr-sabr-madad' (gratitude—patience and
equanimity—altruism) that they had devotedly lived by.
His mother reminded him of the sentiment with which
they had named him Rahim—one of the many names of
Allah that means one who is merciful, compassionate,
kind, loving and helpful. She asked him to choose what
he wanted to remember about his father—the pain, the
kindness, the misery, the generosity. He asked her back what
she remembered, and was amazed with her response—
'I remember and honour all. His pain is just as sacred for
me as his kindness and selflessness. Memory of his pain
only deepens my resolve to help others in pain. I do not
run away from my grief, or bury it under anger. I have let
my grief guide me on the path of forgiveness and kindness.'*

*Slowly and gradually, Rahim let his bitterness dissolve
in the spring of compassion. Over-occupied with his anger,
he had never touched his grief. Washed clean of bitterness,
his grief unraveled his inner grace that knew how to honour
his vulnerability and strength alongside each other. In
helping his Uncle, he felt forgiveness unfolding quietly in
his heart. It took time and immense courage for Rahim to
rekindle his forgotten virtues of kindness and helpfulness.
Eventually emerging a transformed person, he expanded
his parents' life-motto, adding the word 'kaabil' (capable*

*and empowered) to it. Along with his wife and mother,
he founded a charitable trust in his father's memory that
imparted job-oriented skill training to the underprivileged,
taking the focus beyond charity to making the beneficiaries
kaabil, and inspiring them to be compassionate and helpful
human beings.*

—❖—

'*Shukr-sabr-madad-kaabil*' (gratitude-patience and equanimity-altruism-empowerment)—Indeed, what an amazing life-philosophy to live by. And what an amazing transformation to inspire.

GROWTH Mandala
Created by Neena Verma

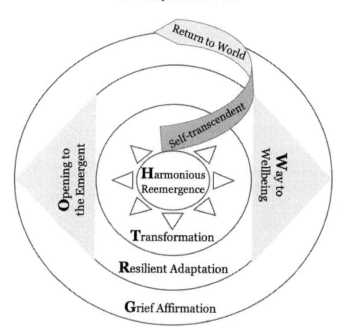

Rahim entered the inner most ring of the GROWTH Mandala that we talked about in chapter three. He transcended the mud of his anger and bitterness, and bloomed anew. Though he had resiliently adapted to his loss-altered new life, his grief was still raw, unhealed and buried underneath his traumatic feelings. As he opened his heart to forgive, it became easier for him to embrace his hurt, and purge his bitterness. With love and courage, he rekindled his virtues of compassion and helpfulness. He entered the dark woods of his grief; faced, accepted and healed the dark side of his emotions; endured his pain; honoured and grew through his grief; and emerged transformed from the gooey remains of his trauma.

Transformation phase of the GROWTH Mandala pilgrimage invokes us to a higher level of consciousness. Having affirmed our grief and resiliently adapted, we emerge in the green valley of healing and well-being, from where we can return homewards with a sense of health and strength to restart our lives in an adaptive way. This is what most of us do. But some of us take the call and choose to take a higher journey to the shrine of transformation. It is an arduous journey beyond the familiar. There is no known path to transit through this Great Pass. Walking in faith, humility and strength, we make our own path and trek to the shrine of our *bodhi* (knowing) self. This journey is represented by the innermost ring of the GROWTH Mandala, the ring of lotus, that sprouts from the mud of pain, blooms and unfolds petals of growth, transformation, emergence and grace. The journey begins as we embrace the twilight of our sorrow and strength, and our grief and growth.

❖

TWILIGHT

'The blue river is grey at morning and evening.
There is twilight at dawn and dusk.
I lie in the dark wondering if this quiet in me now is a
beginning or an end.'

—Jack Gilbert

I have always been in awe of the quiet splendour of twilight. Its infinite expanse is both invocational as well as intriguing. Nothing affirms the transient nature of life more tenderly than the shades of twilight. It is the only time of the day when the light and dark meet and become one. The surreal saffron greys of the dusk, and the ethereal golden greys of the dawn are so similar, yet so different. The interplay of colour, dark and light co-creates the realization that loss and pain are a prelude to growth and transformation. Being in reverent witness of twilight evokes humility, faith, gratitude, hope, resilience, flowing-ness, creative movement and more.

~

'Twilight ...
The confluence of life and death.
The celestial dance of existential and essential.'

—Neena Verma

~

The metaphor of twilight reveals the symbiotic nature of life and death. There comes a twilight moment in our grief journey, when realization dawns that we are stronger than our sorrow. That we have abundant inherent warmth and wisdom to nurse our wound and allow it to become the source of light. That we are both a humble drop as well as the mighty ocean itself. That we must come in empty to drink from the spring of consciousness that Nature kindles in all of us. That we are what poet and philosopher David Whyte calls—'a sun-lit moment, come from a long darkness.'

Here on, begins our pilgrimage to the shrine of transformation. It is okay to feel lost or vulnerable as we step on the threshold of our twilight journey. Like the proverbial hero, we all have an instinctive capacity to enter the zone of sacred transition and emerge transformed. The legendary poet Dante used the word *traviamento* which alludes to 'existential crisis' that puts our whole being on the line. It has the power to change us completely, for better or for worse. The twilight moment of our grief journey brings us face to face with our *traviamento*. We are summoned to make a conscious choice to enter the dark night of our pain. Rahim had the choice to carry on with his life of success and comfort. Nothing would have gone wrong. But he accepted the call to confront his bitterness, purge it and emerge wiser and humbler. He embraced Dante's *traviamento* and put his identity on the line, only to emerge a healed, harmonious, happy and transformed human being.

MY STORY

It was no coincidence that my initiation into vipassana happened at dusk. As if by a deeper design of Nature, I realized that dusk is not just the harbinger of dark, but also marks the confluence of light and dark, just like dawn. Its sprawling dark no longer intimidated me. The metaphor of twilight invoked me to embrace the dark night of my pain and enter it as if it were a meditation. It helped me accept and purge my dark feelings, and allowed my inner light to emerge. I no longer abhorred dusk, thinking of it as the time of the day that had taken my son away, on a Wednesday of a 24th. Twilight consciousness reminded me that dusk was also the time of the day that had blessed me with my son, on another Wednesday of another 24th, 22 years and three months before.

24! Dusk!

The two symbols of time and timelessness had appeared several times in my son's life-script from start to end and in between. A surreal realization emerged that 24 symbolizes cyclic completion. My son had lived his day with meaning and inspiration, and left with the characteristic quiet grace with which he had arrived in this world. Wide awake and fully oriented, Utkarsh had the medics worried when he didn't make the expected baby cry. And filled them with wonder, when he made his first sound as soon as I touched him. The anaesthetist remarked joyfully—'Aw! Such sweet sound. Young man is ringing his arrival.' From the twilight of his arrival to the twilight of his departure, quiet generosity and courage remained Utkarsh's inscape.

It was time for me to make good of the gifts of inspiration that he had left me with. As I entered the twilight zone of transformation, I had an almost epiphanic realization that Utkarsh's famous trust-fall was truly a fall in trust, not just good skill and bravado. It was with amazing grace that he would take the plunge, as if floating in space. I finally understood that I needed to let my baggage fall 'in trust'. It called for immense self-compassion and courage to stand up for myself, assert my need for dignity, well-being and safety, and say a firm goodbye to some tormenting elements in my environment. The timid and submissive me, discovered her courage and strength.

—◆—

METAMORPHIC BLOSSOMING

'His grief he will not forget;
but it will not darken his heart,
it will teach him wisdom.'

—J.R.R. Tolkien

Like the sacred lotus is rooted in the dark muddy waters, our growth and transformation too emerge from the swamp of suffering and fear. As we acknowledge, affirm and transcend our pain, it unravels the seeds of will to meaning and *will to transform*. Petal by petal, the lotus of our growth blooms gently and magnificently on the supple green-bed that emerges over the dark realm of our pain. Eventually, we transform from a seed of sorrow to a flower of strength, and offer the gift of our growth and grace to the world, just like a lotus spreads open to the vast infinite skies. The transformation phase of the GROWTH pilgrimage marks our symbolic rebirth with a higher knowing and grace. We come to accept death as the ultimate form of end. Yet, an end that can and does create new openings and profound change. Whether or not we notice, our loss-altered life changes us, for good or for bad. It is liberating to know that we can consciously choose to create the way and the path of transformative change.

Manpreet, a coachee of mine, had begun college barely four months before his elder brother's and father's brutal deaths in communal violence. He, along with his mother and younger sister, somehow managed to survive the gory night of violence. Supporting his semi-literate mother in making ends meet, he managed to educate himself and his younger sister. Having lived a hard life, it wouldn't have surprised anyone had he chased material wellness. Instead, he didn't just let go of lucrative corporate opportunities, but also kept his heart free of bitterness, and set up a peace foundation that works to build socio-communal harmony, and supports rehabilitation of survivors like him. When he approached me, I wrongly guessed that he wanted grief or trauma counselling. In fact, he left me with many an amazing lesson on grief affirmation, resilient adaptation and deep transformation. Having grown his foundation to impressive heights and engaged a large and diverse team of volunteers and social workers, he actually wanted executive coaching to enhance his strategic planning, stakeholder management and leadership ability.

Manpreet refused to stay a victim, and grew beyond being just a survivor. He became a thriver, reformer, inspirer and a beacon of hope and support for many. Just like Rahim, who chose to grow beyond his grief and hardships, and became an enabler of capability and growth. How did Manpreet and Rahim rise from the muddy pond of pain and bloom like a lotus? How did their growth and transformation come about?

> 'What the caterpillar calls the end of the world,
> the master calls a butterfly.'
>
> —Richard Bach

I hope you remember the second step of *imaginal wisdom* in the RISE framework of resilient adaptation which we talked about in chapter five. The butterfly takes birth from the imaginal cells that emerge from the gooey remains of the disintegrating body of the caterpillar. It is not without reason that these emergent cells of life are called 'imaginal.' Their sacred duty is to imagine life even in the face of the caterpillar's dissolution, or what we can call existential death. This capacity to imagine life is what gives them strength to withstand and overcome the churn of the disintegrating cells of the caterpillar. This is what Rahim and Manpreet did too. They chose to imagine an expanded consciousness, and re-birthed themselves like a butterfly, emerging from the gooey remains of their pain and trauma that had already begun to melt, as they affirmed their grief and adapted to their new life with resilience. Going beyond a life of comfort, they chose to serve the world.

Across cultures and contexts, the butterfly evokes hope and inspires rebirth and renewal. It is said that the walls of holocaust concentration camps had images of butterflies, supposedly drawn by the camp inmates who somehow managed to stay alive, suffering unimaginable, worse-than-death tortures. What must have been going on in the minds and hearts of these brave-hearts! They allowed every emergent moment to guide them to a higher consciousness while continuing to engage with the realities of life. They let their trauma churn them, and waited in faith and hope for something profound to emerge. Their task was to stay put. And they did, however impossibly hard it became to endure the ghastly sufferings inflicted on them, trusting that some higher forces were at work, and that a greater power was taking shape somewhere in the womb of their collective pain. They accepted the call and continued to breathe in faith and hope, striving to stay alive to meet life and light at the other end of their long dark tunnel of suffering. And they emerged stronger, wiser and braver, with an appreciative and meaning-filled perspective on life.

Transformation happens when we let go of the urge to control or fight our circumstances. The seeds of change and growth are sown in the very moment when we accept and embrace our loss and pain, and begin actively engaging with life. Transcending fear, anxiety, pain and worry, we must look beyond our known limits, and keep striving. No doubt, it takes time, faith and hope. Equally importantly, it takes grit and endeavour. Make the effort that only you can and should, and trust Nature to bless the seed of your karma (deed) with the fruits of grace. Allow yourself to dream anew and imagine a transformed you. Create an action map to make it come alive. And act—bit by bit, moment to moment. Transcend, stride on, and let Nature guide you on the path of higher consciousness.

Transformative Tip

Imagine Growth

'Where imagination is alive, possibility is awake.'

—John O'Donohue

- Think of a loss or trauma whose grief and pain overwhelm you.
- Notice and acknowledge what is coming apart. Become aware of the vulnerability and pain of the disintegrating part(s) of your being.
- What would you like to see emerging alongside your pain?
- Tap into and activate your imaginal growth wisdom.
- Imagine a good genie is granting you three wishes to re-author your story of grief as one of growth and transformation. What would you ask for? Why? Think about what you would like to do with the genie's gifts.
- Now fast-forward a year or two in time, and imagine that what you had wished of the good genie is all a reality now.
- Think back and identify the real-time actions you might have taken to make it all come true.
- Create an action-map to bring to reality the wishes granted by the good genie, who, by now you know, is none else but your own will to grow and will to transform.
- Give yourself a happy pat and a warm hug.

TRANSCEND

'This plant would like to grow, and yet be embryo.
Be vaguely vast, and climb, to the tip end of time.
With all of space to fill, like boundless Igdrasil,
that has the stars for fruits.'

—Richard Wilbur

Yggdrasil (or Igdrasil) is a mythical tree in Norse mythology. It is believed to represent the cycle of life, encompassing all its phases of birth, growth, death and rebirth. Yggdrasil is the mighty tree of life that is made of eternal ash, and supposed to contain nine realms of existence including light, darkness, fear, inspiration, creativity and fertility, among others. Yggdrasil holds all the realms of life together as one eternal whole, and together all these realms make Yggdrasil complete. No realm is higher or lower in significance. Each has meaning of its own. They coexist and hold each other, flowing with the sacred order of Nature.

Our emotional landscape is like Yggdrasil in some sense. It is made of different yet interwoven realms. Love, loss, pain, yearning, sorrow, anger, compassion, courage, strength, growth and more. They don't disregard or suppress or preclude each other. Each has its own time that the others must honour and make way for. Nothing can hold space for loss more tenderly than love. And nothing can humble strength more kindly than vulnerability.

At a time when I was still struggling to come to terms with my loss, my younger son gifted me a beautiful pearl of wisdom—'Bhai's (brother's) going is a wound that may never heal. I can't and wouldn't fight with it. Let it heal in its own time and way. His life is an inspiration that I know would always light my path. I am choosing inspiration.' Few months later, a large and diverse audience at the World Appreciative Inquiry Conference, was moved with awe and emotion when my not-yet-19 boy spoke on the intriguing topic of 'Transcending Grief—Deep Appreciation Way'.

Grief! Appreciation! How can the two words even sit together? Your skepticism is valid. So is my son's and many people's faith. They know from experience that when we honour life in its full cycle, our view expands. We begin to see that the broken cup of life continues to be beautiful nonetheless. And we are able to restore and transform our broken cup with the Japanese *kintsugi* (which I hope you remember from chapter five) art of 'golden joinery'. All human emotions and experiences are harbingers of a higher consciousness. Acknowledge each emotion, however painful it may be, receive and affirm its deeper message, make good of its gift of growth, transcend it when the moment is ripe and you are ready, and look for new meanings and possibilities beyond your known horizon.

> *'I am searching for the lost needle out*
> *in the bazaar because there is light here.*
> *So what, if I lost it inside the*
> *home where there is dark.'*
>
> —Rabia, the Sufi saint

We keep busy looking for peace, happiness and strength in the world outside because we fear looking through the dark within. But our light lives within our own dark. This amazing insight surfaced for me while watching the splendid sunrise at Kanyakumari, a holy city at the southern-most tip of mainland India where the three mighty waters of the Indian Ocean, Arabian Sea and the Bay of Bengal meet at a surreal confluence. The blue Indian Ocean, the grey Bay of

Bengal and the green Arabian Sea are distinctly clear—both in their individual glory, as well as in their graceful union. The sunrise at Kanyakumari is astoundingly beautiful. And it evokes an ethereal feeling. In a close to four-hour-long divine experience, you can see the universe quietly changing colours—from the night's black, to the hesitant saffron grey of pre-dawn, the shy pink of dawn, to the majestic golden of the rising Sun that emerges mighty yet serene on the welcoming confluence of the three waters. This was not my first experience of watching the Sunrise at Kanyakumari. But this insight was new. I knew it in my head. But I finally understood it in my heart that the word 'insight' means to see-inside. And I saw my light within my dark, my faith within my fear, my love within my loss, and my growth within my grief.

Remember, the search for light begins within the dark night of your pain. See and seek within. Your light is taking birth in the dark womb of your pain. Stay in reverent witness. The golden dawn is unfolding. Marvel at its glory. Re-author your story of life and light, and spread it in the universe.

Words Create Worlds

Twilight Story

- Recall significant life experiences that have affected and/or shaped you in a deep and profound way. Some of these may be sweet and pleasant, and some others difficult, even traumatic.
- Try to be fully aware in your body, heart and mind, as you recall memories, feelings and thoughts associated with each.
- Think of each of these as different characters in your life-story.

- Give each character (experience/event) a unique name and symbol that represent its significance and special place in your life.
- Now assign your grief the protagonist's role.
- What name and symbol have you given it? What meaning do they hold?
- What fears, pains and hopes drive the protagonist? What do they need?
- What stance/mindset must be taken by the story-writer (you) to help the protagonist (your grief) feel acknowledged, accepted and integrated?
- What plot must the story-writer weave to help the protagonist transcend their pain, and seek a higher consciousness?
- What would help them find a way to grow with meaning and rekindle their light?
- Imagine the protagonist is seeking a soul-partner called 'Growth'. How would you shape the story to ensure the twain meet at the confluence of their dark and light, and co-create twilight wisdom?

Taking cue from the above prompts and whatever else feels important, script the story of the protagonist's (your grief) journey of affirmation, transcendence, metamorphic blossoming, and re-emergence. Be as vivid as possible.

Weave a narrative that inspires and enables you to accept and transcend your pain, and transform it into a higher purpose.

TRAVEL LIGHT

'Afoot and light-hearted I take to the open road.
Healthy, free, the world before me...
leading me wherever I choose.
I ask not good fortune, I myself am good fortune.
I whimper no more, postpone no more, need nothing.'

—Walt Whitman

All our life we keep busy trying to get a grip on life, merrily unaware that life is passing us by. The happiest traveller is the one who carries the lightest bag. While others remain occupied with fussing over their belongings, the light traveller soaks in the true joys of travel.

On one of our jungle safaris in the Bandhavgarh National Park in central India, a family requested us to accommodate them in our jeep since their booking had not materialized. We happily took them on board. But their heavy camera equipment took so much space that we all sat cramped, and I had to literally hold their young daughter on my lap all through the safari. While we were savouring the glorious sight of a mighty tigress leisurely soaking in the sunshine on a winter morning, along with her three young adult female cubs, our co-traveller couple were noisily adjusting their elaborate camera equipment. They were very upset over their failure to capture the prized sighting on their sophisticated camera, which had been bought specifically for this holiday. I felt sad for them. Not because they had failed to film to their preference, but because in their fuss, they missed out on their daughter's awe-filled gleaming eyes and hear her joyful cries—a sight far more precious than a tiger-sighting captured on camera. Later, at the rest point, their daughter told them about the pictures I had managed to get on my phone camera. They were astounded to see the various moods and antics of the tiger cubs. I happily shared it all with them. They enquired about my photography skills. I didn't have any secret formula to share. All that I had done was hold my phone steady and let my hands follow my gaze, while my heart and eyes remained immersed in marvelling at the majestic and graceful movement of the tigress who was indulgently watching over her cubs. Not even the best camera in the world could capture such a preciously endearing sight that I could behold only in the eyes of my heart.

Life is one such precious sighting. Behold it in your heart and eyes. We can't contain water in our fist. We have to make a grateful cup of our humble palms to drink water from the spring of life. The tighter we hold; the faster life slips away. The lighter we cup life in our heart, the sweeter is the taste and aroma of its myriad experiences, pain and joy alike.

Consider going a day without a personal effect that you feel incomplete without. It could be your watch, your phone device, a particular pen or anything else that you can't generally do without. A day or two later, ponder over your experience. How upsetting or liberating was it? Did you notice all your finer feelings beyond the expected discomfort? Is there a deeper message in the sense of something being amiss? Is there a baggage—a fear, worry, guilt, shame, jealousy, resentment, anxiety, memory, prejudice, obsession, desire, belief, a behavioural pattern or any such thing that you have been holding on to, and are now willing to let go? Is there something you can (or should) let go of to travel lighter on the path of life? There is a popular Urdu couplet by the poet Hairat Allahabadi that beautifully makes the point about living without baggage and travelling light.

'आगाह अपनी मौत से कोई बशर नहीं
सामान सौ बरस का है पल की खबर नहीं'

(āgāh apnī maut se koī bashar nahīñ
sāmān sau baras kā hai pal kī k̲h̲abar nahīñ)

Whoever knows the moment of his departure,
No clue of the next moment, worldly effects, you gather.

Travel Light. It frees us up in ways we may not notice, but would surely feel, and if I may say so, enjoy to our heart's fill. Travelling light is about emptying yourself of non-essential stuff and baggage of all kinds—material, emotional or behavioural. It is about emptying yourself of what has lived its time and purpose, so you can refill your cup of life. It is about accepting that we may not have answers to all questions of life, that we may not be able to manage all crises of life, that we must learn to flow with what we can't fix. In Tibetan, the word for body is *'lu'*, which means something that we leave behind, without baggage. As in death, so in life. Easing ourselves of the non-essential baggage is key to rising high without losing our gravitational contact with Earth.

Nine months before my son's departure from the mortal world, he had started his last-semester capstone project training at a coveted research and development institution in India. My husband wanted him to buy some new clothes to look sharply dressed. My son kept avoiding the discussion since he felt that his clothes, though old, were functional and sturdy enough, and there was no need for new clothes. My husband felt his clothes had worn out and didn't look nice. Utkarsh's polite response—*'But I need clothes only to cover myself, not to look good'*—left me amazed, though not surprised. I persisted nonetheless, making a point that he had too few clothes. I was spellbound with his gentle wisdom—*'Travel light, Mamma. Who knows what you have to off-load and when!'*

Travel Light. Indeed. Utkarsh lived his words in every sense. He travelled light, leaving behind a rich lifetime of inspiration, wisdom and love, from a life abruptly cut short. His gift of light and Sufi vision lives on, not just in the form of his corneas, but also through his legacy mission of community libraries for marginalized children, and in many other real and symbolic ways. His life mantra, as shared below, is the simplest yet most profound pearl of wisdom about 'traveling light'. I find meaning and inspiration in it, and have adopted it as my life mantra too.

> *'Breathe quiet. Eat light. Sleep tight.*
> *Share forward what life has given you*
> *in excess of your needs.*
> *Do what you can.*
> *And travel light.'*

—Utkarsh Verma

Travel light. It is that ultimate level of transcendence that helps us go beyond ourselves, and emerge larger than ourselves—humbler, deeper, wiser, more expansive and magnificent. Travel light so you can travel far. And travel light so you can return home warmer and happier. Please remember to create and take home your poetic affirmation as we prepare to embark on the final phase of the GROWTH Mandala pilgrimage which heralds our return home, all transformed, all anew.

—◆:◆—

PATH 8

Poetic Affirmation to Take Home

'Welcome, marvel, avow, behold.
Your Sun is rising, rich in gold.
A livelier light is emerging bright.
A new "You" has begun to unfold.'

—Neena Verma

You are returning home,
healed, grown and transformed.
Adorn your gifts of wisdom and transformation.

9

Harmonious Reemergence

'Come and rejoice, for April is awake.
Life's shoreless sea is heaving in the sun before you.
Plunge into the deep without fear,
with the gladness of April in your heart.'

—Rabindranath Tagore

Bob was born in a small town called Milford in the state
of Ohio in the US. His upbringing was in a Catholic
community, though at a later stage in life he became
nontheistic. Yet he felt drawn to eastern philosophies
of Confucianism, Taoism, Krishna Consciousness, and
Buddhism in particular. This philosophical quest, along
with many other things, influenced his academic interest
in philosophy of psychology, psychotherapy and personality
theory.

Bob's childhood was filled with adventure, what with
a vast woodland right behind his home where he would
play and explore nature in the spirited company of his
younger brother and many friends, developing a sense
of both leadership and community early on in life. He
grew up with a sense of exploration and creativity—
hiking, making up games, playing Cowboys and Indians,
collecting fossils and crayfish in the creek bed, and doing
all those amazing outbound things that children of the

pre-technology era would do. His love for hiking, running and nature has continued, well into the second half of his sparkling sixties.

Early on, Bob became a Cub Scout, and soon a Boy Scout. He began to undertake various self-initiated projects, earning merit badges, and eventually becoming an Eagle Scout at the rather early age of 14 years. His childhood exploration and Scout experience laid a formative foundation for what he was to pursue later in life—research, scholarly and clinical work, and the development of new concepts and practices in his chosen field of psychology.

Unfortunately, Bob's abundantly explorative, creative and loving childhood came to an abrupt and tragic end with his father's suicide. Just 10 days shy of turning 12, life suddenly ejected Bob out of a happy childhood, and placed a heavy load of responsibilities on his young shoulders. The eldest of three siblings, Bob had to grow up fast. He continued to excel in his academics even though he usually had a couple of part-time jobs, which would often become full-time during summer, and eventually converted into professional work as he moved to graduate school. The family's grief and financial hardships were further compounded by his mother's complicated grief that led her to make repeated suicide attempts.

Despite such trying life circumstances, Bob preserved his virtues and further nurtured his strengths of exploratory spirit, research, creativity, love for nature, hiking, focus, sensitivity, cheerfulness, friendliness, sense of responsibility and more. Life was his training ground for hard work, resilience and self-reliance, and his loss kindled in him an earnest sensitivity for bereavement and trauma work. As an undergraduate volunteer at University, he became deeply involved with suicide intervention work at one of the USA's pioneering suicide and crisis intervention services.

How many 12-year-olds can we imagine maintaining the kind of discipline and excellence that Bob did? Working from his boyhood days to support his endeavours, he devoted his life to serving the cause of suicide intervention, grief and trauma, something that had thrown his life upside down at the tender age of 12. Bob chose to remember, honour and celebrate the loving relationship he had had with his parents, rather than let himself go bitter or helpless because of his father's suicide, his mother's complicated grief, and the resultant life miseries. He took his love for people to a higher level, and immersed himself in pioneering research, scholarly writing, teaching, training and clinical practice in the grief and trauma space.

His personal quest and academic exposure inspired Bob to look for and create meaning, even out of the most traumatic experiences of his life. In his close to five-decades-long academic and professional career, Bob created several path-setting frameworks, the most impactful of which is 'Grief Therapy as Meaning Reconstruction' approach, for which he is known and respected the world over. His uniquely inspiring meaning-constructivist approach to grief is being practiced around the globe with immensely transformative impact. An eminent psychologist, researcher, multi-award-winning academician, clinician, author and editor of hundreds of scholarly articles and books, expressive artist and poet—Bob wears his many hats lightly. Above all of his inspiring credentials and accomplishments, what one would most admire and respect Bob for is his amazingly simple, warm, sensitive, secure, cheerful, generous and gracious nature. Perhaps the most meaningful way to

honour Bob's story would be by closing it with excerpts
from one of his moving poems that he had written in a
suicide survivors creative writing workshop.

> *'You make me happy*
> *when you share your sadness,*
> *open your heart's pages*
> *and read the small print.*
> *This is how it is, for us now,*
> *as we stand in the ashes,*
> *only see beauty*
> *where it is laid bare,*
> *stripped of ornamentation,*
> *just the sturdy posts*
> *that still stand,*
> *nudged back into place,*
> *re-centered by other hands.*
> *They give no protection*
> *from the howling wind,*
> *but they endure,*
> *and provide a place of meeting.*
> *A place to rebuild.'*

—Bob Neimeyer

How does one come to terms with the enormity of grief and adversity that Bob endured at such a tender age, leave alone transcending it and emerging warmer, wiser, brighter and stronger on the other side? Growing beyond his pain and vulnerability, Bob self-enabled wholesome personal and professional growth. His pioneering work and wide-ranging accomplishments amaze and inspire. More importantly, it is the human being that he is, that makes Bob unique and much loved by one and all.

Bob is the internationally acclaimed grief expert Dr Robert Neimeyer whose gracious foreword welcomed you to this book. I have also referenced some of his work early in the book. His 'Grief Therapy as Meaning Reconstruction' approach has opened new vistas in the grief therapy realm. I am privileged and grateful to be his mentee, friend and colleague in different spaces of life and work. I feel happy, humbled and honoured that he shared his above-mentioned poetry with me in our very first mail exchange, and gave me the permission to share it with you.

Is there a magic mantra for such profound growth in the wake of loss and grief? Well, if there is one, it is right in your heart and hands. We ourselves enable and herald our harmonious reemergence.

GROWTH Mandala
Created by Neena Verma

Having traversed various phases of the GROWTH Mandala pilgrimage, we return home healed, grown and transformed. Ready to live life anew for ourselves and others, we take the path of meaning and grace. Grief is still a sacred part of our being, but it does not overwhelm or possess us. On the contrary it bestows on us the wisdom, generosity, compassion and grace to go beyond ourselves, and share with the world the nectar of our transformation. What we have to offer to the world now holds greater meaning for us, than what we seek of the world. Welcome to the '*harmonious reemergence*' phase of the GROWTH Mandala pilgrimage, where you make a *self-transcendent return* to the world. This is what Bob did. This is what I did. This is what you too can do, if you aren't already doing it.

RETURN

'It'll be spring soon...orchards will be in blossom...
birds will be nesting.
They'll be sowing the summer barley,
and eating the first of the strawberries with cream.
Do you remember the taste of strawberries?'

—J.R.R. Tolkien

Welcome home.

Having affirmed and transcended our grief, and resiliently adapted to our new reality, we return home to ourselves and the world, with a heart filled with faith, hope, reverence, gratitude, resilience, compassion, meaning, love and more. We return as the same human, yet different being. Our life-view, frames and filters have undergone profound transformation. We know. Others may not know or understand that. The world has been going about the business of life as usual. At some level it may feel strange. At a deeper level though, we have grown and awakened to a higher knowing. This new *knowing self* at the centre of the GROWTH Mandala understands that time and life remain in motion. It guides our harmonious reemergence from grief, with growth, and towards grace.

If you are not yet familiar with *The Lord of the Rings*, I highly recommend that you read or watch the epic-trilogy by J.R.R. Tolkien. Having completed their traumatic journey and delivered on their sacred yet daunting duties, the four Hobbits return home. They are overcome by suffering and grief on one side, and a sombre sense of fulfilment on the other. But life at the Shire (their homeland) is going on as usual. Nobody seems interested or bothered about the trauma these chosen Hobbits have faced and come out of, or the growth and transformation that they have undergone. They would have loved it had anyone cared more. But they don't sit in disappointment or lament. Instead, they choose to flow with the world, rather than waiting for others to notice and honour their journey. They decide to seek life anew. Their grief remains sacred for them. That said, they choose to celebrate life—welcoming spring, growing summer barley and tasting strawberries. They meet their old world with their new wisdom and strength, and share with their community the gifts of grace that their arduous journey of trials, trauma and transformation has bestowed on them.

Such is the nature of Nature. Seasons change. Winter falls when it is meant to. Spring blooms when it must. And summer brings new harvest just when we are ready to savour it. We are inherently gifted with the adaptive instinct to flow with all seasons of life—meeting winter with grit, welcoming spring with grace, and partaking the fruits of summer with gratitude. Bob did just that. Having faced and endured his grief and hardships with resilience, hope and dignity, he met his new life with meaning and purpose. Dedicating himself to bereavement and grief work, he created a path-setting grief therapy approach, led scholarly researches, contributed extensively by way of teaching, writing, training and mentoring, and most importantly helped thousands of people come out of their grief and take the path of meaning-centric growth.

> `You might not start out a hero,*
> *and you might not even come back that way.*
> *But you change. The journey changes you,*
> *whether or not you know it,*
> *and whether or not you want it to.'*

—Kami Garcia

Life holds all the makings of becoming a heroic journey, whether or not we intentionally set out that way, or realize along the way. So is the case with one's grief journey and GROWTH Pilgrimage. Bob started out, a simple young boy in grief, and emerged an inspiring leader of grief therapy, making extraordinary contributions. I began with a small need, just wanting to find a way to live with my grief without neglecting my life responsibilities. Little did I know I would emerge humbler, wiser, stronger, more forgiving, creative and altruistic on the other side of my grief and growth pilgrimage. This is what can and does happen with many who take the GROWTH Pilgrimage path. They transcend their grief and emerge as someone whose purpose in life has grown bigger than their pain.

—◆—

RECONSTRUCT AND REEMERGE

'What I need is the dandelion in the spring.
The bright yellow that means rebirth.
The promise that life can go on,
no matter how bad our losses.
That it can be good again.'

—Suzanne Collins

However shattered we begin, Nature holds the promise of helping us reconstruct life with deeper meaning, even a higher calling. We can and should regenerate ourselves, and harmoniously reweave the fabric of our life, moving from 'misery to meaning', 'pain to purpose' and from 'cry to calling'.

Making sense of the loss is often not easy, more so when it is traumatic, untimely or unexpected. It takes great courage to endure the pain of recalling our loss story, let alone look at it with our new accepting eyes and heart. It is also true that we may not always be able to know the deeper meaning of all that happens in our lives. It may not even be necessary. That said, there is immense value in being able to make meaning of our loss-altered life. Having travelled across various phases of the GROWTH pilgrimage, we feel settled, strong, harmonious and willing to do so. Integrating the death of our loved one and our grief as life-defining parts of our larger story is a helpful step in the direction of finding meaning and purpose in our unfolding life.

Most people are able to reconstruct their story on their own, unless when grief has turned complicated and professional help is needed. There are many things that give soul to our story. The room, bed, clothes, souvenirs and various other belongings of our deceased loved ones hold meaning for us. There is absolutely nothing wrong with preserving what is precious for you and helps you re-anchor your life. Take time to search and curate all the belongings of your deceased loved one that hold meaning for you. Create a sacred space, however tiny, that honours and celebrates their Presence.

MY STORY

My son was a person with frugal needs. He lived off barely five-six sets of clothes and meagre belongings. But there are a few, seemingly rather ordinary things, that held deep meaning for him and now hold special place in my life. The much-relied-upon, tiny time-piece that he had brought home from his hostel room continues to sit happily on his bed-side. Some days after his going, the time-piece stopped, apparently because of cell discharge. I noticed but did nothing for months together, as if I was okay being frozen in time. And then one day, for no clear reason it fell on my hand while cleaning the table. I don't recall how long I sat, all blank, before getting up to change the cell and restart the time-piece. In a symbolic way, it reoriented me to my unfolding life.

As a kid, my son loved playing his harmonica and keyboard. His self-composed melodious renditions were mostly for the private audience of my younger son, and occasionally me as well. His harmonica and keyboard have, over time, kindled a keener interest in music for me.

On his first ever summer camp at 10 years of age, he had spent all of his meagre pocket allowance to buy a beautiful walking stick for my father who was battling cancer at that time. That stick commemorates my son's sensitive and caring nature. I have treasured it in his tiny nook.

My son's exploratory spirit, inquisitiveness, vast spread of knowledge and depth of understanding, quiet and selfless generosity, and so much more, hold inspiration for my younger son and me. He was a pro at complex puzzles. His Rubik's cube is now in the treasured care of my younger son, who has surprisingly developed a greater interest in history and literature, something that my transcended son was keenly into. Books being his only indulgence, he had a huge collection. I still have a large bookshelf full of his most loved books, even after donating nearly 2,000 from his collection.

I used to secretly lament that my son's untimely sudden departure hadn't allowed me to do anything to save and care for my child, not even a goodbye, until one day in a poignant spur of the moment I found myself writing a letter from him to me.

There are so many special moments, memories and things that help me reconstruct my life with meaning, and honour my son's Presence. Most precious of all is his legacy mission of inclusive learning, which has inspired my life-purpose. Of course, I shouldn't have had to pay the price of my loss to become a better human being. I would give up everything without a blink if I could have my son back. Affirming my loss though, I feel deeply humble and grateful for being able to transcend my pain, grow larger than myself, and let my cry become a calling.

While our bond lives in our hearts, there are ways to commemorate it outwardly. Some people create rituals of meaning. Some people set up legacy projects. Taking forward my son's inclusive learning mission, I run a library movement for underprivileged children. We set up a new library every year on his birthday. That is our way of celebrating his birthday. If loss and grief can bring life to a stand-still or regress it, they also open the path for deep transformation. Nature endows each one of us with the spirit and strength to grow from our grief and reemerge with a sense of meaning. Honour both your grief and your growth, and harmonize the two. Re-story your life. Create your legacy mission.

Words Create Worlds

Legacy Plaque

*'The meaning of life is to find your gift,
the purpose of life is to give it away.'*

—Pablo Picasso

- This pearl of wisdom from Picasso held special meaning for my son. Somewhere along the way, it became special for me as well.
- You too might have imbibed, inherited or felt inspired by something that your deceased loved one held dear to their heart.
- Think of all their dreams, causes, interests or pursuits. In what way do they continue to inspire you?
- Do you feel inspired by, share or wish to adopt any of their dreams or pursuits?
- In this moment of conscious contemplation, become aware of what matters the most for you. What gives you a sense of meaning?
- What is emerging as a new life purpose for you that you want to take forward as your deceased loved one's legacy mission?
- Write it as a mantra or a mission statement on a plaque.
- Create the plaque with your own hands. Adorn it the way you like.

- Hang it, pin it or place it in a way that keeps you inspired and focused.
- Now make a concrete action plan to bring your legacy mission to reality.
- Be clear about the broad vision and list specific details of everything you need to do, and when and how you will do it.
- And get going.
- I wish your mission and you, abundant success.

REMEMBRANCE

'If there ever comes a day when we can't be together, keep me in your heart. I'll stay there forever.'

—A.A. Milne

We honour our grief by celebrating our love. Love transcends grief. If grief lives long, love lives longer. It lives forever. Even after our deceased loved ones have completed their mortal journey, their Presence lives on. Let your love and relationship live on because they have not died. Let your beautiful past become a continued part of your life. Let your memories become eternal *Remembrance*. Let what you loved the most about them inspire who you choose to be today. Embody their gifts.

I was introduced to the above quote from Milne's famous *Winnie the Pooh*, by my (then 13 years young) transcended son. I loved it from the word go. I expressed my wish to live in his heart even after my death. Responding with a serene smile, all that he said was, 'Who knows, Mamma.' Indeed. Who knew? Being a bereaved parent is an unimaginably painful and arduous journey that no one should ever have to take. His alive Presence in my heart and consciousness gives me immense strength to persevere. His many small or big gifts continue to fill my life with fun, hope, love, meaning and creativity. From our midnight chit-chats full of teasing, arguing, fighting, sulking, confiding in, indulging and celebrating each other; to several nature sojourns in jungles, on mountains or by the riverside; to poetry jamming; to debates over socio-political matters; to community service—I have countless fun and wisdom moments to cherish and preserve. Instead of letting them fade away as memory, I have created an eternal Remembrance out of a lifetime of special moments and momentoes, and celebrated my son's BEING with his legacy mission.

Love goes beyond Death
The body disappears
The person lives
In Love
And in this Love
Remembrance is born'

—Neena Verma

Time to address the unanswered question from chapter seven. What if your relationship with your deceased loved one was going through a rocky phase? Well the whole of your relationship is precious—both love and hurt. No relationship is ever fully happy, complete or perfect. For relationships to gain true depth and intimacy, we have to allow room for hurt and disappointments, alongside love and care. We receive a lot. And we must also give a lot, bear a lot and forgive a lot. All your emotions towards your deceased loved one have meaning. Welcome and value them all. Savour all the happy emotions, and seek or create a way to let them become remembrance. Acknowledge the unsavoury residuals, and mindfully look for messages that those tough times had for both of you. Try acting upon them, even those that relate to your deceased loved one. For example, if you feel the message about anger-management from a rough fight was more relevant for your loved one, accept it nonetheless as a gift for both of you, and try working upon it. Remember—your relationship does not die. It becomes an eternal bond of love. And love is forever. Viktor Frankl puts it so well—

> Love goes very far beyond the physical person of the beloved. It finds its deepest meaning in his spiritual being, his inner self. Whether or not actually present... or still alive at all, ceases somehow to be of importance.

Our relationship has every right, every chance and every way to become more beautiful, even after our loved one is gone. My relationship with my son is far deeper and happier today, without making light of my grief. You owe your relationship continued nurturance, both for yourself and the one you are grieving. There is nothing delusional about continuing to relate with your deceased loved one. Their *spirit presence* lives on in your heart, mind and life. Talk about your differences with the symbolic presence of your loved one. Resolve them. Restrengthen the relationship. Celebrate it. Savour it with gratitude, and continue to nurture it with love. Bless their soul, and seek their blessings.

Transformative Tip

Re-Member

'My spellbound heart has made and remade the necklace of songs, that you take as a gift, wear round your neck in your many forms, in life after life, in age after age, forever.'

—Rabindranath Tagore

- Find a quiet time and space to be by yourself.
- Take a deep breath. Reminisce your pre-loss life. Recall the precious moments and memories with your deceased loved one.
- Pick one that is particularly evocative in this moment. Relive the experience. Feel your surging emotions.
- Become aware of and welcome all that is surfacing— tears or laughter, sighs or smiles.
- Let yourself be in this experience for as long as it naturally stays.
- Gently and slowly return to the present moment.
- Write a letter to your deceased loved one.
- Share all that you hold dear to your heart about your shared life. Recount beautiful memories. Tell them everything that you love and value about your relationship, and their positive impact on you, in life and death. Shower affection and gratitude for your beautiful shared life.
- Commemorate this special letter. Adorn it the way you like. Pin it at a prominent place or treasure it privately.
- Savour. And repeat with as many memories and as often as you like to.
- Now go down memory lane once again, and allow the unsavoury residuals, if any, to show up.

- Avoid controlling or suppressing. Just witness whatever shows up—anger, annoyance, disappointment, regret or guilt.
- Imagine your deceased loved one in an empty chair in front of you.
- Speak out what continues to bother you. Speak out—literally.
- Listen to their virtual voice. Seek to understand and accept their disappointment of you, if any.
- Allow the consciousness dialogue to continue as long as it happens organically. Clarify and resolve the differences or misunderstandings.
- Seek and offer forgiveness.
- Re-member the bond of love.
- Allow your spring of love to sprout anew and become fuller.
- Create a song of love for your deceased loved one. You don't have to be Guru Rabindranath Tagore to do that. Sit back and enjoy the beauty of your creation. Create one more song. And as many more as you like.
- Offer the gift of your songs of love to your deceased loved one.

—◆—

SHARING NECTAR

'Share quietly and do what you can.'

—Utkarsh Verma

My son Utkarsh was eight years and four months old when he began volunteering at a community outreach, non-formal school for underprivileged girls. Soon he was running his weekend pavement library in a nearby slum. He would carry a large backpack of books from our home library and a rugged mat to spread on the pavement from where he ran his humble but hugely facilitative library. He wore multiple hats as a story-teller, poetry facilitator, curiosity stimulator, thought provoker, hygiene educator and more. On weekdays, some under-resourced kids used to regularly visit our home for help with their science, maths and language lessons. He inspired and nudged me and my younger son also to join in. Later he began volunteering to sensitize the homeless children against substance abuse.

All his service was quiet and almost invisible. Though deeply fond and proud of his altruistic endeavours, I also used to sometimes worry if his selfless nature would make him liable for abuse, which it did quite often. As a young anxious mother, I even tried dissuading him once, telling him that there was only so much he could do in his small capacity. In response he told me the story of the tiny hummingbird that carried droplets of water in its beak to pour over a huge jungle fire. When a lion on the run asked what it was doing, the tiny bird sweetly answered, 'I am doing what I can' and quietly went about doing its job.

'Share quietly and do what you can'—the insight that my young son gifted me that day for a meaningfully happy life, has now become my life mantra. I feel humble and grateful to be blessed with the will and wisdom to serve the disadvantaged. A large part of my time, energy and income is devoted for the same. I know many bereaved people who do similar things, having walked the embers of grief and learnt to emerge warmer and stronger on the side of growth. Elizabeth Berrien puts it well—

> Once you have walked down the grief path, what you have gained on your journey may turn into invaluable advice for someone else.

Rob Fazio, a counselling psychologist and the president of 'Hold the Door for Others' founded the organization in honour of his father Ron Fazio, who literally held the door open for his colleagues to run to safety in the 9/11 terrorist attack. Helping several people survive on that fateful morning, he himself died holding the door for others. Moved and inspired by how his father put others' lives above his own, Rob Fazio and his family decided to serve others in grief and trauma find a way to accept it and grow through it.

Sharing the nectar of your growth with others is a simple and pure way of saying 'Thank You' for what the universe supported you with, in finding and creating for yourself. Think about all those people who helped you traverse your grief and growth pilgrimage—people who held the space for you, or gave you strength, or inspired you, or did random things that you value and feel thankful for. Express your gratitude to them. And think of all those people who need your help and care. Reach out to them. Be their guide. Hold the door for others, and share with an open heart.

Life brings storms to everyone. Some storms, though, are so colossally devastating that we can't and don't get through them without allowing ourselves to be changed and transformed by them. Dostoevsky's wise words, 'There is only one thing I dread: not to be worthy of my sufferings', made real sense to me only when I fell in the ravines of grief, and took my fall as a call to pilgrimage. Indeed, in grief or in crisis of any nature, there is no safe middle path. The frightening void that we face is the liminal space that holds within it seeds of healing, growth and grace. Sooner or later, most bereaved people return to life with a restored sense of strength. But to return with the gifts of grace that the GROWTH pilgrimage can bestow on us, we need to 'be worthy of our sufferings', and make the immensely trying journey.

Embrace life in all its splendour—the storm and the sunshine alike. The marvel of grace is waiting to unravel itself to you as you prepare to re-emerge in the world—healed, harmonious, grown larger than your pain, and ready to share the nectar of your transformation with the world. As we move towards that, let me gently remind you to please create and take home your poetic affirmation.

PATH 9

Poetic Affirmation to Take Home

'The long dark night,
has found its light.
Dawn is seeking you,
bathed in resplendent twilight
Welcome yourself as you return,
to the spring of your own light.'

—Neena Verma

Celebrate your growth and reemergence.
And prepare yourself to take the path of GRACE.

Part 3

MARVEL OF GRACE

10

Forgiveness ...
The Self-transcendent
Path to Grace

'Forgiveness is the way out of darkness and into the light.'

—Gerald G. Jampolsky

Savi was married off at 19 years of age. A promising student, she had studied on scholarships, despite coming from a conservative family that didn't think much of educating girls. Being a timid and compliant girl, Savi submitted to her parents' decision to marry her off early, and suffered all her life at the hands of her alcoholic husband who was a far cry from what her parents had hoped, and definitely not a match she deserved.

Raising four children, Savi was forever tight on money because of her husband's alcohol addiction. Though she managed her circumstances with dignified stoicism, on some rare occasions she felt sad over the loss of her youth and a good life's prospect, had she been able to complete her studies. Keeping her own pain aside, she had invested all her energy in raising her children well and arranging the best possible education for them despite her financial constraints. Her eldest son, Sajal, was an exceptionally bright kid. Her third son, Mitul, and the youngest of the lot, her daughter, Rupal also did well. But her second son, Vipul, caused Savi much worry. He had been expelled from school for his unruly conduct and failing grades. She managed to shift him to another school but his waywardness and poor performance continued. Despite her best care and positive parenting, he eventually dropped out. An indifferent and unavailable father, her husband did little to keep his son from straying.

Savi was in acute distress seeing her dear child fall in to bad company. Even worse, like his father he also took to alcohol at a rather young age. Savi felt as though she had failed and was distraught but kept trying. She got him counselled to start rehab. Her eldest son, Sajal, stood by her side, filling her with hope and strength. Apart from managing his own studies, he took up a part-time job to pay for his dear brother's rehab. Together they endured all hardships and made sure that Vipul returned to normal life, stayed sober and resumed studies. Unfortunately, due to excessive consumption of country liquor, Vipul's tender liver had developed cirrhosis and he died a painful death at the young age of 20 years.

Savi was shattered to the core but stoically managed to live on. She felt filled with gratitude, hope and pride for her other children. Most of all, for Sajal who didn't just maintain a brilliant track record at his own studies and career, but also kept his younger siblings Mitul and Rupal in his care, ensuring that they too did well in studies and went into good careers. Overall life had begun to unfold positively for Savi and her children. Her grief over Vipul's tragic death notwithstanding, she had decided to keep her chin up and keep herself busy with her other children who had all become successful professionals in their respective fields.

For some people, though, clouds of loss and grief always keep lurking. Savi's life was swallowed by such dark clouds when Sajal got killed by a family who were upset over his relationship with their daughter. The so-called upper-caste family did not approve of a lower-caste boy seeing their daughter. When they saw the couple determined to marry, they decided to eliminate Sajal. An epitome of selfless love, he died at the hands of the agents of hatred. In a matter of little over five years, Savi had lost two of her children at the prime of their youth. While she could still console herself over Vipul's death because of the understandable reasons, she couldn't make sense of Sajal's brutal murder. Her entire world came apart. She fell into a numbing silence that worried and scared her two younger children. Her husband, though saddened by the loss of two young sons, didn't do much. Himself struggling with liver cirrhosis, he worried for his own life especially after Vipul's painful death. It was now on Mitul and Rupal to take care of their distraught parents. But they were themselves no less vulnerable. Nonetheless, with their love and care, slowly and gradually Savi began to reengage with life, enduring her engulfing grief and pain.

Even as her pain gnawed at her, Savi continued to affirm life, and selflessly cared for one and all. Over time, encouraged by her daughter, Savi began to volunteer at a rehab. Taking notice of her sensitive and resilient nature, the organization got her trained as a community counsellor. She had successfully counselled three people out of addiction, when she heard about two families in her neighbourhood getting into a violent tiff over their children's inter-faith relationship. An otherwise timid person, Savi bravely tried to pacify the two hostile groups, dissuading them from violence and encouraging them to accept their children's relationship. In the scuffle she got injured. Scared to the core, Mitul and Rupal called in the police, who mediated and counselled both sides to sanity.

Meanwhile, having heard about Sajal's killing, the mediating police officer later came to meet Savi. He was curious to know how she managed to accept her loss and live with her grief. Her simple and brief answer was— 'I forgave'. He was stunned and so were her children Mitul and Rupal who had attributed her dignified adaptation to her compassion, resilience and affirmative attitude. But they could never imagine forgiving Sajal's killers. In fact, they both secretly hated the family that had stabbed their beloved brother to death. Forgive! Why? How? Savi's response was unfathomable even to her children. To the police officer, it was puzzling.

How can a mother forgive the killers of her son? How can anyone forgive the kind of life that Savi had lived? But Savi did. She had forgiven all her pain. She had forgiven a life that only kept her on a hook and heaped loss after loss upon her. Why? How?

Because hatred and bitterness were too heavy a burden to carry which Savi chose not to add to her already grief-overloaded back. Because she realized that she could nurse her wounds only with love, not resentment. Because she knew that Sajal's murderers' crime belonged to them and it was not condonable in any way, but her pain belonged to her and she could ease it some bit only by letting love occupy her heart, not bitterness. Because she found her anchor in healing, not hating. Because she wanted Sajal's memory to be associated with what he represented—love and care; not the hatred that he fell prey to. Because she wanted her children, Mitul and Rupal, to continue trusting and upholding humanity. And because forgiveness was the only way she knew to honour the universe's grace in the face of grief. Savi forgave.

—◦:◦—

FORGIVENESS
THE SUPREME HUMAN VIRTUE

The realm of forgiveness is both sensitive and strong. It is both inspiring and intriguing in ways that we can't understand from the lens of logic or reasoning. It is a realm of faith, acceptance and love; and of healing. However deep be our wound, however intense our pain, forgiveness shepherds us gently down the tricky and treacherous slopes of agony, angst, resentment, fear, hatred and bitterness. Forgiveness takes us beyond ourselves. Forgiveness ushers us on the path of meaning and grace.

Forgiveness is understood in myriad ways—as a virtue, an emotion, a humanistic strength, an experience, a process, or a transcendent state. Let us begin understanding forgiveness by clarifying what it is not. Forgiveness is not about denying, forgetting or suppressing the pain. It is not about condoning or justifying the wrong. Nor is it necessarily about reconciliation or restoration of relationship. It is natural to feel hurt, scared, indignant, resentful, even revengeful as a result of being wronged. But we don't deserve to carry the wound of others' wrongs in our heart.

Savi did not condone the murder of her son. She left it to the law to do the needful. She chose not to let this feed or fuel her anger. She was alive to her pain, anguish, sorrow, her sense of being a victim of hatred. She just chose not to be a prisoner of her victimhood. She acknowledged her pain but didn't think of bitterness as a useful medicine. She had a thousand valid reasons to blame and lament. She did, of course, feel the urge to seek retribution. But she didn't fight with or kill her urge.

Nor did she come down harshly on herself for feeling such an urge. Instead, she chose to understand the deeper message of her urge, and decided that forgiveness was a better portal to healing, well-being and a future without hatred for her family and herself.

Unlike reconciliation, which involves both sides, forgiveness is a private matter. And one should have full freedom to decide whether to forgive or not. No one should be under any religious, moral, emotional or relational obligation to forgive. A forced, conformed, obligatory or unwilling act of pardoning or excusing is far from forgiveness. One may have a thousand and one solid reasons to not forgive. And we should not judge ourselves or others for that. That said, if there is even one faint hint from our soul to consider forgiveness, we should give it the respect, reflection and consideration it deserves. Savi noticed that tiny hint even though it was buried under layers of several valid reasons to not forgive.

Forgiveness is a subjective experience, private and internal to each one of us. It is a profoundly personal experience that arises from that deep place in our psyche, heart and soul that shows us a way beyond ourselves. It is a matter of choice, of heart and mind. It involves acknowledging and feeling one's pain, making sense of the same, stepping beyond it, invoking radical compassion and empathetic understanding, and eventually taking a decision and acting upon the same, whether by externally verbalizing or by a quiet expression within ourselves. At each stage, our deeper conscious wisdom guides and propels us forward. Forgiveness, as Savi knows, takes *will of heart* and will to meaning. And forgiveness, as Savi's children, Mitul and Rupal, came to understand takes time, conscious effort and *will to heal*. Forgiveness, as we all deep inside understand, releases us from the prison of our pain. Savi chose to delink her pain from her right for justice.

She honoured her pain by transcending it. She chose to forgive and allowed her pain to heal in a truly abiding sense.

There is enough research and evidence to confirm various psychological and health benefits of forgiveness. People who have taken this path would also vouch for its socio-relational and spiritual positive effects. Forgiveness may or may not result in the restoration of relationship. Yet, it does weaken the impulse to resent. Based on my humble understanding, personal experience and professional practice, I would say those who take the path of forgiveness, do so more for their inner peace and well-being, rather than any external benefit. There is deep peace, meaning and grace to be found in forgiveness, even in the face of grief, and we realise this only by taking this path.

Pause and Ponder-1

- Find a quiet time and place to sit in a contemplative state.
- Take a few deep breaths. Relax. Try to turn your attention inwards.
- Think of a hurting event or a person that you haven't been able to forgive.
- Notice your body sensations, feelings and thoughts. What happens to your physical and emotional state as you recall this event/experience?
- Take a few deep breaths. Relax.
- Focus on your heart center, the seat of compassion.
- Imagine all your energy is preparing to bring forgiveness to the fore of your being.
- Notice your body sensations, feelings and thoughts.
- What difference, if any, do you notice in your overall state?
- Think again of the same hurting event or person. What would you like to do with your hurt? What does your

> inner sage advise you to do?
> - Bless yourself and the event/person you forgave.
> - Bless yourself, nonetheless, even if you haven't been able to forgive. And think of returning to this practice at another peaceful moment in time.

FORGIVING THE UNFORGIVEABLE

Forgiveness is not easy. Not even for small hurts. Nor even when the transgressor is offering an apology and seeking reconciliation. But how does one forgive in the face of grief, especially when loss is by violence or crime? How does one forgive the suffering, anger and grief caused by such traumatic loss? It is not easy to find closure or resolution for grief even in normal death. But in the face of violent loss, it can forever remain irreconcilable. It would be justifiable to remain caved in lament and bitterness—even hatred—in such a situation. Paradoxically, even in the face of loss by violence or trauma, forgiveness can and does heal grief and create an opening for deeper existential and spiritual growth.

Two families in different cities in India lost their young sons to socio-communal violence in separate unrelated incidents in 2018. Transcending their grief, they both rose in the moment of their gravest pain to forgive the communal hatred, and appealed for peace and social harmony, dissuading their respective communities from retaliating. A few months later, one of them even organized prayers for the other faith community, and sent messages of love and peace. This is an exceptional expression of forgiveness, coming from rare courage and compassion—knowing that the wrong done to them cannot be forgiven, and yet choosing to forgive anyway.

Forgiveness researcher, Fred Luskin, had women from Northern Ireland who had lost their sons to religious-political violence, undergo a forgiveness project called HOPE (Healing Our Past Experiences). These bereaved mothers didn't just report significantly reduced intensity of their pain and grief, and a growing sense of peace and hope, but also returned to serve as guides to subsequent participants. Such is the healing power of forgiveness. It allows the emergence of a transformed self that poet David Whyte wisely calls 'a larger identity than the person who was first hurt'.

Priyanka Gandhi, the daughter of former prime minister of India, Rajiv Gandhi, who was blown to pieces in a terrorist attack, talked in a TV interview of her transformation from being 'furious with the world' to becoming a 'forgiving daughter'. In a private visit to the prison to meet the convict of her father's assassination, she felt her own victimhood disappear the moment she understood that the convict was a victim too of her own conditioning and circumstances. When asked for his reaction to the killing of the terrorist who had masterminded their father's assassination, Priyanka's brother, Rahul Gandhi, voiced dismay at the way the slain terrorist's corpse was being ill-treated. He also expressed compassion for his children, stressing that he 'understood deeply what it meant to be on the other side of that thing'. Both Priyanka and Rahul Gandhi represent radical forgiveness, rising above their grief and taking a profoundly compassionate view of the transgressors.

The whole world, including her own children, couldn't understand what made Savi view her son's killers' crime from their perspective. She did because she was able to take a larger view of the situation that included their anger and hatred, however wrong it was. And because she was willing and able to step beyond her own pain and acknowledge even her offenders' agony, however improper it was.

What explains the kind of radical forgiveness that Savi, the two families mentioned above, the Irish bereaved mothers and Priyanka and Rahul Gandhi epitomize?

---◆:◆---

SELF-TRANSCENDENCE

Self-transcendence is the secret kernel of forgiveness. It is the ability to rise above and beyond own feelings, needs, urges and perceptions, and seek understanding from other's world-view. It comes from a space of greater inclusive sensitivity. It is more than just overcoming bitterness, resentment, vengefulness or other such feelings associated with loss, hurt or injustice. It is about transcending such feelings, and coming to a space of shared healing. Viktor Frankl affirms that we all have our own 'inner concentration camp that we must deal with ...with forgiveness.' Viktor Frankl knows better. He is not just the founder of logotherapy—a meaning-centric approach to psychotherapy— but also a holocaust survivor himself who lost his entire family to Nazi barbarism. Yet he chose to find meaning in his suffering.

Forgiveness calls us to step beyond and rise above our injury and pain, without suppressing or disregarding the same. It doesn't mean we neglect ourselves or leave ourselves behind. Of course, our internal defence mechanism needs to remember the source of hurt so as to guard us better in future. Forgiveness doesn't preclude such self-care. That said, stepping beyond oneself initiates a profound process of self-cleansing. It not just facilitates our well-being, but also helps us realise immense transformative potential at a personal, relationship and social level. Forgiveness is a transcendent response to our sense of loss, injury, injustice or offence, that enables reframing of our hard feelings into a more humane or life-giving form. It takes immense courage to let go of own pain and assertion for justice, and empathize with the transgressor, and understand the wrong from their point of view. In the process, we expand our story beyond our bereftness and allow it to move towards grace.

Self-transcendence enables the capacity to let go, release the suffering, take an empathetic perspective and choose the path of compassion. It helps us grow larger than our pain. It strengthens us to choose love over lament. Jain philosophy asserts that *uttam-kshama* (supreme forgiveness) is an inherent attribute of the essential benevolent nature of the soul. Honouring its transcendental nature, the Jain community dedicates the first day of their 10-day-long annual spiritual festival to forgiveness. They celebrate it as Kshama-vani Diwas (Forgiveness Day), seeking and offering unconditional forgiveness as a process of purification and spiritual evolution. No doubt we all are naturally endowed to grow beyond our pain, take the path of forgiveness and become whole again.

Pause and Ponder-2

'Forgiveness is the journey we take towards
healing the broken parts.
It is how we become whole again.'

—Desmond Tutu

- Think of a trauma or transgression that left you feeling broken.
- How would you like to acknowledge and address your feelings? Through art, writing, talking to someone you trust or even yourself, spending time in nature, doing yoga, meditating or something else that helps. These are only suggestions. Please choose the way you find most appropriate and facilitative for yourself.

- As you look through the clouds of your feelings, what else do you see?
- What new wisdom emerges for you as you take a larger perspective beyond your pain?
- Hoping you are able to transcend your pain, and forgive, how would you help another person in similar turmoil?
- Imagine you are invited to share your wisdom about forgiveness as the way to wholeness—what would be your one-sentence message?

FORGIVENESS IN THE FACE OF GRIEF

'The only way out of the labyrinth of suffering is to forgive.'

—John Green

Grief, as we know, doesn't come alone. There are several difficult emotions that occupy the crevices of our broken heart. It is relatively less difficult for us to sense our sorrow, pain and fear. But anger in grief is often unspecific. Whether in acute or even normal grief, we might experience intense anger. We feel angry at our loss but don't know who/what to direct our anger at. It is not uncommon to resent God, destiny or nature for taking away our loved one. Such angst gets further compounded when we are heaped with platitudes like 'God knows better'.

When you are writhing in grief, you can't be comforted with a nicely worded cliché. Remember, when it comes to forgiving unkind reality, or what we may call fate, it is a difficult journey. We can't forgive unkind life circumstances in just one brave leap. Our cup of anger and pain takes time to empty.

And it also takes us time to refill our cup with fresh water of forgiveness. Many bereaved people I work with, confide in me their anger with God. I myself had a thousand angry questions for God. We hide our anger with God from others for the fear of unkind judgment. And we wonder if and how as humans can we forgive God. Why not?

God is first and foremost a feeling in faith, whether a spiritual phenomenon of our own making, or influenced by religious or cultural conditioning. The only God we know first-hand is the abstract God-figure within us. Divinity lives in humanity and vice versa. Our anger at losing our loved one is normal. And our act of forgiving God (or God-figure within ourselves) is sacred. Remember, forgiveness is a gift of grace. It happened to me on the morning of the first birthday of my son after his departure. I woke up at dawn feeling a surreal warmth soaking every pore of my body. And I heard myself say to my God—'*I forgive you. I love you.*' Forgiveness had been throbbing in my heart and mind. But like most people, I also found the idea of forgiving God irreverent. And then it happened—not by my intent alone, but more as a higher grace. The grace that is bestowed upon us, we can surely gift that back to God, the ultimate source of grace. There is no definitive 'how' to it. Invoke state of prayerfulness. Express love and gratitude. Bless God—yes you can. God needs our blessings as much as we need Hers/His. Do what feels natural and comfortable. Take the weight off your chest.

Sometimes we might secretly be upset with our deceased loved one, especially in case they have been neglectful of their health or have taken their life. It could get worse if our relationship had been in some stress, in which case we are left with unfinished business for the rest of our life. Caught in our despair and not knowing what to do with our anger, we can sometimes unconsciously mislay it on random people, like

Sheeba (chapter four) felt anger at the organ-donation appeal team. Sometimes our anger is a bit more complex. Remember Tanya (chapter two) who felt let down by doctors, was upset with her father for his apathy, secretly felt angry at God, and also felt guilty herself. Such multi-layered anger might actually be hiding our despair, fear, pain or even guilt. We need to recognize, address and heal this concoction of open, concealed or suppressed anger. Whether our anger is specific or undirected, it tends to add further weight and pain to our grief and makes us more prone to suffering. When allowed to simmer unconsciously, our anger can turn into bitterness and cause secondary adverse effects such as health problems or relationship disharmony. It is important to recognize and process our anger, and allow it to melt in a healthy way. With forgiveness, we find a way to release our anger and allow our pain to heal.

Savi had every valid reason to hold on to anger and resentment. But she knew it wasn't going to help her or her family to sit in resentment. She knew, for her grief to be affirmed and harmoniously integrated, she needed to delink it from her valid anger towards the killers of her son. She needed to heal her wound, which couldn't have been treated by anything except the balm of forgiveness. She didn't suppress her anguish. She didn't condone their crime either. She trusted that justice would eventually prevail. But she didn't wait for it to forgive the offenders. She released them from her right for retribution, and realised that her own suffering got released in the process.

MY STORY

My son Utkarsh had inspired me to pledge for cornea-organ-tissue donation barely seven weeks before he transcended the mortal world. His going, by silent heart-attack, was unexpected and untimely. It was so sudden that medics could hardly do anything. I was driving back home when my husband called to break the dreaded news that no father should have to utter, and no mother should have to hear. I have no recollection of how my reflexes drove the 20-odd kilometers to the hospital.

We, the distraught parents, were completely overcome by shock and grief. In such daze and frozenness, my son's characteristic gentle voice suddenly started buzzing in my heart. I have no logical explanation for what I experienced in that moment. I distinctly heard him calling me to 'donate'. And we decided to honour his call. His being a cardiac death, only corneas and tissues could be retrieved. In the absence of necessary logistic support, we could only donate his corneas, but not without going through a hellish ordeal at the hands of some relatives. It isn't easy to put in words the unimaginable distress that I was subjected to. It was, perhaps, the first time that these people could do something for us after having enjoyed my quiet service for many long years. But here they were—acting hostile. Eventually, with some well-wishers standing by us, the cornea donation happened.

It was natural to feel wounded or bitter. And we did experience anger for some time. There was some more untellable and insufferable harm that I was subjected to in the months to come. I was so broken that in one passing moment my woundedness felt stronger than my wisdom. Thankfully, instead of unconsciously slipping into the dark abyss of bitterness, I chose to witness my feelings without judgment. And an intense and profoundly transformative churn ensued in the process.

Caught between feeling broken and wanting to regain my sense of wholeness, eventually my warmth took care of my woundedness. As I came face to face with my pain,

> *I could see that the weight of bitterness was too heavy a burden on my already traumatized heart. The voice of the sage that quietly lives within all of us nudged me to let go of my pain and forgive. I chose not to wait for apology or regret. It never came by. But my healing did. My grief wouldn't have eased with a word of apology. But it didn't have to get worse because of others' wrongs. I chose love over anger, forgave the violative transgression, and sent those people my prayer of well-being.*

But my journey of forgiveness didn't end there. I needed to seek forgiveness from people whom I had caused hurt. Sometimes preoccupied with our own distress, we unconsciously say or do things that hurt others. I too had been improper in my conduct with some people. Regret was not enough. I needed to seek forgiveness. And I did. It was a deeply cleansing experience to acknowledge my wrong and seek forgiveness.

—◆—

START BY SEEKING FORGIVENESS

'And throughout all Eternity,
I forgive you and you forgive me.'

—William Blake

Sometimes even when we intend to, it may not be easy for us to actually put our intention to forgive to action. It may not be easy to forgive even when we mean to. And sometimes, even when we think we have forgiven, our hard feelings may come back on rebound. It is OK. While some people are more naturally attuned to forgive, most people need time to be fully alive to their feelings, process their pain, understand their true intention, and put it to action. Forgiveness is a long pilgrimage. Even with good intentions, sometimes we may struggle to practice forgiveness.

A good way to start is by seeking forgiveness for the wrongs we have committed and the hurts we have caused. Often it is easier for us to be more consciously attuned to the harm or the wound that we have suffered. In contrast, we tend to have an unconscious selective omission bias for our own offences and misdoings. We are likely to react more strongly to our own pain and suffering, than be willing to acknowledge our own wrong. I was no exception. I too had kept my own hurt above the ones that I had caused. As I began to recall life-events I noticed quite a few occasions when I had been rough or wrong. There were many people I needed to seek forgiveness from, most of all my children who have on occasions borne the brunt of my bottled pain caused by the unrelenting adversities that I have had to put up with in my life.

I decided to begin with the paramedic at the hospital whom I had shouted at. He was handling my son's discharge. He had carelessly dropped my son's hand with a clinical coldness that he might have become used to in his routine handling of dead bodies. This landed my son's hand on the side iron-bar of the bed he was laid on. The mother in me screamed in horror at what I saw in that moment as his lack of sensitivity and dignity. I angrily asked him to lay his hands off my son's body. The kind man quietly stepped back, handing over to a colleague.

It was extremely painful for me to visit the hospital from where I had brought my lifeless son home. But I needed to make this visit to seek forgiveness for my rough conduct to a person who was doing his duty, a duty that not many mortals would have heart to serve on. He had no intention to hurt. My son was already gone. He couldn't have been hurt. There was no one to be hurt, except my broken heart. This man was actually helping in his own way. And instead of thanking him, I had shouted at him. I loitered in the hospital compound for over an hour before I could gather courage to enquire about him. I didn't know his name. I didn't even remember his face. The front office executive checked records and located three paramedics whom he thought might have handled my son's discharge.

Before I could, the man I was looking for, recognised me. He gently greeted me with a Namaste, and enquired about my well-being. I could barely mutter something in response. He expressed regret over his handling and thanked me for helping him learn the importance of sensitivity and dignity on such occasions. I was stunned. What was I supposed to do or say? I had no better way to respond than to receive his grace with grace. Instead of verbalizing my apology, with my head bowed in gratitude, I just handed him the brief letter that I had written seeking his forgiveness and expressing my gratefulness. My bare words, 'Please forgive me. God bless', said much more than my letter. Something melted in the moment, and I felt an eternal bond with him even though we never met again. Such is the magic of forgiveness.

Words Create Worlds

Therapeutic Writing

This being a therapeutic writing exercise, please do it when you can be in a quiet reflective state by yourself. As requested before, please try to write—(a) by-hand; and (b) in a dedicated notebook.

- Think of a wrong that you have committed or a hurt that you have caused to someone.
- Allow the experience to fully come alive as you recall the details.

- Notice your body sensations, feelings and thoughts.
- Acknowledge your act of wrong to yourself.
- Once again notice your body sensations, feelings and thoughts.
- Now prepare to write a letter of apology. Avoid explaining or justifying your action. Just express your feelings of regret and seek forgiveness.
- You may or may not want to post the letter, though it would feel better if you did. You can think later what you want to do with that letter. For now, just focus on seeking forgiveness with all your heart.
- You may or may not want to restore/rebuild the relationship. It is OK.
- Just be in the moment, and seek forgiveness with sincerity and grace.

—◆:◆—

FORGIVE FOR GOOD

'We are not responsible for what breaks us,
but we can be responsible for what puts us back together again.'

—Desmond Tutu

To heal our pain, we first need to acknowledge its presence, and feel it in its fullness. We need to allow the experience of pain without denying, suppressing, distorting or discounting it. Our difficult feelings can't be replaced just like that with the pleasant ones that we would rather want in their place. We need to know our pain to be able to work with it. We need to face and embrace our difficult feelings to be able to heal and transcend them. There are many ways to understand

and give our pain a healthy expression. One beautiful way is through expressive arts.

Mandala Art

Paint Forgiveness

This as you know is a meditative arts exercise. Please do it when you can be in a quiet reflective state by yourself.

- Gather some art material of your liking—a drawing sheet or a canvas, and some crayons or pencils—and place on the worktop in front of you.
- Arrange a soft cloth that you can comfortably wrap around your face.
- Take few deep breaths. Relax. Take time to feel present in the moment.
- Think of an experience/person that left you feeling wounded and hurt.
- Allow yourself to face and touch your feelings of woundedness and pain.
- Wrap the cloth over your eyes as if it were a blindfold.
- Pick up the colours and let your hands paint your pain.
- Suspend worry, judgment or anxiety about how a drawing under blindfold would turn out to be. Let your fingers do their work while you stay focused on witnessing and feeling your wound and pain.
- Let your hand flow for as long as it wishes to. No censoring. No sneaking. No stopping your hand before it wants to stop on its own.
- Notice the ebb and flow of your feelings as your hand continues to draw or paint. Notice their changing form and intensity. Maybe you feel more pain than when you started. Or maybe you feel less. Observe like a detached witness. No questions. No value judgments.

Just notice what emerges, acknowledge it and let it go its own way.

- Slowly bring your fingers to rest as and when you naturally feel complete with your work of art.
- Remove the blindfold, and gently open your eyes. Take a compassionate non-judgmental look at your creation.
- How does it feel—strange, 'not-me', 'so-me', 'why so', 'what do I do'?
- What does it say of your feelings? What meaning do you make of it?
- What does it evoke in you—anger, pain, guilt, sadness, fear, peace, love, faith? What do you wish to do with these emergent feelings?
- What are you being called to do?
- Once you feel fully grounded in the awareness of your pain, acknowledge it to yourself in a way that feels healthy.
- Become aware of your emergent feelings, thoughts and overall state.
- Ask yourself—'where do I wish to go from here?'
- Hoping your answer is 'forgiveness'—take action and begin walking in that direction.

Maria Popova, the founder and generous curator of Brain Pickings, and the author of *Figuring* puts it simply—'In any bond of depth and significance, forgive, forgive, forgive. And then forgive again'. Forgiving, thus, is an act of grace. Our job is to participate in it. We do that by opening our heart and mind to what wants to happen.

'Forgiveness comes from an open heart, and it comes without condition, or it does not come at all.'

—From the movie *Amish Grace*

Forgiveness is the gift of an open heart that doesn't ask anything in return. The human heart is naturally programmed to be kind and forgiving. The heart knows how to honour our wholeness. Of its own accord, the heart would always choose what is best for our healing, health and harmony. It has far more compassion and love than all the hard feelings put together. Left to itself, the heart would choose forgiveness and love over anger and bitterness. Let us be willing to trust our heart and follow its lead.

We need our mind also to be a friendly partner in our journey of forgiveness. In some ways, opening our mind can be a little more difficult than opening our heart. It is said that the human brain has a default negativity bias. Nothing wrong with that. It is with the valid purpose to prepare and protect us against potential harm. But sometimes we tend to take it far, attaching a lot more importance to hurtful experiences than they reasonably deserve. The result is, we unconsciously allow quite a bit of anguish and pain to collect inside. Irrespective of the label (positive/negative) they carry, all our feelings and emotions belong to us and together make us whole. We need to discern which ones to nourish with our energy and which ones to let go.

Sometimes we tend to get stuck over small, if not petty, or trivial matters. Our unforgiving stance can harm not just our relationships, but also our health. Let us remember that forgiveness is as much relevant in small everyday matters, as it is in the context of big wounds. Richard Carlson wisely puts it as—'Don't sweat the small stuff...and it is all small stuff'. When you feel stuck with a hurt or failed expectation, ask yourself how would it matter in the larger scheme of things one year from now, or even one week from now. If it genuinely feels like it will matter big—by all means go ahead and seek resolution (not retribution). And if it is a small matter, follow Richard Carlson's advice and stop sweating.

All said, let me also underline that our safety and well-being come before forgiveness. Sometimes there could be a sustaining hurt or harm, or serious abuse. Remember, your safety comes first. It is entirely for you and you alone to decide whether you want to, and are ready to, forgive the abuse. Please don't be under moral pressure to forgive if it comes by risking your well-being. And if the harm is in the nature of a crime, you shouldn't ignore it. Do the needful. You may forgive the pain and release the suffering of ruminating over your hurt but let law take its course, like Savi did. It is great if you have in your large heartedness forgiven the transgressor. But in the interest of your safety and well-being, there is practical wisdom in maintaining distance and guard, and not explicitly conveying your forgiveness to an unrepentant transgressor.

—◆—

FORGIVE YOURSELF

'To forgive is to set a prisoner free and discover that the prisoner was you.'

—Lewis B. Smedes

Lastly, but perhaps most importantly, let us be forgiving towards our most lovable person (ourselves) who needs the most reliable shoulder (ours) it can safely lean on. In grief, any small or big hurt breaks us to the core. Sometimes it is hard to stay coherent. We are short on strength. Yet we need to stay put. The least we can do to comfort ourselves is not add more pain to our already distressed heart. Tanya (chapter two) stressed herself, feeling guilty for not being able to save her mother from dying. However irrational it may sound to a detached onlooker, her guilt was real for her. That said, she would have caused herself more harm by holding on to such feelings. It is only when she forgave herself that she found the strength to live with her grief and pain.

I hope you recall from chapter two how I loathed myself for not fulfilling my son's wish of a particular dish for breakfast on the day that was to be his last. His last wish of me, a small wish, that too after a long time, and I didn't fulfil it. I punished myself with guilt forever. It took a long time for me to be able to forgive myself and release myself of guilt. I wouldn't credit all of my subsequent health improvement to self-forgiveness. But I am very sure of its good impact.

We can't forgive others with a heart that begrudges itself. We need to first cleanse our heart of the laments we hold against ourselves before we can forgive others for the hurt they have left us with. We find our strength the moment we own our vulnerability. And forgiving ourselves is one of the important steps in that direction, if not the most important step. No one deserves our compassion more than we do ourselves. Forgive yourself and set yourself free from the prison of your guilt, anger, remorse or shame.

LET THE LIGHT IN

'Wound is where the light comes in.'

—Mevlana Rumi

One of the many folklores about the great Sufi Saint, Junaid, has it that he once reached a small village in the evening hours. As he was looking around for someone to guide him to a night shelter, he saw a young boy walking with a lit candle, apparently to place it at the temple door. Junaid asked him—'Can you tell me from where the light comes? You have lighted the candle. So, you must have seen. What is the source of light?' The boy blew out the candle, and asked Junaid—'You have seen the light go. Can you tell me where it has gone? If you can, then I will tell you from where it came, because it has gone to the same place. It has returned to the source.'

Our wounds, pain, sorrow, joy, love and faith—all emerge from and return to the same source called *grace*. Let us bow in faith and put up the prayer flags of gratitude, reverence for life, compassion, and essence of life on our temple of grace. As you sit to pray, remember to compose and take home your poetic affirmation.

PATH 10

Poetic Affirmation to Take Home

'Let the morning rise fresh with light and dew,
Even when the darkness is enveloping you.
Honour your hurt that is in a bitter brew.
Forgive the wound and begin anew.'

—**Neena Verma**

Look inside your wound
Let go of the hurt and pain
Light the lamp of forgiveness
Let yourself take the path of grace

11

The GRACE Way

'Sorrow surrenders its crown to a throne called grace.'

—Aberjhani

Once upon a time, it was a green and beautiful world. All beings were happy and healthy. One day, the Creator who created by thinking what will be, thought of cold, and the Snow-spirit descended and covered the entire world with mist and frost. For a while, it was a novelty. All creatures played in the snow and had fun. But soon many creatures died of the biting cold, and those who survived feared for their lives.

The wise owl decided that someone would have to travel to the abode of the Creator and plead Him to un-think cold. The question was, who should go? Owl itself could see only in the dark and would have been blinded by the radiance of the Creator. Turtle was too slow. Coyote, although fast and smart, wasn't going to be wise in a way that would gain the Creator's positive attention.

Then the Rainbow Crow, the most beautiful of all the birds, the one with a uniquely enchanting voice, spread its magnificent rainbow-hued feathers and spoke mellifluously, 'I will go.' Indeed, only the one with such a mesmerizing appearance, melodious voice, gentle manner and wisdom, should make an appeal and talk to the Creator. Thus chosen, off flew the Rainbow Crow, up and beyond the skies, the moon, the stars and the sun, braving torturing winds for three days and nights, stopping only at the abode of the Creator. In his mellifluous voice, he called out to the Creator—'Help'. But the Creator was busy thinking and creating new things, and wouldn't hear the Rainbow Crow's call. So, it began to sing, drawing the Creator's curiosity. Pleased with his soulful rendition, the Creator asked what gifts He could offer to the Rainbow Crow.

All that the selfless and compassionate bird had on mind was the misery of his people. He asked the Creator to un-think Snow. But once thought by the Creator, the Snow-spirit had already come into existence and couldn't be destroyed. Reassuring the dejected Rainbow Crow, the Creator offered to think of Fire which would warm all creatures and melt the Snow. Delighted and grateful for the Creator's gift, the Rainbow Crow quickly left carrying the stick of Fire, taking the same three-days-long arduous journey. Along the way, the Fire grew hot, and as he flew past the Sun, his tail caught fire and burnt his splendid feathers. Undeterred, he kept flying. As he leaped through the clouds, the smoke choked his throat and his sweet voice. The most beautiful and melodious of all the birds, the Rainbow Crow returned home ugly and hoarse, all black in body and nothing but a husky 'caw' in place of his enchanting croon. Yet his sense of gratitude for being able to save fellow creatures remained stronger than the grief of losing his mesmerizing persona.

Happy with the warmth of the Fire-spirit and the melting of the snow, all creatures began to rejoice. Sad and embarrassed over his blackened feathers and hoarse voice, as the Rainbow Crow sat alone grieving what felt like his symbolic death, he felt The Creator's presence in the form of the whiff and touch of breeze, and heard Him say—'Do not be sad, dear Bird. This end is not the end. You begin anew as a bird that all will honour for selflessness, compassion and courage. Men won't hunt you any longer since your flesh is now made of smoke, and your hoarse voice would keep them from caging you. You will be a free spirit.'

The Grace revealed itself to the chosen bird, as he heard the Creator say—'Beneath your lost outer beauty, your inner beauty is eternal. Just spread your feathers and look within. The iridescent hues of your goodness will always radiate.' The Rainbow Crow saw with amazement that all the rainbow colours were dazzling inside the black of his burnt feathers.

And so, it has been since the start of universe, and so it shall be forever. No matter what, the rainbow colours of Grace shall always continue to sparkle from within the darkness of grief.

The Rainbow Crow folktale comes from the Lenni Lenape (meaning 'true people') tribe of the Native American Indians. Various versions of the folktale are in circulation. I heard the above version from my younger son. I do not claim its accuracy. Instead, I invite your attention to the message of the tale.

There is always something unknowable that continues to bless and guide life even in the face of loss and trauma. Faith, strength, love and grace never die. They reflect even brighter in the mirror of pain, just as the burnt feathers of the Rainbow Crow continued to radiate all the resplendent colours of the rainbow despite turning black as tar. The same is true of human spirit. It continues to affirm life with reverence, gratitude, compassion and meaning, even when overwhelmed with grief, and sometimes actually because of grief and pain.

'All things of grace and beauty such that one holds
them to one's heart have a common provenance
in pain. Their birth in grief and ashes.'

—Cormac McCarthy

True indeed, that it is hard enough to grieve a loved one's death. Imagine one's own symbolic death. How does one grieve that? The Rainbow Crow was chosen to do that. His journey, especially the return, above and beyond the skies is a metaphoric representation of his unique grief and growth pilgrimage. As he annihilated his attachment to his mesmerizing persona and voice, and transcended the grief of losing the same, his true abiding grace emerged from beneath his burnt feathers.

Grace is a transcendent phenomenon. It inspires us to look for deeper meaning in our suffering. Such is the blessing of grace. It stays with us, in sorrow and joy. It gifts us openings to heal, transcend, grow and reemerge. It fills us with light that shines within and radiates outside, all so quietly. It invites and inspires us to partake the splendour of Nature. Let us step into the temple of grace that rests on the sacred pillars of gratitude, reverence, affirmation, compassion, meaning and essence.

❖

GRATITUDE

'...and then, I have nature and art and poetry,
and if that is not enough, what is enough?'

—Vincent van Gogh

Living in gratitude is one of the most beautiful graces that Nature bestows on us. The blessed sense of *enough* that Vincent van Gogh finds in nature, art and poetry, is something that we all can and do feel. Believe you me, nature and life are abundantly rich with things that fill us with serene joy, meaning and appreciation, even in the face of loss and trauma. Gratitude continues to live in our appreciative eye and heart, however hard be our life journey. It shows up as acknowledgment that life has beauty and meaning even in the midst of all the brokenness and misery.

There is enough research evidence to suggest the positive effects of gratitude on our body, mind and psychology. It has been found that deliberate practice of gratitude can influence our brain behaviour in a positive way. The best thing about gratitude is that it is a simple and sure way to create a virtuous loop of affirmative energy around us. The more we experience and express gratitude, the more it grows. It acts like a beacon that continually attracts positive energy and influences in life.

It is okay if you find it hard to imagine how someone in grief could feel gratitude. Such doubts of the mind are understandable. But the heart knows. It knows that grief and gratitude have a deep enduring relationship. I have seen many grieving people experience, embody and express a deep and warm sense of gratitude. No doubt, in grief, sorrow takes the centre-stage. But yearning is not just about pain alone. It also evokes a sense of nostalgia, joy and thankfulness for the beautiful life that we had with our loved one. Invoke their 'Presence' and express your gratitude for the life that you shared, for all the small or big joys, and for the gifts of wisdom or purpose that they have left behind as a legacy.

Kristin Granger wisely avers—'Gratitude for the turning of the seasons. May we attune our hearts to their enduring message of renewal.' When we see life with a heart of gratitude, we understand that everything in nature is both timely and timeless. Each season arrives at its own time, and quietly weathers away when it is time for the next. In the process, decay makes way for regeneration. Like all things in nature, we humans too have an intuitive sense of timing. Our inner sage knows when and how to invoke the season of gratitude, so what if the season of grief is still abiding. The path of grace urges us to feel and express gratitude for the life that our loved one had before death came calling. Whether it was a simple life, a privileged life, or a trying and tough life—their life calls for affirmation and celebration. And the fact that they shared their precious life with us is reason enough for us to bow in gratitude and love.

Gratitude is the sacred bell at the temple of grace. It echoes far and wide. When we express gratitude for the good that we see, we feel inspired and invited to do good ourselves. A noble and beautiful embodiment of gratitude is to feel and express it on behalf of your deceased loved one. Think of the people whose kindness or generosity came as a blessing to your loved one, whether in life or on death. Convey your gratitude to them for all they meant and did for your loved one. You will be amazed to see the spring of gratitude and love that sprouts out.

MY STORY

On my son, Utkarsh's, birthday (yes—birthday, not birth anniversary) in 2020, I had founded a legacy endeavour at his university.

With the pandemic keeping us all indoors, we planned a virtual dedication ceremony. With a couple of his friends' help, I sent out the invitation to as many people as we could trace, personalizing each invite, expressing warm appreciation and gratitude for what each one meant to my son and us. I had personal information about only a few. For those I didn't know well, I nonetheless expressed gratitude for being my son's co-travellers in life. Given his reclusive and introverted nature, I wasn't expecting even half as many people as were invited. And here we had nearly twice as many on a sultry summer evening.

Everyone had something personally meaningful to say. Many people remembered with fondness how he always made it a point to acknowledge and thank people for all their small or big acts of kindness and goodwill, including even the easily missable things such as lending him a pencil. Almost everyone spoke with fondness about his heartful 'Thank you', apart from his other commonly lauded virtues of helpfulness, sharing spirit, inquisitiveness, vast knowledge, deep understanding, resilience, wit and more. Though no one knew about his quiet and invisible community service, almost everyone felt awe-inspired by the extraordinary selflessness that he embodied. Several people stayed back to reminisce so many fun, happy and pensive moments with him. We celebrated his whole being, warts and all, strengths and wrongs together.

What else would a (bereaved) mother's heart ask for?

Despite his reclusiveness, my son lives on in so many hearts.

Such is the radiance of gratitude. It is eternal. It is an innate human virtue, strength and emotion. It is great if gratitude comes naturally to you. If not, there is no reason to feel disheartened. We can consciously cultivate and practice gratitude. In fact, I would encourage everyone, including those for whom gratitude is a natural strength, to consciously practice it as a worthy life-habit. I share below, one of the simplest and most effective gratitude practices. Please feel free to improvise and create your own.

Words Create Worlds

Gratitude Journal

- Create a Gratitude Journal. Buy a new notebook or hand-craft one by sewing together loose sheets. Personalize and decorate it the way you like.
- Give it a name. I call mine '*Abundance*'.
- For 15-20 minutes each time, at least three-four times a week, pour your expressions of gratitude into your journal.
- Make sure you write your reflections by-hand. Healing and growth are embodied experiences. Make them sensory, and the effect will go deep.
- Write about one or two things that you feel grateful for at the moment.
- If you find it difficult to recall or notice big blessings of life, start with seemingly simple things from your everyday routine—good sleep, fresh morning, wholesome meal, warm clothing, compliment at work or home, rejuvenating time in nature, a happy evening out, or an unexpected meeting with an old friend. The list goes on.
- Go deep into the experience. Savour the feeling. Believe me, the feeling of gratitude is profound even for seemingly ordinary things.
- Notice all nuances of the touch and the impact of the feeling of gratitude.
- Avoid jump-starting the exercise, or doing it in a hurried, abrupt or regimented way. Enjoy being in the moment and relish the process.
- Take a pause. Relax and soak in the energy of gratitude expression.

- Now reminisce the life you shared with your deceased loved one. Let things unfold naturally. Go only as deep as you wish to or feel comfortable with. Avoid tasking or stressing yourself.
- Allow, acknowledge and welcome whatever emotions or experiences surface, including tears and sighs. Each has a message of its own.
- Become aware of the memories, recollections and feelings that fill you with gratitude. Pick one that you want to write about in this moment.
- Let your pen flow. Allow words to appear on paper in the stream of consciousness. Avoid censoring or conditioning yourself.
- Express gratitude to your loved one for your shared life. Go deep and be specific, especially about things that you feel particularly grateful for.
- And now, on their behalf, express gratitude to yourself. Easy—of course not. Therapeutic and heart-warming—immensely.
- Relive the experience in this moment. Bring it alive in your being and your writing. Try being specific.
- Savour the process of writing about it. Soak in the experience.
- Slowly and gently return to your routines.
- Remember, gratitude is not a task or target. It is an experience. Let it happen in a natural way. Avoid stressing, especially when overwhelmed by grief.
- Finally, there is no right or wrong way to gratitude journaling. It is your private pursuit, and entirely your choice whether or not you share it with anyone. Create your own unique way that taps into your inner flow and feelings. Stay consistent. Just do it.

REVERENCE FOR LIFE

'In the midst of all your pain and heartache,
you are surrounded by beauty, the wonder of creation,
the sounds of laughter and love, of whispered hopes and
celebrations, of new life and transformation.'

—William Paul Young

Life never ceases to reflect Nature's radiance. It can be seen and felt in every particle of the universe. The Rainbow Crow felt and heard the Creator's presence in the touch, whiff and sound of the breeze. The rainbow colours that sparkled from inside his burnt black feathers were a reflection of his reverence for life. The Rainbow Crow endured burning, so he could bring the warmth and life-energy of the Fire-spirit to his fellow beings, only to find that the fire that burnt him also blessed him with the iridescent light. All that he needed to do was to seek within, to see the light and colours of grace that quietly hid beneath his burnt feathers. And he did, in faith and reverence.

Reverence for life is an expression of pure innocence. It lights up everything. It is that glimmer of light, however tiny or hazy, that guides us through the dark tunnel of our pain. The light of Supreme Grace keeps shining without fuss. It quietly walks beside us, gently nudging us to notice and admire the myriad hues of Nature. And as we begin to see with eyes of wonder, we realize that life is beautiful, simply because it is alive. The movie *Nebraska*, depicts a touching story where the already much-stressed protagonist volunteers to take his father on a long cross-country journey, just because the father believes that he has won a million dollars, based on a bogus sweepstakes letter that he had received. An ailing, adamant, foul-tempered and almost senile man whom nobody in the family likes, the father is determined to travel a thousand-mile-journey all by himself, on foot. The protagonist's own life has been coming apart. His worried mother and disapproving elder brother do not support his decision to go on a pointless long journey that he can ill-afford. But a poignant moment with his parting girlfriend, who advises him to continue watering the plant if he wished to keep it alive, leaves him with an epiphanic realization that despite all his bothersome and unreasonable ways, his old and vulnerable father deserved to be loved and cared for. Life is exactly like a plant. And reverence and love are like water. No matter what storms beat the plant of life, we need to keep nourishing it with the water of love and care.

Even the nastiest mess has some meaning. It is okay if you can't see it yet. Life holds the promise to unfurl its gifts upon you. You need to accept it in its entirety. Marvel at its glories, and engage with the trials with faith, humility, curiosity, fortitude and sense of meaning. See the light in the dark, always and already there. Every one of us has an eternal spring of love and light within. We need to enter the dark cave of our pain, willing to see and accept all that is unfolding. Hard indeed. Begin by avowing and beholding in wonder all that you see around in nature—chirping birds, blooming flowers, fluttering butterflies, twinkling stars, the smile of an infant, gay abandonment of youth; and also, the wise crinkle of old age, falling leaves, silence of the moonless night. Storm and the sunshine, affirm and celebrate them both. Nature is waiting in a thousand guises to hold you in trance, and heal your broken heart. Meet life in its eyes and say, '*I love you*'.

Anne Frank writes in her famous diary-memoir, 'I don't think of all the misery, but of the beauty that still remains.' Your light is taking birth in the womb of your pain. The Supreme Grace awaits you. Join the adventure. Life continues to be beautiful even when broken. Affirm it *as-is*. Say, '*YES to life*', in its entirety, no matter what.

—◆—

AYE
SAY YES TO LIFE

'To love life... even when you have no stomach for it.
When grief sits with you... hold life... between your palms.
A plain face, no charming smile, no violet eyes.
And say, YES, I will take you... love you, again.'

—Ellen Bass

The only true events of life are birth and death. In between, the drama of life unfolds. And this drama is action-packed. There is romance, comedy, philosophy, action, mystery, thrill, trial and tragedy. Each has its own unique place and timing. Each complements and completes the others. Each has meaning for its own sake. Each deserves a grateful applause. We can't enjoy one without affirming the others. Drama of life does not come in isolated chapters or parts. We need to say 'YES' to it in its entirety. Saying 'YES' to life is about trusting that life can still be whole and worth living again, however shattering be our loss, trauma and pain.

As soon as they entered the concentration camp, the holocaust prisoners were subjected to the most dehumanizing experience that no one should have to bear. Stripped to their bones in full view of each other and the brutal Nazis, their whole existence was reduced to stark nakedness, both literally and symbolically. And this would only be a tiny preview of what they had to endure at the concentration camps. What could keep a person from not wanting or trying to end their life in the face of such horrendous torture and indescribable dehumanization? It is what Viktor Frankl calls, 'the last of all human freedoms—the freedom to choose our attitude, and say "YES" to life no matter what.' Frankl knows this first-hand. He said 'YES to life' despite all its insufferable goriness, and searched for meaning in his suffering.

Saying 'YES' prepares us to see what lies beyond our pain, without suppressing or disregarding the pain. It calls for affirmative surrender to the Supreme Grace. Not resigning in despair or haplessness or giving in to pain, rather facing and embracing reality *as-is*. It is about trusting that Supreme Grace is watching over us, that some good is always waiting to unfold, and that our job is to keep at it and keep striving. Not easy indeed. Essential, nonetheless. Faith is the key to the door of life, where the nameplate reads—Say 'YES to life', as it is.

Affirmative surrender is an act of faith that comes from believing that life is in flow even when it feels turbulent or still. It is about pronoia (opposite of paranoia)—believing that deep down everything in nature has a good intent to support you. Not naivete, but aware, wise faith that Supreme Grace is at work and is guiding things on the path that they are meant to take. It is about understanding and trusting that it is our grief itself that will guide us through and out of its maze. As we accept this, we feel humbler and better able to honour life. Faith is the quiet alchemy that prepares us to say 'YES' to the drama of life in its entirety. It is the invisible string that holds it all together. It is the only thing that works when all else seems to have come apart, even though reasoning may fail to explain why and how it works. Faith is about honouring both life and death. It is about transcending grief by affirming life in wholeness—cry and celebration, lament and love, woe and wonder, grief and grace—altogether.

Faith is the gift of Supreme Grace. It comes to us all. Not all of us, though, partake of it. We need to be present to see it and receive it. Go in humble. Trust. Wait. Witness. Allow the grace of faith to touch you and strengthen you. Marvel at its quiet glory. Receive it with gratitude and say 'YES' to life, loss and love together.

—◆:◆—

COMPASSION

'Love yourself…
as if you were a rainbow
with gold at both ends.'

—Aberjhani

The path to courage leads through and with compassion. The Rainbow Crow's journey began with compassion for other creatures. And it became a pilgrimage, the moment he held his own grief and pain in self-compassion. That is the beauty and power of compassion. It doesn't just melt pain, but also unravels the gift of courage.

The book and the movie *Amish Grace,* explore the Amish Community's astonishingly compassionate response to the horrific 2006 shooting at their Village School in Lancaster County, Pennsylvania, USA. The Amish Community didn't just choose to forgive the shooter who killed several little girls from their community, but also showed radical compassion by extending support to the bereaved family of the shooter who had shot himself also dead. Theirs was an act of exemplary courage that is made possible by grace of compassion. The Amish even attended the funeral of their transgressor, which was avoided by most from his own congregation. In an interview, one of the bereaved parents shared that although he had forgiven the shooter in the immediacy of his loss, it was more in the spirit of honouring his community elders' decision. It was only after he felt pure compassion in his heart for the shooter's family that his true will and strength to forgive, emerge. He let his compassion heal his wound.

> 'When wounds are healed by love,
> the scars are beautiful.'
>
> —David Bowles

Compassion takes birth and grows in the silence of love. It does not need a voice. Its light and fragrance radiate themselves. Compassion takes us beyond ourselves, while still staying rooted at our core. Compassion is that self-transcendent expression of love and grace that liberates us, and transforms our brokenness and bitterness into profound beauty. Of course, it is hard to invoke or feel compassion when one is in grief. The amazing paradox is that it is only with compassion that we prepare ourselves to bear witness to our grief, and embrace our pain. Self-compassion is perhaps one of the deepest soul-fulfilling experiences. A heart in grief, Rumi says, can be 'the garden of compassion.' Let your compassion be friends with your pain. Allow it to heal your sorrow, balm your heart, transform your pain, and fill life with love.

Partake the grace of compassion.

ESSENCE OF LIFE

*'Ultimately, man should not ask what the meaning
of his life is, but rather must recognize that it is he
who is asked what the meaning of life is.'*

—Viktor E. Frankl

A life of meaning and purpose unfurls deep abiding happiness that goes beyond material joys or worldly pains. What we can't change, we must accept, with humility, grace, adaptiveness, and will to meaning. Viktor Frankl offers three wonderful 'A's to realize and fulfil the meaning of life—appreciation, attitude to respond and acting with purpose. He emphasizes that we alone hold the responsibility to discover meaning in our suffering and choose our response. I would humbly add that we need to appreciate and accept life in its wholeness, to be able to see and uphold its essence, and fulfil the call it holds for us, of us. Appreciation is much more than just praise. It is an expansive phenomenon, that encompasses opening up, noticing, acknowledging, affirming, understanding, seeking meaning, valuing, adding value, growing, transcending, taking to a higher level, creating an upward spiral, and becoming 'appreciation' yourself. Appreciating life in its wholeness is about recognizing and honouring what life expects from us. And discovering in the process the deeper meaning of our dark, and the higher purpose of our light.

There is no way to celebrate day without accepting night, no way to welcome the radiant sun without marveling at the celestial grandeur that only shows up in the night sky. All things have a unique beauty and meaning. It is in the iridescent colours inside his burnt black feathers, that Rainbow Crow discovered his inner light of compassion and selfless service. As he embodied deep appreciation, his hoarse caw and blackened appearance didn't shame him anymore. Rather, it became a symbol of the sacred sacrifice that he had made to save his fellow beings. He chose his response to his symbolic death, and his attitude towards his new life. And in doing so he discovered that his higher call was to serve.

See with an appreciative eye. You may find the majesty of the Rainbow Crow in your neighbourhood crow that quietly cleans your surroundings of discards, and selflessly raises the cuckoo's offspring, so you can enjoy its lilting song. Hear with a warm heart. Perhaps the caw that you find annoying, is the crow's call of affection, for affection. In Hindu belief, the crow is considered a messenger from the worlds beyond. On the day of shradh (the annual ritual to offer prayers and meal to the departed ancestors), the crow is invoked to partake the meal on behalf of the departed ancestors. To me, the crow represents endurance, kindness, simple happiness and rainbow grace.

Become the Rainbow Crow of your life. Fly past the blazing sun of your sorrow. Dive into the dark smokey clouds of your grief. Embrace what frightens you or pains you. Let your heart cry. Let your tears wash your wounds. Receive with gratitude every emotion and experience, happy and sad alike. Celebrate and put to good use, the new wisdom they gift you. Affirm. Heal. Transcend. Grow. Rise from the ashes of your pain. Choose your response with wisdom and integrity. Adapt with grit and poise. Discover the splendid colours of the meaning and purpose of your life. Create something of larger value that continues to serve even after you are gone.

Indeed, the noble dharma (duty) of life is to discover its essence, to find meaning in our life-journey, and to dedicate ourselves to a larger purpose. My son loved poetry. One of his most favourite poems was the classic 'If' by Rudyard Kipling. The deep meaning and message of this poem was made even more profound by Utkarsh's evocative recitation. It was my go-to mantra to cheer myself up and get inspired to face and engage with the trials of life. He would never tire of reciting it one more time for his crazy mother. One day he insisted that I recite it myself. Here are the lines I loved reciting the most—

> 'Dream—and not make dreams your master;
> Think—and not make thoughts your aim;
> Meet with Triumph and Disaster,
> and treat those two impostors just the same.'

A year after his passing on, I was sorting Utkarsh's books for donation. Landing my hands on the collected works of Kipling, I was transported back to times when he would recite 'If' for me. Reminiscing his mellifluous recitations, I read and recited the beautiful poem one more time, only to discover my higher purpose in the following lines,

> 'If you can force your heart and nerve and sinew,
> To serve your turn long after they are gone.'

I am sure Kipling had a gentler meaning for 'force'. To me, his words inspire strength in vulnerability, love in loss, meaning in suffering, and purpose in pain. While inspiring me to pledge for cornea-organ-tissue donation, Utkarsh had said, 'true appreciation is to appreciate life, even in death.' What could be a more evocative expression of reverence for life. Utkarsh's quiet wisdom and his Presence in my heart and life, inspire me to serve those in grief and trauma. Through counselling, meaning-reconstructive grief therapy, poetry, therapeutic writing, arts and more, I help them walk their journey, and transform it into GROWTH pilgrimage.

I am sure you, too, must be serving a higher purpose in life. And if not yet, I hope this book inspires and supports you in finding your call and devoting yourself to it. As you close this book, I invite you to make a new beginning. Appreciate the essence of your life. Fill it with meaning. Make life the sacred offering of compassion, gratitude, resilience and meaning. And let it unfold growth. Seek to live in faith. Keep striving, do what you can and must, and know that life will reveal its true essence. Each of us is chosen for and entrusted a unique journey. Create meaning in yours.

I wish you good health, meaning, joy, abundance and love. Remember to create and take home your eleventh and final poetic affirmation.

PATH 11

Poetic Affirmation to Take Home

*'The darkest of the night
is bowing in surrender to
the light of grace.
The Sun is rising with a new promise.
The morning bird is singing hope.
Chime in the new day with
faith, hope, love and grace.'*

—Neena Verma

Nature is grace personified.
Become your own Sun.
Unfurl your petals, and bloom.
Feel your inner grace.
And offer it to the world.

The Prayer

May we embrace our pain with a sense of purpose.
May we meet adversity with a world-view of abundance.
May we heal our wounds with the warmth of our wisdom.
May we see and create meaning in our suffering.
May we grow strength in the garden of sorrow.
May we cradle our loss with love.
May we savour our dark with our light.
May we serve the purpose we are chosen for.
May we share the nectar of our growth with others.
May our journey of grief become pilgrimage of growth.
May we partake Nature's grace and spread ours in the world.

—◆—

And
The rest
as Shakespeare says
is
Silence.

Recommended Readings

Adams, Kathleen (2009). *Journal to the Self: Twenty-Two Paths to Personal Growth*. New York: Hachette Books.

Bonano, George A. (2019). *The Other Side of Sadness: What The New Science Of Bereavement Tells Us About Life After Loss*. New York: Basic Books.

Calhoun, Lawrence G. & Tedeschi, Richard G. (2013). *Post-Traumatic Growth in Clinical Practice*. New York: Routledge.

Frankl, Viktor E. (2004). *Man's Search For Meaning: The classic tribute to hope from the Holocaust*. London: Rider (Penguin Random House).

Frankl, Viktor E. (2020). *Yes To Life: In Spite of Everything*. London: Rider (Penguin Random House).

Joseph, Stephen (2012). *What Doesn't Kill Us: The New Psychology of post-traumatic Growth*. New York: Basic Books.

Kessler, David (2019). *Finding Meaning: The Sixth Stage of Grief*. New York: Rider (Penguin Random House).

Lewis, C.S. (1994). *A Grief Observed*. New York: HarperOne.

Neimeyer, Robert A. (Editor) (2012). *Techniques of Grief Therapy: Creative Practices for Counseling the Bereaved*. New York: Routledge.

Pennebaker, James W. & Smyth, Joshua M. (2016). *Opening Up by Writing It Down: How Expressive Writing Improves Health and Eases Emotional Pain*. New York: Guilford Press.

Rendon, Jim (2016). *Upside: The New Science of Post-Traumatic Growth*. New York: Touchstone (Simon & Schuster).

Richo, David (2007). *The Power of Coincidence: How Life Shows*

Us What We Need to Know. Boston: Shambhala.

Stang, Heather (2014). *Mindfulness & Grief: With Guided Meditations To Calm Your Mind And Restore Your Spirit.* London/New York: CICO Books.

Tedeschi, Richard & Moore, Bret A. (2016). *The Post-Traumatic Growth Workbook: Coming Through Trauma Wiser, Stronger, and More Resilient.* Oakland, California, USA: New Harbinger.

Verma, Neena (2016). *A Mother's Cry .. A Mother's Celebration.* Chennai, India: Notion Press.

Worden, William J. (2009). *Grief Counselling and Grief Therapy: A Handbook for the Mental Health Practitioner.* New York: Springer.